One Last Goodbye

Sometimes only a mother's love
can help end the pain

KAY GILDERDALE

EBURY
PRESS

1 3 5 7 9 10 8 6 4 2

First published in 2011 by Ebury Press, an imprint of Ebury Publishing

A Random House Group company

Copyright © Kay Gilderdale 2011

Kay Gilderdale has asserted her right to be identified as the author of this
work in accordance with the Copyright, Designs and Patents Act 1988

The Random House Group Limited Reg. No. 954009

Addresses for companies within the Random House Group can be found at
www.randomhouse.co.uk

A CIP catalogue record for this book is available from the British Library

The Random House Group Limited supports The Forest Stewardship
Council (FSC), the leading international forest certification organisation.
All our titles that are printed on Greenpeace-approved FSC-certified paper
carry the FSC logo. Our paper procurement policy can be found at
www.rbooks.co.uk/environment

Mixed Sources
Product group from well-managed
forests and other controlled sources
www.fsc.org Cert no. TT-COC-2139
© 1996 Forest Stewardship Council

Designed and set by seagulls.net

Printed and bound in the UK by CPI Cox & Wyman, Reading, RG1 8EX

ISBN 9780091939144

To buy books by your favourite authors and register for offers visit
www.rbooks.co.uk

This book is dedicated to my inspirational daughter. Not only because it is her story, a story of unimaginable suffering, but because it teaches us the meaning of love, tenacity and perseverance and that sometimes letting go is not a frail or cowardly act, but one of incredible courage.

CONTENTS

PROLOGUE

A court usher put her head round the door of the waiting room. 'They're coming back,' she said. I began to tremble. This was it. The moment of truth. After an hour and 45 minutes of deliberation the jury was about to return to court and tell me whether they thought I had deliberately set out to murder my beloved daughter, Lynn.

My son, Stephen, squeezed my arm and gently said, 'Are you okay, Mum? Shall we go?' My brothers and sisters and other members of the family who had been there, supporting me, throughout the nine-day trial clustered round me, bearing me up.

Lynn's dad – my former husband, Richard – had such a look of anguish on his face. He'd spoken so eloquently in court about the heartbreak of Lynn's 17-year struggle with the crippling disease of ME – the disease that had stolen her life and left her completely bedridden, unable to walk, talk or even swallow. But now Richard looked like he was about to collapse. Clutching the hand of Jeanette, his new wife, he followed me through the lobby of the building to Court Number One.

I felt enveloped in love and concern, yet I had to face this judgement alone, as I had acted alone. It was I who had helped my daughter find the one thing she'd desperately

1

wanted more than anything else: peace. Even so, I still could not quite believe that I was there, in Lewes Crown Court, facing a charge of attempted murder, confronted with the possibility of spending that night and the rest of my life in a prison cell.

The anger I felt when the charge was originally put to me had mostly gone. Back then, I had been overwhelmed by a surge of indignation and outrage at the idea that anyone could possibly associate the word *murder* with the relationship between me and Lynn. My love for my only daughter was so strong, it was indescribable. She was my world. I'd dedicated my life to her. *'How could they have come to this?'* I'd asked myself over and over. *'It's totally wrong. I have to show them that that isn't right, that I would never hurt Lynn.'*

I was calmer now but still bewildered. This historic court in the ancient Sussex town of Lewes had seen the trial of so many evil people, including the 'acid bath murderer', John George Haigh, who dissolved his six victims in sulphuric acid, and of Roy Whiting, the paedophile who abducted and killed eight-year-old Sarah Payne.

I did not belong among such people. I was just an ordinary mum. I'd acted out of love, not evil. I was on trial because I'd helped my precious daughter end her life. Something she'd asked me to do and, even more importantly, something she'd needed and longed for with all her heart and mind.

My defence barristers, who had conducted the case in a way that made me feel grateful and proud, smiled encouragingly as I climbed the three wooden stairs to the dock. The court was wood panelled in the Victorian style, surrounded on three sides by a gallery from which hung an old-fashioned gas lamp. In front of me were the lawyers' desks and to the right two press benches, rapidly filling up with reporters who were setting out their notebooks and opening their pens in anticipation of getting a big story. Behind me were about five tiered rows of benches for the public, where my family and friends were filing in and nervously taking their seats.

Once we were all in place the court usher banged her gavel. 'Court rise,' she boomed. Everyone got to their feet to greet the arrival of the judge, Mr Justice Bean, who came through a door behind the judge's bench, set above and opposite where I was standing in the dock, wearing his familiar scarlet robes and grey wig.

When he was settled he gave a nod and everyone except me sat down. Then another door was opened and the jury filed into the two rows of tiered benches on the left of the court: the six men and six women who were to judge my actions and, ultimately, decide upon my fate.

Every nerve within me was strung to breaking point. I was so tense, I was worried I might faint. I touched the two lockets I had kept with me throughout the trial: one, a heart shape made of silver, contained a tiny portion of Lynn's ashes. The other was oval and made of white gold and was fitted on one side with a miniature picture of Lynn and on the other with a few strands of her hair.

She was with me. She was always with me. I did not need the lockets to feel her presence watching over me, though, as my fingers closed round them, I was glad of the comfort they gave me. I had felt her with me so strongly as the trial unfolded that sometimes I could almost see her. I knew how much she would have hated that I had to go through this, how she had tried her best not to involve me. And how the last thing she told me before she died was that she was frightened of what might happen to me.

I stood there, telling myself to be strong, like Lynn. I had no clue which way it would go. I was longing to turn round to my family who were so pent up that the whole atmosphere felt charged with their emotion. But I thought, '*I can't. I must just stand here and face up to whatever is going to happen.*'

The debate about assisted suicide and euthanasia and whether the law should be changed had been raging for months in the media and in Parliament. This was going to be the first time that the British public, in the form of a jury of ordinary men and women, would get the chance to show where their sympathies lay for people caught up in such cases. It is one of the strengths of our legal system that changes in public opinion about profound moral dilemmas can be reflected in this way.

But I was not thinking of any of that as I waited, with Lynn in my heart and by my side. This moment was about what lay ahead for me, yes, but what was far more important to me was that it was about Lynn's dignity as a human being and her right to have sovereignty over her own life and death.

'Foreman of the jury, have you reached a verdict on the charges against Kay Gilderdale on which you are all agreed?' asked the usher.

'Yes,' came the reply.

'On the charge of attempting to murder her daughter, Lynn Gilderdale, how do you find?' I held my breath…

CHAPTER ONE

AN IRISH CHILDHOOD

I was born in Dublin in 1954 to the most colourful, bois-
terous family you could imagine. Named Bridget Kathleen,
but known as Kay, I was the youngest of ten children. Six
boys – Jim, Nicky, Paddy, Noel, John and Vinny – who
were, to say the least, lively; and four girls – Marie, twins
Rosemary and Dolores, and me. So there was always a lot
going on in the house when I was small. My eldest brother,
Jim, was 16 when I came along and was my godfather. He
was like a second father to me.

My father, also called Jim, was a strong, hard-working,
self-made man. He left school young and worked in the
market to save enough to buy his own van which he drove
all over the country delivering fruit.

He worked from dawn till dusk to build up the business until he had a good number of lorries and shops. He
imported fruit that had never been seen in Ireland before
and brought in specialised equipment to keep it at its best.
He made a lot of money and had a large, elegant house in
the city. They held grand parties attended by politicians

and other important people. My mother, intelligent and vibrant, was a superb hostess, and my father, with his good looks and good voice, entertained their guests with music and storytelling, whilst the young ones sneaked out of bed to catch a peek at all the goings on.

My elder brothers went to private school and there were maids to help my mum in the house. But around the time I was born the business took a battering and my father had to sell the house, the lorries and the shops and move to the suburb of Mount Merrion, a few miles to the south of Dublin City.

The boys had to leave their private schools and help Dad in the business. It was an awful blow to them to leave the schools they loved and the rugby they adored. I was only six months old so never knew anything about the anguish of adjustment. All I knew was Mount Merrion, a leafy, spacious, middle-class suburb near enough to the city to go shopping and close to the coast. It was a very nice place to grow up. We had a semi-detached house with a big living room and a dining room and a sizeable garden but it only had three bedrooms so it was a bit of a squeeze until the older ones started to move out. There was always a lot of coming and going with the boys getting home from work or school and smartening themselves up ready to go out on dates. There was never a shortage of girlfriends for six handsome lads with a sense of fun and good humour.

When we were all at home together there was never a quiet moment. We loved music and singing. If we were gathered around the dinner table or doing chores, like polishing the big wooden floors (which would usually involve sliding along in our socks, acting the fool), someone would start up a song.

My brother, Nicky, had the best voice and could play anything on the piano, so he'd give us a tune while others played the spoons or banged on the table. We sang everything – traditional Irish songs, country, classical, pop, ballads. The house vibrated to the sound of music and when my parents bought my brother, Vinny, a whole set of drums for his birthday (a decision they must have later regretted!), the poor house almost disintegrated, like the shattering of a chandelier when the operatic soprano hits her highest note. Come bedtime, I had to share a double bed with my twin sisters, Rosemary and Dolores, whom we nicknamed Rosie and Dolie. It was a bit of a squeeze, but I'd always be so exhausted from the day's fun and games, I'd still sleep.

My oldest sister, Marie, loved to fuss over me like I was her own living doll. She and her friend spent hours dressing me up and tying ribbons in my hair. Marie always used to say how lovely little girls were and I think it was her that instilled a dream in me for my own baby girl to dress up and dote on one day.

Being the annoying little sister, I used to torment them and my closest brother, Vinny, which inevitably occasionally ended up in a fight. I remember Rosie chasing me round the flowerbed in the front garden one day and me thinking, '*If she catches me, she is going to kill me*.' Luckily, being the younger and blessed with two strong long legs, I tore off down the road and escaped.

My mother, Rose, was pretty relaxed and she let me have a lot of freedom. Childhood was very different in those days anyway. We didn't watch TV much, instead we were always playing games that would be considered dangerous nowadays like tying each other up in wild Cowboy and Indian battles or throwing our make-believe spears at each other, pretending to be Geronimo or some such brave warrior.

Three of my grandparents died before I was born but my maternal grandfather was still alive and we used to spend holidays at his cottage near the historic town of Kells, County Meath, some 40 miles north of Dublin, where he had about an acre of land. The cottage was primitive by today's standards but commonplace in that area at the time. There was no running water – you had to get it from a water well pump down the road. If that ran dry you crossed the field to a stream – crystal clear and sparkling, yes, but imagine the challenge of trying to cart a full bucket of water back across a muddy field! The toilet was something else for us 'townies' to experience – an earth closet in a shed out the back.

All around the cottage there was nothing but fields. We children played for hours, running, riding horses, sliding down haystacks. The freedom of it was heaven; it was one big adventure. We were always outside, away from the watchful eyes of adults and having fun together.

My grandfather was a great storyteller who beguiled us with his tales of fairies and leprechauns. When I was eight he couldn't manage any longer on his own in the cottage and came to live with us in Mount Merrion, where sadly he died about six months later. But even at death's door he mesmerised us with enchanting stories I fully believed were real.

These memories have stayed with me and in many ways it was an idyllic childhood. Until I was nine I had no cares at all and no reason to think it would change.

I remember quite vividly the day that it did. It was a lovely sunny morning and I was in the front garden messing about when a police car pulled up outside our house. The Garda – the name for the Irish police – who climbed out seemed tall and stern as they walked up our winding path. But when the taller of the two spoke, his voice was surprisingly gentle. 'Hello there, little one,' he said. 'Can you tell me, are your mammy and daddy at home, please?'

'My mammy's here,' I replied.

He knocked on the door and Mum answered it. I remember the look of surprise and foreboding on her face as she took in the two Garda standing before her.

'We have something to tell you. Could we come inside?' the tall officer asked gravely.

Curious, I made to follow them as Mum opened the door wider but she wasn't having it. 'You go and play,' she ordered.

Sensing something was wrong, I stood waiting in the garden under an apple blossom tree with a sort of shivering in my stomach and a weakness in my knees. Then, after a few minutes, the door opened again, my mother emerged and, white-faced, climbed into the back seat of the police car and was driven away at speed, sirens sounding. The officers had told her that my brother, John, who was 16 at the time, had been in a terrible accident and was on the brink of death.

John had been a passenger in a car when something went wrong with one of the tyres – maybe it blew out. The car smashed into a lamp post, which toppled over. John in the front and his friend in the back were thrown together, their heads crashing into each other with great force. His friend was killed and John's brain stem was crushed. The driver had minor injuries but was terribly traumatised by what happened that day.

Before the accident John was a handsome, lively teenager, full of plans and ambitions. He adored Elvis Presley and used to style himself on him when he went out. His good looks won him roles as an extra in a number of films and he would have loved to have been an actor. His back-up plan was to be a radio officer and he had just completed a college course studying Morse code.

Now he was in a coma, covered in bandages and tubes. All day my mother sat by his bed, prayed and talked to him constantly, willing him to come back to life. One day a doctor asked her, 'Why are you praying for him? I am afraid that, if he survives this and wakes up, he will be a vegetable.' That was the awful term they used in those days for people with brain damage.

'I am praying for God's will to be done, whatever that may be,' my mother, whose Catholic faith was unshakeable, calmly replied.

The rest of us tried to think of things to read to John or say to him that would bring him back to us. We asked the nurses to play his favourite Elvis tracks like 'Wooden Heart' or 'Blue Suede Shoes' but it wasn't until 100 days after the accident that he gradually regained consciousness. To our joy, he recognised us all.

It took him a year of recovery in hospital until he was well enough to come home but he could not sit up or do anything for himself and could only speak in a way that was difficult to understand. His voice was low and fragmented and he said words so slowly that you had to listen very carefully to make out what he meant.

My parents converted a room downstairs, in which they put in a hospital bed and all sorts of equipment. We had nurses coming in 24 hours a day to help with lifting John, turning him, washing him and doing some physiotherapy to try to get his body moving again. The dynamics of the family changed completely, of course, as my mother always had to put John's needs first. But I don't remember being frightened by what had happened to him, or resentful of the time and attention my parents devoted to him. As children do, we just adjusted to how things were.

Just as some semblance of order had come back into our lives, the family was hit by another blow: my brother Paddy had a horrific accident on the same stretch of road as John. He had just turned 21. With several broken bones and severe internal injuries, there wasn't much hope of survival. The doctors and nurses who had worked so hard to save John were now doing the same for Paddy and, miraculously, he pulled through. Several operations followed but Paddy's grit and determination resulted in him walking out of the hospital a year later on crutches and he has lived life to the full ever since.

As far as John was concerned there was nothing more that could be done medically so it was a matter of rehabilitating him as much as possible. The best place for that was Stoke Mandeville Hospital in Buckinghamshire, where he spent eight months. I was only 11, so I came over with my mother and we stayed in a hotel in Earls Court in west London. And, while Mum spent her days at the hospital, I went to a convent school.

At one point the doctors despaired of John ever improving but gradually he began to move rather like a robot, jerky and slow. It took about three years for him to get to the point where he could sit in a chair, then in a wheelchair. Later he was able to stand in a Zimmer frame and go on an exercise bike to build up the muscles in his legs.

Not surprisingly, for the first few years he was sometimes bad-tempered and found it very frustrating when he couldn't do something or make himself understood. He was quite hard to live with for a while as he tried desperately to come to terms with how his life had changed.

He never lost his faith, however, which eventually helped him to accept the situation and he began to get some joy out of life again. His compensation payout was 65,000 Irish pounds, the highest award there had ever been in Ireland for a car crash, and he was able to buy a bungalow and have his independence, albeit with a lot of help.

John loved having his own home and he got very adventurous. He used to push himself up the road to the shops and God help anyone who got in his way as he freewheeled down the hill in his wheelchair at breakneck speed. If there was a do on he insisted on getting up and dancing. He stood in one spot and one of us would hold his hands to keep him steady and move him, like in a jive.

My mother continued to organise everything for him and went back and forth between his house and hers. After a few years he began to have more frequent falls; sometimes his carers arrived in the morning to find him lying on the floor where he had been for several hours. When my mother died 22 years ago there wasn't anybody who could stay with him on a regular basis, and though he was very reluctant to give up his freedom, he was forced to bow to the inevitable and move into a nursing home, where he still lives.

John gets as much out of life as he can under the circumstances. He never moans and doesn't dwell on what might have been. Watching him live his difficult life taught me that you have to reconcile yourself to the things you can't change, otherwise it drives you crazy. As I saw him making the transition from angry young man to acceptance, I admired his courage and determination. I also learnt that you have to enjoy your life today because you might not be able to do so tomorrow.

CHAPTER TWO
FALLING IN LOVE

Throughout my teenage years fun was high on the agenda. My grandfather had left the cottage in County Meath to Mum and she decided to move out there. I was the only one left at home by then so I went with her and had to adapt to the change from the 'big city' to the wilds of the countryside. Dad divided his time between there and his business in Dublin.

I already had friends I had made in the summer holidays and I also found I was an object of interest, having arrived from the big city, so I slotted in easily. It didn't take me long to make more friends and I took happily to rural life. Mum was going up and down to Dublin to help John in his bungalow, so from about the age of 14 I was occasionally left on my own in the cottage.

Mum was unhappy with this no matter how many times I said it was fine so she decided to send me to board at a nearby convent. I loved some of the things about boarding school, but not the rules and restrictions. I was always getting into trouble for one thing or another. After about six months the mother superior, exasperated, called my mother in. 'I really think Kay would be better off as a day girl,' she said.

This suited me much better, not least because I had such a great time at the weekends when there was nearly always a dinner dance in a hotel or a disco in the village hall and a crowd of us would go. There were no buses so we girls would ring each other up beforehand. 'Have you got a date? No? Well I've got one and he has a car so we will pick you up.' We'd dance every dance, which was no mean feat as the jive was the in dance at the time, then get the boy with the car to drive us all home, exhausted but happy.

Besides having fun, your teenage years are when you are supposed to work hard to get the qualifications to set yourself up for life. I was never especially ambitious and didn't have the sense to see it that way. I just took each day as it came and did the minimum necessary to get what I wanted, which was to be a nurse, get married and have lots of children. I didn't think anything about the type of man I would want or how to find the right one. I just assumed it would happen in the natural order of things. I guess the idea of being a nurse came from watching the girls who looked after John, plus my sister, Rosie, was a nurse in England, and it was exciting to think of going there.

In September 1971 I left Ireland to start my nurse's training in the hospital that Rosie worked at in Watford. It was no great wrench; I had heard so much about England and thought it sounded *the* place to be. I had my own little room in the nurses' home attached to the hospital and the other nurses were a great bunch of girls.

My brother, Paddy, ran a pub in the City of London which had a lively trade, especially at lunchtime. I worked there on my days off and loved people watching, studying all the City gents and ladies – it was a side of life quite different to rural Ireland or Watford.

One day, as we were clearing up, a young policeman came through the door. My heart always skipped a beat whenever a policeman turned up unexpectedly, because that is how we got the news about John.

The policeman walked towards me and cracked a gorgeous smile. '*Wow!*' I thought. He was tall and thin – maybe a little too thin – but very good-looking. 'Hello, I am Richard Gilderdale,' he revealed. 'I have just come to check that everything is okay here.' I offered him a drink of juice and we got chatting.

After that he often popped in at closing time to make sure everyone had left and we were not having any trouble. We chattered away as I finished clearing up and it soon became obvious that we got on well and rather liked each other. Paddy was also quite friendly with Richard and sometimes invited him to join us for a Chinese after the pub shut, which was another opportunity for he and I to get to know each other better.

After we had been out like this a few times, Richard invited me to go with him one Sunday to Hayes in Kent to meet his parents. He drove me down there; we took the family dog out for a walk and went for a meal in the local pub. That was our first proper date and then we started going out to dances in Leicester Square or to shows or pop festivals. Or sometimes we just drove to the country and walked and talked.

We had only been going out about three months when I went to Ireland for a week. I had been there a couple of days when I got a letter from Richard. '*Dear Kay, you may be surprised to hear from me so soon…*' he wrote. In the envelope he had enclosed a picture of an engagement ring that he had cut from a magazine. I guess it was meant as a hint about what was to happen next because when I got back he asked me to marry him and I said yes.

It was risky to jump into marriage after we had known each other for such a short time. I was only 18 when we met, 19 when we married, and he was 20. But our marriage did work out for a long time. I felt Richard was good for me: he was sensible and made me stop and think about things in a different way; I was completely carefree and quite imma-ture as I had always had people looking after me.

We were married in a register office in December 1973, and for the first few months of our marriage lived with his parents in their three-bed semi in Hayes. But the commut-ing and the expense of city life were not what we wanted long term so Richard decided to leave the City of London Police and apply to Sussex. He soon got a job in Hastings, which came with its own police house.

This was the first home of our own and when we moved in we were blissfully happy. We had nothing much in the way of furniture so anything we did get pleased us no end. For instance, we both loved music but had nothing to play our records on. Out shopping in Hastings we spotted a second-hand record player with its veneer peeling off so we bought it and got some of that 'teak effect' sticky stuff people used to put on their kitchen worktops. We stuck this on and were mightily chuffed with our smart new music system.

Partly for the money, as police officers were badly paid in those days, and partly because I decided I missed nursing, I applied to restart my training. I was accepted and was just about to start when I got some news I thought they should know about. 'I have just found out I am pregnant,' I announced, trying to control my delighted grin. 'Will that affect my training?' The response was, basically, 'Thank you very much and goodbye' and that was the end of that. There were no equal rights for women in those days.

We hadn't planned on having a baby so soon, but then, we didn't really plan anything. It didn't matter – we were overjoyed. I remember how we laughed and skipped down the street when we came out of the surgery after the doctor had told me the good news. I sailed through pregnancy and Stephen was born in October 1974. Both of us felt absolutely ecstatic and extremely proud of our precious little son. We had very little money but we didn't care at all.

Motherhood suited me; I was still only 20 but I took to it naturally. I was perfectly happy to stay at home with

Stephen, or Steve as we sometimes called him, and didn't mind about the restrictions having a baby put on our lives, maybe because I had had so much freedom as a teenager and because being a mum was the only thing I had ever truly wanted.

Our house was one of a cluster of police houses, which made for a very sociable community. We all understood the strains of the job and were always popping in and out of each other's homes as well as enjoying ourselves at the regular police social events.

Richard liked the idea of being a village policeman and I liked the thought of living properly in the country, so when the post in the East Sussex village of Burwash came up, he applied and was accepted and we moved into the police house there when Stephen was two.

Life as a village bobby and his wife was quite different: we were always on call. Richard knew everybody and everybody knew him and also me as his wife, though I didn't necessarily know them. People came to the door any time of the day or night and would expect an answer. If Richard was out I would do my best to deal with the caller, but I didn't always understand the importance of information I was given. Something that seemed to me to be quite trivial could turn out to be of great significance.

We made some great friends and enjoyed village life very much, although it could be strange on occasions for Richard carrying out his duties as a policeman, arresting somebody one day and socialising with them the next. It doesn't apply so much now, but at that time even I felt a sort of responsibility to behave in a sensible, sober fashion because I was the policeman's wife.

Stephen was two when I found out I was pregnant again. I was absolutely delighted and I was really hoping I would have a girl this time. Although I had once wanted many children, Richard only wanted two and I had agreed though I didn't know what I would do if this second baby was not the little girl I longed for.

Around my due date I thought I was in labour and went into hospital all excited. Nothing much happened over the next few hours. Eventually the doctor said, 'Go home, Mrs Gilderdale. Your baby is not ready to come into the world just yet.' I felt a bit of a fool.

Another couple of weeks went by and nothing happened at all except I got bigger than ever. Then they decided enough was enough. 'You had better come in and we will induce you,' they said. It turned into a long, difficult and painful labour involving a forceps delivery and various complications.

But all that was forgotten when they laid the baby in my arms. As I looked down at the squirming little bundle, my breath caught – it was the little girl that I'd so wanted. I was overwhelmed with delight and love and relief. She weighed a healthy six pounds ten ounces and to me was the most beautiful baby girl I had ever seen. In an instant, my family felt complete. Life could not be more perfect.

CHAPTER THREE

MY LITTLE CHATTERBOX

Lynn was born on 20 September 1977, and grew up to be everything you could ever wish for in a daughter: beautiful, bright, lively, loving, accomplished, eager for life and all the delights it had in store for her. Richard was enchanted by his beautiful baby daughter. All her life she was a daddy's girl and although we were both quite strict with her, she had a way of getting around us, especially her father.

It took a little while to name her. We wanted to find a name that was as pretty as she was so Richard and I pored over many lists searching for just the right one that would also go well with Gilderdale. When we came across Lynette we both thought it was lovely, though when she got a bit older she insisted on being called Lynn.

Lynn was very lively as a little girl, full of mischief – not bad mischief, but she liked playing tricks on us. One day we were out shopping in a huge furniture store and we suddenly realised: 'Where's Lynn?' We looked all over for her, round the shop and outside where there was a busy road. There was no sign and we started to panic. We kept calling her name and told the staff who put out a call over the Tannoy. Eventually, after a good 15 minutes of searching, we found her hiding in a wardrobe.

'Did you not hear us calling?' I demanded, a bit sharply, and she just sat there, killing herself laughing.

'Yes, I did,' she said, grinning.

'So why didn't you come out?' I asked, crossly.

'Because it was funny,' she squealed. 'I could hear everyone calling my name and I had to try really hard not to laugh out loud and be found out.' She was so delighted with her trick, you couldn't stay mad at her for long

I have a photo of her sitting with her chin in her hands on the steps of a villa in Portugal, having a strop. I laugh every time I see it because she was trying so hard to look cross and we were laughing and taking pictures of her. She soon realised she wasn't getting anywhere and gave up on the sulk.

Now when I rerun these two episodes in my mind, I can see why laughter is so important and why later it became an indispensible coping mechanism for us. Sometimes when everything is going wrong or you are in some painful situation, it is truly better to laugh rather than cry.

Lynn was around six months old when I started working as an auxiliary nurse doing short, four- or five-hour shifts two or three days a week. I joined an agency in Tunbridge Wells and they sent me everywhere – to NHS or private hospitals, nursing homes or patients' own homes, anywhere that somebody needed a person to look after them.

With Richard and I working opposite shifts, we didn't need to hire childcare. We worked it out so one of us was always at home. If Richard was on early, I was on late, and so we went on like ships that pass in the night.

We had a few arguments in the beginning. I would leave things ready before I went to work – dinner cooked, the children in their pyjamas, place tidy – then if I came back and found something not done I would nag. But it was just an adjustment period and Richard soon became a real hands-on dad and looked after the children brilliantly. We had all the normal stresses a young family experiences but we were happy and felt pretty blessed with our lives.

I was so pleased to finally have a little girl to dress up. Lynn had some really beautiful little dresses which my mother brought back from her trips to America to visit her sister. They were made of velvet or cotton, satin or silk, with ruching or piping or little puff sleeves and tiered skirts. Pretty embellishments like embroidered flowers made them extra special and they were often finished off with a lace band or a sash tied in a bow at the back.

I wish I had kept some of them but when she grew out of them I gave them to charity shops or passed them on to friends or relatives. She wasn't always in pretty dresses, though, she liked to be a tomboy too and could often be found in Steve's hand-me-down jeans and T-shirts playing swing ball in the garden or hurtling down the longest slide in the park.

Her hair was lovely, long and silky. Sometimes she would practise hairstyles on a toy version of the kind of head trainee hairdressers use to learn on. It had long hair and came with style instructions, hair bands, combs and curlers – she called it Matilda.

'Mummy, please can you do my hair like *this*?' she wheedled, showing me some unusual plait or ponytail she had devised.

'You want your hair like *that*?' I'd query, incredulously.

'Sure. No problem! Just give me a moment to perfect it!'

And she would get a fit of the giggles and say, 'Mmmm... actually, it's okay, Mum. I think I'll wear my hair down today.'

Lynn was blonde until she was six or seven. Her eyes stayed blue for ages too and only gradually changed to a hazel-green. She had a sprinkling of freckles across her nose and cheekbones that came out stronger in the summertime. I loved them; she hated them.

'Look, Mummy, just look at me. I've got thousands more of these horrible things,' she would declare.

'Don't exaggerate. There's only a few more and they look really cute,' I would reply.

'Cute? No way. There must be something I can rub on to make them disappear.'

Before I'd get a chance to answer with some quip or other, she'd find something far more interesting to be doing and off she would go, freckles and all, until the next time.

She and her brother, Steve, played well together and shared many happy times, although of course, like all children, they would sometimes quarrel. Lynn liked organising people and sometimes people just didn't want to be organised.

From the age of three Lynn followed her brother to a playschool in a lovely big, old, country house with a huge garden. It was run by a former teacher who adored children and Steve and Lynn had very happy times with her. Both of them could read and write by the time they left her and started infant school.

We went to see *E.T.* when it came out in 1982 and Lynn, who was five at the time, had her hair in bunches and was wearing a stripy jumper just like the little girl in it, played by Drew Barrymore. Full of excitement on seeing this, Lynn exclaimed: 'Look everyone, she looks just like me. I could do that. Please let me be in a film with E.T.' We all loved the film – I still remember the tears and the laughter and Lynn going all coy when we kept teasing her about being a film star.

The 'E.T.' experience must have made a lasting impression on her because she loved being theatrical and dressing up and dressing up her friends or cousins, smearing their faces with make-up for a laugh. If she had a friend to play they would make-believe all kinds of things or pretend they were somebody famous, recording all their nonsense on a cassette recorder.

Sometimes they performed a play they made up as they went along, using different voices. Or Lynn pretended she was a radio presenter called Maria and her friend played a fictitious famous guest called Jennifer Usafacorn. 'Maria' interviewed 'Jennifer', breaking off now and then to play bits of music. While the music was on the two of them chatted and giggled away in the background. They also told stories and silly jokes like: 'What stops the moon from falling down?' 'Moonbeams!'

They invented funny 'facts of the day' and weather slots. Even the family cat, Lucky, had to do his bit and play a part. This usually entailed him being dressed up in a doll's dress and being fed milk from a baby's bottle, which he cooperated with quite happily. Lynn had a great imagination and I just adored hearing her giggling away.

In the early years, Richard and I moved around a little. When Lynn was a toddler we decided to take the plunge and buy our own house in Burwash. The day we moved in to our neat townhouse, we were blissfully happy again, just as we had been with our first-ever home. This was actually our very own home, even if we did owe the building society every penny, and it was such a special feeling when we closed the front door for the first time and knew we wouldn't have people knocking at all times of the day and night. Living in a rent-free police house you belong to the community, now we only belonged to each other.

We moved again when Lynn was nearly eight. We had always liked the village of Stonegate, which had an excellent Church of England primary school, and luckily enough a bungalow in a pleasant cul-de-sac came up for sale. We looked at it and fell in love with it and this is where Lynn spent the rest of her life.

Just like my childhood home, there was rarely a quiet moment in this house. Lynn was a real little chatterbox. She had to tell you about everything that had gone on at school, who said what to whom, without even taking a breath. 'Mum, you'd never guess what happened in Mr King's class today. Sam sent me a note to say that Martin really liked me and that Sam really liked Nicola and Mr King saw us giggling and read the note and Sam was sent out to stand in the corridor…'

And later at secondary school, 'Mum, do you know we had the most brilliant lesson with Mrs Carmichael today. I really enjoy her classes and music was so cool I want to join…Oh, and is it okay for Heather to come around because we had a big argument about something she said which is absolutely not right?' Her river of exuberance flowed on and on.

Steve, not being quite so compelled to share every detail of his daily experiences with Mum and Dad and his little sister, didn't discuss all the finer points of his school day. Lynn was having none of this and would be a real pest until she felt satisfied that she had extracted from him what he did, how he did it and if he liked it.

Both the children were very energetic, active and loved the outdoors. As a family we went out on cycle rides together or went for walks and picnics. In the summers we practically lived on the beach at Eastbourne. Lots of our family photos are of Lynn and Steve in the sea because they adored messing about in the water. It was fortunate they enjoyed playing in the sea so much as we didn't have the kind of money that would have allowed us to splash out on expensive entertainment.

Lynn and Steve's childhood was like mine in that we all enjoyed being outdoors and being very active, but the similarities ended there. I was just 23 when Lynn was born while my mother was 44 when she had me. My parents were not involved in what I did, whereas Richard and I spent most of our spare time with our children and brought them up with more structure and discipline than I had experienced.

They started swimming lessons in Eastbourne when they were very young, partly because Richard's mother taught swimming at a private school there, and became very strong swimmers.

They joined the sailing club and learnt how to roll a canoe, how to sail a Topper – an 11-foot single-handed sailing dinghy ideal for children – rigging the sails, steering, tying knots and so on. Later on they did windsurfing too. Sometimes freezing, their teeth would chatter with the cold, but they didn't mind. Richard and I would sit on the beach, enjoying watching the two of them totally absorbed in what they were doing and having a great time.

We bought a motorised dinghy that we took with us on our holidays to the South of France. One summer's day we set out in good weather and headed for a beauty spot we had heard of about an hour's sail away. As we approached we had to navigate our way through a lot of yachts and small vessels anchored close together.

The weather suddenly changed and the wind picked up. The sea became choppy and all the little boats were being thrown around in the water. We couldn't use the motor for fear of bashing into the yachts so Richard rowed into the beach. Suddenly, one of the oars was whipped out of his hand and went bobbing off on the waves. He, Steve and I sat there, frozen in shock, thinking, '*What are we going to do now?*'

But Lynn didn't hesitate an instant. Before we could stop her, she jumped up, divéd over the side of the boat, swam after the oar, brought it back, handed it to Richard and saved the day. That was her; she just acted and got it sorted while the rest of us were still thinking. She was physically confident, quick thinking and a bit too fearless for my peace of mind.

Her other great love was ballet and modern dance. She started classes in Burwash village hall, with Jane Coleman, when she was six and adored it so much she was soon going three times a week. She had excellent posture and she learnt to go up and stay *en pointe* very quickly.

With the ballet and acting in school plays, she was in so many productions I lost count. I remember the *Wizard of Oz*, and she was the White Rabbit in *Alice in Wonderland*. I sometimes made the costumes – they looked okay so long as you didn't examine them too closely. There was one where Lynn and friend Liz had the main parts and Lynn was in a bright yellow dress with her hair all fluffed out and long nails. She looked like a strange cross between a witch and a fairy. Generally Lynn didn't get the leading parts but she was usually fairly prominent and anyway she was happy just being part of it all.

There was a time when she and her friend, Chloe, had to come up with a ballet routine for a choreography competition and choose appropriate classical music to go with it. They worked really hard together, taking turns to go to each other's houses to practise. They listened to pieces of classical music over and over, trying to match the right notes to a particular movement.

As they argued, Lynn adopted her most convincing voice. 'No, that is not right, it's definitely missing a beat. Can we do it again, Chloe?' she persisted until they finally managed to reach an agreement. I went about my housework, pretending I was not watching, but I could not help quietly revelling in their love, enthusiasm and appreciation of music and dance.

When they came closer to settling on their performance they asked Chloe's mum Wendy and me to watch and be critical. 'Come on, Mum, I need you to be honest and tell me what you really think. Don't try to be kind. Tell me what I'm doing wrong,' Lynn demanded. And I didn't try to be kind but the absolute truth is that these two girls not only knew more than I knew about these classics, they also each had talent that enthralled me. I believed in constructive criticism but I didn't have any to offer; to me their dance was a beauty to behold. The competition judges agreed – they won the trophy.

Lynn never actually wanted to be a ballerina. There was an annual trophy for the person who performed the best over the year and Chloe, who eventually won a place at the Royal Ballet School, usually got that with Lynn a close runner-up.

Everything Lynn did was mostly driven by her; we didn't push too much. For instance, when she wanted to learn the piano and clarinet, she asked, 'If I learn these instruments do I have to do exams? I would really rather just do them for enjoyment. I'd hate if the pressure of exams took that away.' I told her she didn't have to if she didn't want to. She got up to Grade Five but didn't take the exams.

Steve was excellent on the violin and was told to practise every night, which he didn't because he had lots of other interests. A supply teacher at primary school got exasperated and called me in to tell me: 'You have to make your son practise more on the violin. He could be really good.' I said: 'But he doesn't want to. It's one of a number of things he enjoys and he doesn't want to spend all his spare time on one thing.'

She was not happy and reported me to the headmaster but when I went to see him, he agreed with me that Steve was outstanding at lots of things and should be allowed the time to pursue the many different activities he enjoyed.

The same philosophy applied to Lynn. There was never any pressure to practise; she did so because she loved to and I took great joy in listening to it. Her piano was in her bedroom, she would go in and close the door and this wonderful music would fill the house. Sometimes she would play the same piece over and over again, trying to perfect it, but even when she did that, I never tired of listening.

The clarinet was a bit more like hard work. She had to be disciplined in the beginning when the sounds that seeped through her bedroom walls were more like a banshee wailing than the notes of sweet music. But she stuck with it. The first time she played a perfect 'Stranger on the Shore', I cried. I still do when I hear that haunting tune.

Even though she was full of fun, if you gave Lynn a responsibility, she took it seriously – she had more sense than I had at the same age. In primary school she became a prefect and also captain of the netball team.

Academically, I wanted to be stricter with my children than my parents had been with me. I wanted them to fulfil their potential. Steve was always very self-motivated whereas I had to prompt Lynn to do her homework. Once she got down to it, she did apply herself and was quite particular if something wasn't just right and would do it again. She loved history and English and religious studies.

Lynn had four best friends at school, Michaela, Laura, Gemma and Nicola, but lots of other friends too – there was one next door and another a few doors down who called for each other and played in the Close together. Other friends lived in villages around the area or in Tunbridge Wells so ferrying children around and having her friends over for sleepovers was the norm.

When she got to 13 she wanted more independence. 'Mum, can't I go on the bus to town to meet my friends?' she pleaded. At first I said no, worried about her safety. I seemed to have forgotten how much freedom I had as a child and teenager with no ill effects.

While I was thinking about it she got a bit impatient and grumpy. 'Oh come on, Mum. I'm a teenager now after all, not a baby. I'm quite capable of looking after myself. It would be so unfair if you don't let me. All my friends are allowed,' she pleaded.

This may or may not have been true but, either way, I knew she was right. I talked it over with Richard and we realised that it was probably time we let go a bit. Our little girl was growing up and she had to live her life.

Some of my happiest memories from that time were when Lynn was by her dad's side. She and Richard had a similar sense of humour and he was always messing around when we were out. He might suddenly burst into song and do a funny walk while going down a crowded street. Or we might be in a clothes shop looking for a new dress for Lynn or trousers for Steve and he would pick up a woman's blouse, hold it up to his chest and shout out in a really loud voice, 'Lynn, don't you think this is just *perfect* for me?'

Everyone would turn around and look. 'Oh Dad, you are *so* embarrassing,' Lynn would mutter under her breath and she and Steve would move swiftly away, pretending they didn't belong to this strange man. We had a lot of laughs together as a family but as she got towards her teens, Lynn was not so amused. 'Dad, stop it. I will never come out with you again,' she'd whisper, fiercely. She didn't really mean it; she would look at me as she said it and grin.

Her first love was a boy from down the road, a nice chap, with a lively character. 'He really likes me. He wants to buy me a present for my birthday!' she told me excitedly one day. The next day she showed me the present – a heart-shaped locket. She was really chuffed. 'He's lovely,' she sighed. 'He's the best person in the world. I love him. What do you think I should buy him for his birthday?' Eventually, they went on to new adventures and new loves.

She didn't have a fixed ambition about what she wanted to do for work when she grew up. 'Maybe I will be a music teacher,' she sometimes mused after she had particularly enjoyed a lesson. She also spoke about becoming a nurse but I think that was only because I was one. The one thing she was sure about – just like me – was that she wanted to have a family.

It was very important to her, more than anything else. She would drop it into everyday conversation. '*When* I am married and have children…' she'd say. It was never: '*If* I get married'. She loved the fact that she came from a big Irish family. 'Family is the most important and precious thing in life,' she proclaimed.

Lynn was growing up, becoming a proper teenager and loving it. She was not frightened of anything; she was eager to plunge into whatever life had to offer. She still loved being with us too, doing all the activities we had always enjoyed. We had a really happy life. We didn't realise just how happy it was until we lost it.

CHAPTER FOUR

SICKNESS
TAKES HOLD

It was autumn term; an ordinary morning in the Gilderdale house. Terry Wogan was chatting away on the radio in the kitchen. Richard had left for an early shift, I had got up at about 7.30 a.m., dressed for work and got breakfast ready: a poached egg for Steve, cornflakes, toast and Marmite for Lynn, tea for everyone.

Breakfast over, Steve and Lynn collected their school bags and left the house at 8.25 a.m. to walk to the village to catch the school bus. Steve was 17 and doing fine in the sixth form, Lynn was 14 and in her second year at the same mixed comprehensive and she didn't have any problems, except for chatting and giggling too much in class.

Friends of Lynn's lived in the Close and came out of their houses to join her as the two passed by. I could hear their bright young voices mingling, happily starting another day of teenage nattering. Everything was normal and happy; I didn't have a care in the world.

It was in the early afternoon of that day, 13 November 1991, that someone popped their head round the door of the room at Burwash Laundry where I was at work on some mundane admin task and said: 'Kay, there's a phone call for you in reception.' I went through and picked up the receiver to find it was the secretary at Lynn's school.

'Please could you come and pick Lynn up,' she said. 'She is not feeling well.'

I never would have guessed that that call marked the end of the life my family had known until then. At the time I didn't think anything of it and certainly wasn't worried. It was not unusual for a parent to be called to the school because their child had come down with some bug. I got permission to cut short my shift, picked up my coat and drove round there.

I arrived at the secretary's office to find Lynn looking pale and sorry for herself. 'I'm sorry to drag you from work but I feel sick and faint,' she said.

'Oh, that's okay,' I replied. 'Maybe you're getting the flu that your dad has just had,' I said.

That morning Lynn had had the BCG jab that all teenagers are given to protect them from tuberculosis. She had begun to feel ill an hour or so later but at the time I didn't make any connection between the two.

I brought her home and she lay on the settee for most of the afternoon feeling grotty. But the next morning she said she didn't feel too bad so I sent her off once more to catch the school bus.

Again it was early afternoon when a call came telling me she had been sick and I immediately left work to pick her up. She had the rest of the week off but by the weekend she thought she was okay again and went swimming as usual. As she headed up the pool, her usual strong strokes faltered as she suddenly felt like she was going to pass out. Seeing she was in difficulty, her swimming instructor quickly got her to the side of the pool.

'Ooh, I feel really weird,' Lynn groaned as she sat beside the pool, white-faced and shaky. I gave her a piece of choco-late, hoping it would give her a quick energy boost; it didn't. It crossed my mind that she might be taking after me. As a teenager I used to faint frequently. But the difference was that I was essentially well, whereas I was beginning to realise Lynn was not.

Then she really did get flu and oh, how it raged like nothing I had ever seen before. Sweats, high temperature, terrible aches in all her limbs. She had not completely recovered from that when she got bronchitis. That was followed by tonsillitis, then glandular fever and then another chest infection. She was on strong antibiotics for months; it was like her immune system was shot.

I grew more and more worried by all these infections she was getting, one on top of the other, and the fact she couldn't shake any of them off without the use of antibi-otics. We tried making her do without them for a while but she just got a lot sicker.

When she was at her worst she stayed in bed but if she felt up to it at all she came to sit and chat to me while I did some household chore. She didn't like being on her own.

She missed her friends terribly but when they called round she was too ill to see them. Even on good days ordinary tasks like getting up and dressed took longer. Everything had slowed down; everything was an effort.

I went to the school and fetched work for her, which she tackled when she felt able to concentrate. Richard and I pushed her a bit to do more; we got her out in the garden whenever it was fine enough and took her on short outings to the local village or town.

But Lynn was no longer the daughter I sent off on the school bus on that November day and my stomach was in a constant knot of worry. By now she was suffering from total exhaustion, dizziness, a permanent severe sore throat, headaches, pain in all her limbs, swollen glands and constant infections that somehow seemed to have total and free access to her body. She was also growing increasingly sensitive to bright light or any kind of loud noise.

I hated to see her like this and could not understand why it was happening or how I could help her. Whenever she seemed a little bit better I seized on any opportunity to encourage her to do some of the things we used to enjoy so much together. I was so anxious for her to feel normal again.

Foolishly, I thought I could override her noise and light sensitivity with a spot of retail therapy. All teenage girls love shopping and Lynn was usually no exception. Just before Christmas the new Victoria Centre opened in Tunbridge Wells and I suggested a trip. 'I don't really feel up to it, Mum,' she said.

I tried to jolly her along. 'Oh, you'll be fine when we get there. It will make you feel better,' I insisted, hiding my dismay at her words as best I could. How wrong I was.

The new mall was absolutely gorgeous, shining and smart with brightly coloured Christmas lights and carols playing over the Tannoy. I parked the car and led her in, chattering away inanely about what present we could get for whom to cover up my anxiety. Lynn summoned up a smile and tried to join in to please me. I glanced over to her and saw her looking at a dazzling window display and literally flinching in pain. 'I'm sorry. It's too noisy. It's too bright. I can't stand it. Please take me home,' she cried. I realised with a sinking heart that a treat the old, healthy Lynn would have loved was now pure torture for her poor sick body.

When Christmas Day came Lynn had a rare and precious day where she was able, despite feeling so very ill, to enjoy a little normal frivolity. We sat down to dinner, pulled the Christmas crackers and read the silly jokes out to each other, laughing with our party hats on.

After dinner Steve challenged Lynn to a game of Uno – a card game that isn't too demanding energy-wise. Before it ended Lynn needed to rest and went to her room for a sleep but afterwards she managed to join us again to watch *Only Fools and Horses*, something that had become a Christmas tradition in our house. It was a lovely day that allowed me a brief respite from my sense of rising panic but Lynn paid the price for those few hours of fun: for days afterwards she was completely wiped out.

In between the infections she tried to go back to school. She was still pale and had lost her usual energy but I thought it would be good for her to see her friends and do ordinary things. I took her there twice. Each time, I got the dreaded phone call in the middle of the day to come and pick her up. The last time was in January 1992, two months after she fell ill. When I got her in the car she broke into a storm of tears. 'Oh Mum, what's the matter with me? Why can't I get better? I am missing so much school!' she cried.

She was never to return to school again.

Not long afterwards I was in the living room when I heard a thump in the corridor leading to her bedroom. I rushed out and found Lynn had collapsed unconscious on the floor. She came round quite quickly and had not hurt herself but she was feeling very unwell.

It was about that time that she wrote me a note as she lay on her bed one day. I was shocked by her handwriting. Normally her writing was very neat but this was scrawled messily across the page. It was devastating to see that she had so little strength she couldn't even control a pen properly.

Hello, Mum. How are you? I hope you're okay. Today the weather, so I've been told, is sunny and warm. I haven't really noticed though because I'm still not very well, in fact, pretty awful, but never mind. Sorry about the writing. It's easier to write like this when I haven't

got much energy. I don't know what's wrong with me.
Love Lynn.

At the time I didn't understand the significance of it, I said something like, 'Oh, that's lovely. Thank you for writing me a note.' When I thought back to that day later on, I realised she must have been beginning to get really frightened. To write down how awful you are feeling, to someone who is there in the next room, shows how much you want those close to you to understand how very sick and scared you feel.

I was starting to be afraid that there was some horrible, serious, underlying problem that was making Lynn so vulnerable, like cancer of some kind, maybe leukaemia. Our local GP, Dr Jane Woodgate, did a series of blood tests but they came back saying that there was nothing wrong with her.

It was incredibly puzzling and completely frustrating. Questions kept chasing each other round and round my head: What can it be? Why don't the tests show something? Lynn was never like this before. They have to be missing something. Where can we get more help?

Before long Lynn was passing out regularly. She could be walking across the living room to fetch something from the kitchen when her legs would suddenly buckle from under her and she'd hit the floor, often bruising herself in the process. When she came to, she'd feel nauseous, dizzy and confused.

My work generously allowed me to take as much time off as I wanted but I tried not to take advantage so sometimes would rely on Steve to look after his sister. He was terrific but he was only a teenager and he was frightened by Lynn's symptoms. We all were. If she passed out when he was with her he'd ring me immediately. 'Mum, I don't know what to do, Lynn's collapsed again,' he'd tell me worriedly, and I'd rush home.

By February she was passing out every day, was totally drained of energy, couldn't concentrate on her schoolwork and was growing increasingly confused. Her throat was red raw and very painful and she had awful headaches. Walking any distance became impossible and she was in so much pain in her limbs and joints that she cried out in the night.

Richard and I sat with her for hours, trying to comfort her. 'What's wrong with me?' she sobbed. 'Why aren't I getting better? Please, please help me.'

We would hug her and offer pathetic reassurances we were finding it ever harder to believe. 'You're just having a run of bad luck getting all these bugs one after the other,' I soothed. 'We'll get on top of it, you'll see. Dr Woodgate says you'll be okay. It's just taking its time.'

My beloved lively chatterbox had now missed so much school that we had to get a home tutor, Mrs James, to come in for a couple of hours a day twice a week. This was a bit of a blow for Lynn; she was totally fed up with staying at home alone all the time and fed up of feeling sick. It wasn't that she felt sorry for herself; like anyone in her situation she was desperate to know why she was feeling so rotten.

I couldn't stand not being able to find anybody to give us the answer. The stress was so constant and draining that I could hardly eat or sleep. Richard was just as upset and worried as I was. We were all running on nervous energy. It was dreadful to watch my beautiful, feisty daughter losing her faculties one by one; she was so clearly ill, yet nothing showed up on tests to give a reason for it and no one knew what to do. All we could do was stand by and watch, feeling utterly helpless and desolate, while the only thing anyone said to us was: 'Wait a little while longer.'

One Sunday Lynn had an especially bad time. She was just getting over tonsillitis when all her glands swelled up and her temperature control went haywire: she was raging hot one minute, freezing the next. She had been crying most of the night, racked with pain throughout her body.

By the morning, I was absolutely desperate. I felt so sorry for her suffering and was exhausted from lack of sleep that only added to the awful anxiety and bewilderment that were my constant companions ever since Lynn had fallen ill. I thought to myself, '*This* can't *go on. We can't wait any longer. The doctor* has *to do something.*' Our lively, healthy girl had been dreadfully sick for over two and a half months and it was *not* going to be okay. I knew there was something terribly wrong.

First thing that morning I jumped in the car and drove to the surgery to catch Dr Woodgate on her way in. She could see the state I was in but she said she couldn't see me then. She gave me an appointment and promised to do more tests on Lynn. 'Try not to worry too much. It will probably turn out to be glandular fever,' she urged.

A week or so later I was in the kitchen preparing a casserole for the evening meal. I could see Lynn sitting at our dining table in the living room cutting out pictures and putting them in a folder. I heard a thud: Lynn must have got up to stroke Lucky, who was stretched out on the windowsill, and then collapsed in a heap on the floor.

I rushed over. This time was different to her other faints; her whole body was jerking in violent spasms. She seemed to be having trouble breathing. I swept her into my arms, trying to still her flailing arms and legs. 'Lynn, Lynn, wake up!' I cried but she was unresponsive. I grabbed the phone and called Richard and he immediately phoned for an ambulance.

Though it was awful to see her stretchered off in an ambulance, it was also a relief because I thought that in hospital they might be able to find out what was wrong. She was taken to the Kent and Sussex Hospital in Tunbridge Wells, where they kept her in for a couple of nights to run blood tests and a chest X-ray. She was glad to be in there – it gave her hope they would solve the mystery of what was happening to her.

When we arrived to find out the results, half fearful that we would hear something dreadful and half hopeful that at last we could start her on some effective treatment, we encountered an attitude that we were to find all too common over the coming years and which was to make Lynn's and our ordeal ten times worse.

The doctor in charge of her case called us into his office. It seemed that once again the tests had not found any cause for Lynn's condition. 'She hasn't been in school since November? Nearly three months? Why?' he demanded in a challenging tone.

'She has had one bug after another,' I explained.

'What about when she didn't have the bugs?' he persisted.

'She has still been very sick between the bugs. She tried to go back but each time she had to come home again,' I pointed out.

It was clear that he didn't believe us. 'It's disgraceful,' he barked. 'Get her back to school. Her tests are fine. There is nothing wrong with her.'

We were literally astounded by his attitude, not to mention furious. Just because his scientific tests did not reveal the cause of Lynn's illness he had made up his mind she was school-phobic or something else was going on, instead of listening to his patient and seeing for himself the symptoms she was experiencing. He was insulting us as well, treating us as if we were terrible parents. Did he really think we would keep her at home if she wasn't sick?

But worse than all this was the crushing disappointment. We were consumed with terror and distress and had gone to the hospital believing in the expertise of doctors and longing for some explanation, and in return all we got was scepticism. The doctor didn't believe that our daughter was terribly ill. We were dismayed.

The one useful outcome of that episode was that Lynn was referred to a paediatrician. We had medical insurance with reduced premiums through the police so we decided to go private to speed things up. Towards the end of February we took her to Pembury Hospital near Tunbridge Wells.

On the day of the appointment, Lynn was very low. She was quiet and pale, feeling unwell, exhausted and deeply despondent. She sat wrapped in her winter coat, giving short answers to the consultant's questions and not volunteering anything. I think she was scared but didn't want to admit it.

A week later we went back for the results. The consultant looked pretty pleased with himself. 'You will be happy to know I am able to make a diagnosis of what I think the problem is. Lynn has got ME,' he announced. Turning to Lynn, he went on brightly, 'You are lucky because you have got a very fashionable illness.'

Perhaps he meant it kindly, but telling her she was 'lucky' made us wince then and has rankled ever since as we watched her suffer from this devastating illness. 'I've seen other young people with ME and they are just like you,' he reassured her. 'They come in with their heavy coats on and their pale faces, not wanting to talk. And they all get better. We will put you on a programme and you will be fine.'

ME stands for myalgic encephalomyelitis. Myalgia means muscle pain and encephalomyelitis means inflammation of the brain and spinal cord. I had heard of it because a few other children at Lynn's school had it, including a boy whose mother I spoke to occasionally. I thought it was some kind of post-viral tiredness but other than that I didn't know much about it.

I actually felt cheered at the time. At last we had a name for this horrible thing that was making Lynn so ill. I didn't think the diagnosis of ME was as bad as some of the life-threatening conditions, like cancer or leukaemia, that had been swirling round my head and now we could start looking for the right treatments, or so I thought.

I had never come across ME while I was nursing so decided I had better find out more about it. I dug around and soon discovered that when it was referred to in the media it was usually called 'chronic fatigue syndrome, also known as yuppie flu'. It was probably this nickname of 'yuppie flu' that the doctor was referring to when he talked about it being a 'very fashionable' illness.

I read on and found out that the nickname 'yuppie flu' was dreamt up by the American magazine, *Newsweek*, in 1990 and reflected the complete misconception that it was a form of burn-out suffered by 1980s City types or highly strung women. I thought this certainly didn't apply to Lynn as she wasn't old enough to be a yuppie and anyway we lived a simple life. We weren't wealthy or into designer clothes or consumerism. Lynn didn't fit the description at all.

I also found out that the World Health Organisation had recognised that ME was a neurological disease way back in 1969 but that the ignorant attitude that it was more to do with stress or psychological problems, rather than having a physical cause, still persisted among many health professionals and respected medical journalists.

Finally we were given a form of treatment to try and I was determined to make Lynn stick with it. The paediatrician put her on a programme of 'graded exercise' in which her day was divided up into chunks for different activities so that she did a little bit of everything, like school work, social time and walking for exercise. Even if she had been awake all night, screaming in pain, I was told not to let her lie in so her body clock did not go out of sync.

As a nurse, I knew that this was what you usually did with other illnesses so I blinded myself to her suffering and did my best to make her follow the doctor's advice. Lynn was already finding it increasingly difficult to walk any distance. Sometimes she couldn't manage to get from the living room to her bedroom, yet I believed it would be good for her to follow the programme.

Part of it was to walk every day for about 20 minutes, which she found increasingly hard to do. I insisted she make it as far as the end of the Close no matter how bad she was feeling. It was only 30 metres or so. I could not understand how she would not be able to do it.

Richard or I went with her. I'd put my arm around her waist and she'd lean against me, dragging her legs like a dead weight. It was heartbreaking to have to prop up this pale, floppy girl who just three months earlier had been flying along this road on her roller skates.

'My legs don't want to do this. It's really hard,' she'd complain, but I kept encouraging her, telling her to keep trying, telling her the consultant knew best. After a couple of weeks of this, by the time we turned round at the end of the Close to come back she could barely make her legs obey the command from her brain to move. I had to half carry her to the door then drag her across the living room to flop on the settee.

I bitterly regret having forced Lynn to do more than she felt capable of because I later found out that not only does it not work with ME patients, it usually makes them worse. Above everything else, patients need rest, especially in the early stages. I beat myself up about this for years until I realised I did not have the energy to spare on feeling guilty. I needed every vestige of my mental strength to care for Lynn so I had to learn to forgive myself for following the advice of the 'experts'.

One day when her tutor was leaving at the end of a lesson, Lynn stayed on the settee instead of getting up as she usually did to see her out. 'Why didn't you see Mrs James out?' I asked her.

'Mum, I can't feel my legs! I can't stand up!' she cried.

I went cold inside and a wave of panic threatened to engulf me but I forced myself to pretend to be calm. 'You're exhausted,' I said. 'Sleep a while and you'll be fine.'

She lay her head down on the arm of the sofa and went into a deep sleep. When she woke, she could feel her legs again. I breathed a sigh of relief but the deep fear that gripped my stomach had not abated. I lived in a state of continual suspense, waiting for the next disaster.

The consultant had advised Lynn to keep up her social contact so I invited her friends round one at a time. They were more than happy to come and Lynn would be over-joyed to see them, but shortly after they arrived, she'd become exhausted and too ill to go on. Her friend, seeing how poorly she was, would say: 'I'll go now; I'll come back another time. Lovely to see you. Get better soon. We miss you.' Lynn felt embarrassed that she was not even capable of having a girly chat with her best friends. I had to go some-where by myself and weep at seeing the one-time champion chatterbox so severely altered.

It was all so strange and so very different to the life we had been used to with Lynn that we found it terribly diffi-cult to understand or to know what to do for the best. If it was a sunny day we would carry her out into the back garden. 'You *have* to be out in the sunshine. It will do you good,' I gently insisted. All my instincts told me that sunshine and the beauty of nature would help her heal.

But Lynn begged us to carry her back inside. 'I just can't stand it. Please take me in. I can't look at light. It hurts me,' she moaned.

'But how can it hurt you?' I asked, completely puzzled. Yet I saw that it did, severely, and that sound hurt her too.

She would go 'Shhh,' when we were just talking normally and the music that she once loved so much now hurt her.

Once we were out in the garden and an aeroplane flew overhead. She winced with pain and clamped her hands over her ears. As it came closer the noise caused her such agony that she passed out for a few seconds. I rushed over and scooped her up. I felt so sorry for her and so powerless. As a mother I yearned to make her suffering go away, to make everything right for her, but none of the usual rules applied in this illness. How could I protect her from the sound of an aircraft passing overhead?

Lynn's illness was progressing with terrifying speed. Her fainting episodes developed into horrendous fits that lasted for hours. You'd be talking to her or she'd be doing something she enjoyed, like reading a magazine or watching TV, and suddenly her eyes would flicker and roll back in her head, and her body would be racked by violent spasms: her legs thrashed, her fists clenched and her arms twisted around in all directions. It was absolutely dreadful.

Richard, Steve and I were completely traumatised by watching her relentless suffering and shocking deterioration and the utter helplessness that we felt. We talked endlessly about what we could do to help her, which was exhausting and demoralising because we had absolutely no answers.

We tried to think of ways to make her more comfortable. For instance, when she went into spasms, her nails dug deep into her palms. Even when she came round, her fists did not unclench straight away and she was left with painful red marks. In anxious discussion somebody suggested buying fingerless gloves to protect her palms. I rushed out the next day to find some. It was pathetically little to do for her but I was glad to be doing something.

Steve hated seeing the sister he had had such happy times with reduced to this awful state and wanted to help. Richard and I talked openly in front of him but we didn't want to burden him too much so we encouraged him to go in his room and listen to his music through headphones so he would not hear her crying.

Life for Steve had changed completely too. We never again went anywhere together as a family. There was not much we could do about it but we tried to be semi-normal sometimes. Richard started teaching him to drive and we encouraged him to go out with his friends and let his hair down.

There were mornings Lynn couldn't get up after being awake in the night with pain or sickness. And the more we pushed her to do her exercise, the more frequently she was unable to use her legs. We started with two walks a day, which we had to reduce to one, then she could not even manage that.

While she was doing the 'graded exercise' she kept a diary in a red, spiral-bound exercise book to record her programme of activity for the doctor. Written in blue biro in Lynn's firm, round, still childish hand, a typical entry showed how her life became a timetable of mundane tasks.

But while they may sound trivial to an ordinary person, each and every little thing was a big ordeal for Lynn. She found the simplest things so difficult, which left her completely distraught.

WEDNESDAY, 26TH FEBRUARY:

10.25 a.m.: had to be woken up, having slept all night. I still felt very sleepy.

11.30 a.m.: got up and dressed having had one slice of toast and a cup of tea for breakfast.

1.00 p.m.: had a pasty for lunch.

2.20 p.m.: walked to the shop and back in 15 mins.

3.00 p.m.: got a pain in my chest and then I had difficulty breathing. Felt sick and was shaking a bit. Lasted for about 20 mins. After that attack I felt very tired and dizzy.

4.25 p.m.: started a project on Mozart. Didn't find 10 mins too much.

6.30 p.m.: had another attack. It started off with a bad pain in my chest which got worse and then I had difficulty breathing. I felt sick and started shaking. It was worse than this afternoon. It lasted for about 45 mins.

8.15 p.m.: had vegetable soup and bread for dinner.

10.00 p.m.: was very tired, so I went to bed. After my 6.30 p.m. attack I found it hard to walk and couldn't do so without help.

Reading the entries she wrote about her attacks was terrifying in itself, so I couldn't imagine how scared Lynn was.

I was gasping for breath and the pain in my chest was excruciating. I was crying out and felt very agitated. It lasted for about 25 mins.

Gradually, as she became sicker and sicker, Lynn's entries became shorter and shorter. She constantly complained of a sore throat, how her whole body ached and how she was always fainting or having fits. Sometimes, she could only manage a single line:

While I was walking down the hall, again my legs gave way and I hit the floor pretty hard or I couldn't walk so Mum and Stephen carried me to the sofa.

Her last entry was on Wednesday, 18 March 1992, when she was 14 and a half years old. It ends:

3 p.m.: walked to the end of the Close, got back at 3.10 p.m.

After that she was too feeble to even lift a pen. My little girl was losing all control of her body and no one seemed to have any idea how to stop it happening.

CHAPTER FIVE

CONFUSION AND PANIC

It wasn't just Lynn who kept a diary. In the midst of the confusion, I found myself reaching for a pen to make some sort of sense of what was going on, or to find some pattern that might provide the key to the mystery of what was ravaging her body.

'*Got wheelchair*,' says the first entry. It's a very bald statement for what was a devastating event – picking up a wheelchair from Eastbourne General Hospital because our 14-year-old daughter had become paralysed. We had been arguing about it for a while because she hated the idea of being in a wheelchair.

I hated it too and felt sick at the thought. When we went on our family bike rides, I was always the one at the back puffing away, trying to keep up with Steve and Lynn as their strong young legs flashed in the distance ahead. Now Lynn was weak and helpless and I would have to push her around. By this time nothing was working properly; it was like her whole brain was misfiring. And all the time the area on her arm where she'd had her BCG jab was red, raised and painful.

That first night after she got her wheelchair, I lifted her out of it and got her into bed then fell into bed myself soon afterwards, worn out with the shock and horror of it all. It seemed like no sooner was I asleep than I heard a thumping and thrashing from Lynn's room. Grabbing my dressing gown, I ran along the corridor to find her convulsed in a fit, her head thrown back, her body shaking violently and her arms lashing out. I stood by the side of her bed to stop her falling out and quickly propped pillows against the wall on the other side to stop her flailing arms bashing into it. It would have hurt her if I had tried to hold her still. All I could do was stand there, helpless, just being with her and trying my best to make sure she didn't come to any harm.

Richard stumbled into the room. 'What's happening?' he asked.

'She's having another fit. I will stay with her. You try to get some rest so you can take over later,' I urged him.

After about half an hour the spasms died down and she came to. Then she started crying out, 'Oh, it hurts. My head hurts. My throat is sore. The pain is awful. Please make it stop. Mum, Dad, help me, I'm frightened. What's happening to me? What's the matter with me? Please make it go away.'

Weak with exhaustion, I sat down. My arms ached to wrap her in a big, warm, comforting hug. I longed to stroke her and soothe her as only a mother can. But I had to force myself to keep my hands still; everything hurt her so much, she just couldn't even bear my touch.

'Shhh. It will be all right. Calm down. Try to sleep,' I whispered, fighting to keep calm myself and swallowing my own tears. She continued sobbing for what seemed like hours and then, to my horror, slipped into another violent fit. I jumped up and stood once again by her bedside, watching her thrashing around, unable to do anything to help her. I could hardly bear it. It was so terrible to see her like this.

Hearing the thumping, Richard rushed back into the bedroom. 'Call the doctor,' I cried desperately. 'Her body can't take any more of this. She needs some rest.'

Half an hour later the duty doctor arrived and injected her with a sedative. We would have many nights the same, with Richard and I taking it in turns to keep Lynn safe while the other tried to snatch a few minutes of sleep, then calling the doctor when we had reached the end of our tether.

The next day Lynn woke late in the morning and was very groggy. I managed to get her up and wheeled her into the living room, where she sat looking bewildered. I pressed my hand into her left leg. 'Can you feel that?' I asked. She shook her head miserably. 'Or that?' I asked again, pressing the right leg this time.

'No, I can't feel anything.'

I felt panic-stricken and desolate. Was this going to be permanent? She could barely sit up straight. Her top half had gone floppy as if her bones had lost their strength. Suddenly her head fell backwards like a rag doll's. What kind of illness made a 14-year-old girl lose all the power in her muscles and nerves? I could barely breathe with the stress and anxiety of it all. I didn't know what to do, where to turn.

At around 6.30 in the evening, she passed out. I sat on the sofa, stroking her forehead, talking to her, desperately wanting to hug her and comfort her as over the next two hours she drifted in and out of consciousness. When the fit finally passed she opened her eyes and looked around vacantly. 'Where am I? What's going on?' she whispered.

'You are at home, in the living room. You have been unconscious. It's okay now,' I replied softly.

By this time Lynn was unable to follow the graded exercise regime. She had been to see the consultant paediatrician at Pembury a few times, taking her diary. He didn't allow Richard and me to come in the room with her and she felt the consultant was quite rude to her. He basically told her it was her attitude that was the problem. 'You can make yourself a lot better if you do as I say,' he declared. In other words, 'Pull yourself together and do more.'

She told him that she had been doing her best to follow his instructions but she was just feeling worse. No matter what he said about knowing about ME, he was obviously treating it as a psychological condition, not a physical illness, as he was only offering a management regime and no medical treatment. 'He doesn't believe me,' Lynn said, which she found doubly upsetting on top of feeling so vile.

It dawned on me that the usual avenues you go down when someone is ill – going to your GP for referral to a specialist at hospital – were not going to give us the answers and I had to start trying to find them myself. From that time on, I never stopped searching and asking and chasing any tiny bit of information that could possibly lead to a clue about how to help her.

I found the number of the ME Association and through them got in touch with a local support group. I told a volunteer at the other end of the phone about Lynn, the awful spasms and how her legs were paralysed and asked if she knew where we could go. Were there *any* doctors who knew what to do?

'Are you sure it is ME? I have never heard of anybody that ill with ME,' she replied. Then I was wondering: '*What if it isn't ME? What could it be instead?*' So we asked for a referral to a consultant paediatrician at Eastbourne General Hospital for a second opinion. We also got the name of a doctor at a private clinic in north London who was well known in the field.

There was a waiting list of six months at the clinic. I rang them in a panic. 'We can't wait six months!' I snapped. We really felt Lynn was going downhill so fast, her very life might be in danger. They promised to see if they could get her in more quickly and in the meantime she was admitted to Eastbourne to be assessed. This was on 7 May 1992, two and a half months since she had been diagnosed with ME and six months after she first fell ill.

She was in there for about ten days while they did a whole battery of tests: blood tests, X-rays, a CT scan of her brain. They all came back normal but she was still getting worse. The fits continued and every day her top half was getting weaker. She would be sitting in a chair and she would suddenly flop over. And her voice had faded to a tiny whisper.

The medical team at Eastbourne said that the fact they could not find anything medically wrong was 'a good sign'. It didn't feel that way to us because they were going to discharge her in an even worse state than when she went in. They confirmed the diagnosis of ME and prescribed anti-viral drugs and beta-blockers. Then they said, 'There's nothing more we can do. Take her home.'

Crestfallen at how little treatment she had been offered, Richard went to collect her. It was a bright spring day; he put her in her wheelchair and pushed her out of the hospital, chatting to her about going to find the car. Wincing from the brightness of the sun, she turned to him and asked, 'Daddy, what's a car?' It made his heart miss a beat.

Once in the car he said, 'Put your seat belt on.' She stared at him blankly, not understanding what he meant. He had to do it for her. As he was driving home, she lost consciousness and flopped sideways, strapped in the belt. Later he told me that that it was then that he felt deep down that she would never recover to be the happy, healthy girl she had once been, though he didn't share this fear with me at the time.

Once she was home things got more frightening by the day as Lynn's cognitive and physical powers rapidly deteriorated. I settled her on the sofa in the living room. 'Would you like to watch TV?' I asked. She gazed at me blankly. 'What's TV?' she replied.

A shiver ran down my spine. How could she not recognise an ordinary object she had seen every day of her life? It was totally beyond my comprehension and very frightening.

With hot tears stinging my eyes, I picked up the TV control and showed it to her. 'Turn it on and you'll see people talking and acting in that box over there.' She laughed at me, thinking I was joking with her. 'Go on, turn it on.'

'You do it, Mum. I can't remember what to do. Sorry,' she whispered.

From then on, her memory grew worse and worse. She did remember how to do some things but mostly I had to explain what things were for and show her what to do with them. Other times she knew what something was for but couldn't remember what it was called. If she was cold and wanted her cardigan she pointed to it and called it something else. Everything seemed muddled up in her brain, like she was the victim of a stroke.

One afternoon, Stephen came home from school and went over to say hello. She looked round for me with questioning eyes. 'Who is this?' she whispered.

My heart breaking, I said, 'It's Stephen, your brother. You know Stephen.'

She shook her head. 'No. This is not my brother.'

Another time, her beloved cat, Lucky, jumped up on her knee and instead of delightedly burying her face in his fur as she used to do, she gazed at him suspiciously. Cocking his head he went 'meow' and she squealed in fright. 'Mum, what is it? What's it doing?' she cried.

'It's your cat, darling. It's Lucky. You love Lucky. There's nothing to be afraid of,' I said, feeling gripped by a panic that was by now horribly familiar.

Later her dad came home and bent to give her a kiss. Again she looked bewildered and fearful. 'Who are you?' she whispered. He turned away in despair, unable to stop his tears from flowing.

A few days later she seemed a little brighter and my hopes rose slightly, but her memory was still failing her. She now referred to Steve as 'that boy' and to Lucky as 'that cat'. I kept talking to her about familiar things, trying to find something that would reconnect her with the girl she was, but relatives, neighbours, friends, favourite foods, pastimes were all forgotten. The tutor had stopped coming because Lynn could no longer remember anything; she did not even know how to read any more.

Still, she managed to flick through a few magazines and we watched a bit of TV. I even began to hope that her fits would not come on at the usual time of early evening. But that was a hope too far.

One day, at around 6 p.m., she suddenly keeled over, unconscious. I sat holding her limp body, stroking her hair and talking to her soothingly for about half an hour until, just as suddenly, she came round. I gave her a welcoming smile and she stared at me, uncomprehending, panicking.

'Who are you? Where am I?' she screamed, looking around frantically. 'Mummy, Mummy, where are you? Help me!'

'It's me, I am here. Lynn, Mummy's here,' I pleaded, tears springing to my eyes.

'No, not you; I don't know you. I want Mummy, Mummy! Please help me, I'm frightened.'

I continued pleading with her, trying to soothe her and she gradually calmed down though she continued to be vague all evening. I felt shaken to my foundations. Not to recognise her own mother! My poor girl was disintegrating before my eyes.

The next night after she came round from passing out she started talking jibberish. I answered what she said as though I understood, but one I obviously got wrong agitated her as she tried to explain. I started guessing. 'Are you cold, do you want another blanket? Is something hurting? Do you need something for pain?' Everything I suggested was wrong, then I thought, '*Toilet. She wants the toilet,*' but that wasn't right either. Eventually I got it – she wanted a drink.

It went on like this every day with Lynn feeling extremely ill and having these awful attacks and begging us to help her. She needed me, Richard or Stephen with her 24 hours a day. We were reeling with exhaustion, bewilderment and terror.

On top of all this she began to have great problems swallowing. I tried feeding her soft foods and processing everything. It progressed over two or three weeks to where she could not tolerate anything lumpy so I fed her on the kind of liquid food you usually buy for a baby. As she struggled to eat it, I could barely swallow either. Somehow the clock had been turned back 14 years and I was forced to treat my big, strong girl like a baby again. Then it got to the point where she could not take fluid. She could not even swallow water. I had to force it down her a teaspoonful at a time.

Our beloved daughter was being destroyed before our eyes. We were in a complete panic. We did not know what to do; nobody else seemed to know either. I got on to the clinic in north London. 'We are absolutely desperate now,' I said. 'Lynn has not had any proper food for a couple of weeks and now she can't even take water.'

Much to our relief, the consultant agreed to take her in. '*At last*,' I thought, '*She will be in the hands of real experts in ME and surely they will know how to help her. Surely.*'

CHAPTER SIX

BEGGING
FOR HELP

The paramedics gently carried Lynn along the corridor from her bedroom, trying to cause her as little discomfort as possible. The top half of her body was completely floppy now and she was no longer able to sit up. By the time they got her out of our front door and laid her on a stretcher, she was unconscious.

She came round as she was being taken into the ambulance and blinked in pain as the strong sunshine poured through the window. Even when she put on her sunglasses the light still hurt her eyes. One of the paramedics immediately jumped to his feet and pulled down the blinds. 'Is that better, Lynn?' he asked. 'You tell me if there's anything you want and I'll get it for you. Okay?'

I was standing at the door of the ambulance and she pointed to me, asking, 'Can Mum come with us?' He smiled and said I could.

We drove to the clinic in convoy, Richard following behind in the car. We were both anxious and exhausted from the stress of it all. Neither of us wanted to admit to each other how much hope we were investing in this clinic in case they too could do nothing to help. And we knew we could not cope on our own any longer. We were at our wits' end.

We arrived at 4 p.m. on a bright summer day. Lynn had found the journey incredibly difficult, flinching with pain every time the ambulance went over a bump. They had to stop a few times en route while she was being sick. But now we were here she smiled at Richard and me as much as to say, 'It's going to be all right.'

The place was reassuring – beautifully appointed and it seemed well run. The friendly nurses had pleasant manners and greeted us with smiles. We were told that the consultant would speak with us the following morning and answer any questions we might have. After spending about an hour with Lynn, we left her to get some rest. She didn't seem anxious, just exhausted and weak.

When we made our way to Lynn's room the next morning, we found her in tears with her hands clamped over her ears. There was the most horrific drilling noise from building work right outside her room. Richard immediately went to find the nurse in charge. 'There is an awful racket going on outside Lynn's room. You do realise that she is extremely noise sensitive, don't you?' he demanded.

'Yes, we are. But it will only be for a few more days,' she informed him complacently.

Richard was astounded. 'There is no way Lynn can stand that noise for a few more hours, never mind a few more days,' he fumed. 'She will have to be moved.'

With great reluctance, they agreed and Lynn was moved to a room at the other end of the building. I couldn't believe that a clinic that specialises in ME did not know how noise sensitive patients could be. It shook our faith in the place a little but we still hoped they would be able to help her.

Soon afterwards the consultant arrived wearing dark trousers and a navy blazer with gold buttons at the cuffs. A middle-aged man with an air of self-confidence, he listened to what we had to say with a degree of impatience and then told us that Lynn had 'encephalitis (inflammation of the brain) of unknown origin'. He anticipated she would need to be in the clinic for a few weeks.

There were strict rules at the clinic – parents were only allowed to visit for half an hour each day. Sometimes we broke them by pretending we had just arrived when we had already been there half an hour or we sneaked back for a second visit.

The staff tried to sit Lynn upright by strapping her in a chair. Just as at home, she fell unconscious so they had to keep her in bed. While assessing her ability to swallow they gave her fluids through a vein. When they found she could not swallow anything at all, they inserted a nasogastric tube.

This was a fine, flexible tube that went down her nose to deliver liquid food straight to her stomach. When we saw it in place we were relieved. 'At last you are getting some decent nourishment,' Richard said to her. 'It will do you good. It means they can build up your strength again and get you back on your feet.'

We did not know it at the time, but Lynn was never to eat proper food again.

Only a couple of days later we arrived just as the nurses were leaving Lynn's room. She was crying. I had to lean very close to her to hear what she was saying as by now her voice had dwindled to a pathetic little whisper. 'They keep telling me I'm pretending,' she sobbed.

'What do you mean? How can they think you are putting this on? What are they saying?' I exploded.

'It's the nurses. They say to me "You *can* sit up. You *can* swallow. Why are you doing this?" One of them started laughing at me and called me a "silly little girl". They keep telling me to behave. Honestly, Mummy, I am *not* pretending. I don't want to be like this. I hate being ill. Why do they say I'm pretending?'

I was furious and wanted to weep for the psychological pain she was being put through on top of her terrible illness. With every other illness you get kindness, sympathy, care and encouragement to show your feelings and that is what Lynn deserved and what we needed, but it just wasn't there. All she got were accusations that she was faking it, which just added insult to injury. I fought the impulse to cry in case they misinterpreted my actions too and concluded I was an 'overprotective mother, reacting too much'.

Richard and I demanded an immediate interview with the consultant. We had to wait two hours before he came to Lynn's room. Bottling his fury, Richard said, 'I want to know what medical treatment you are planning for Lynn. I want to know why she is being accused of pretending when she is clearly very seriously ill.'

Steepling his hands together, the consultant replied, 'Well, you know, Lynn's fits are very odd. It is most strange that they occur at roughly the same time each day. Please don't worry, Mr Gilderdale. We are doing a very wide range of tests and I am sure we will have the answer before long. But if you want me to look after your daughter, you must do exactly as I say.'

I assumed he meant physical tests but unknown to us, he had decided to conduct a psychological experiment. The next day we arrived to find her confused and tearful. 'I'm frightened, Mum,' she cried. 'Where am I? It's been such a long time since I saw you.'

Richard and I looked at each other in dismay. The room was dark with heavy curtains drawn to block out the daylight. Then Richard spotted something was missing. 'The clock. Where's your little coloured clock we brought from home?' he asked. Lynn stared at him blankly.

Once again, Richard sought out the head nurse and demanded to see the consultant. 'I'm afraid that is not possible, he is not in the clinic. But we are only following the doctor's instructions,' he was told. He insisted they hand over Lynn's clock and treat her with respect from now on.

It turned out that the consultant had ordered the nurses to shut out the light, no TV or radio or phone calls from us, she had no way of telling whether it was day or night.

The consultant's theory was that she was staging the fits at particular times and now they would stop. Despite all these measures, the fits continued at the same times so his theory was disproved. But what harm did he cause Lynn by his experiment and his disbelief? I hate to think, but what I do know is that when soldiers want to break prisoners of war, they put them in isolation and deprive them of light and time to disorientate them. What place did this technique have in treating a person – a child – who was so desperately ill?

Richard and I were staying in accommodation locally. Steve was in his first year of sixth form and studying hard so he stayed at home or with Richard's parents. Between visits to the clinic we wandered aimlessly around the north London streets feeling dazed and bewildered. In the evenings we would go to a pub and just sit there, the two of us worn to a frazzle, going over everything, asking ourselves what we were going to do.

Endlessly we went around in circles. Who could help us? What was wrong with our little girl? Why was this happening to us? But each time, we'd come away without any answers. Instead, we'd feel even more confused and upset. Richard felt terribly frustrated that he could not fix this; as a father, he could not protect his family. All my nurturing and mothering skills counted for nothing too. We felt devastated and bewildered at being robbed of all our power as parents.

Over the last six months we'd seen so many people – doctors, nurses, specialists – yet we'd never felt so alone. Maybe we needed counselling to help deal with the terrible change that had happened to our lives, but counselling for us didn't come into it. All that mattered was finding answers for Lynn. At least we were able to support each other. Some families with a child with ME are torn apart by the stress, especially if the father is out of the house for most of the day and doesn't see what the child goes through. He might then suspect the doctors are right and the child is somehow 'pretending', which puts the parents in conflict. Because he worked shifts, Richard saw the reality of how Lynn was suffering. It meant we were both dealing with the same torment.

One afternoon I came across a middle-aged female patient, also suffering from ME, who invited me into her room. I went in and chatted, interested in her story, and she told me how wonderful the consultant was. She confided that every three months or so she came to the clinic for a good rest when she was feeling tired. 'How lovely it is to be served on hand and foot and the food is so delicious,' she sighed.

I began to wonder what this clinic was really about. Did they have the necessary medical expertise at all? With a sinking heart I thought that if this lady was typical of the type of people they treated, maybe they didn't have any experience of helping someone as sick as Lynn.

We kept asking to see the consultant without any success. One day we were sitting disconsolately in the lounge waiting for the nurses to tell us we could go up to Lynn when he came in and started to talk to us. 'I am afraid all our tests have come back negative. I have never seen anyone with ME fit like this and I have never seen anybody this bad with it,' he announced.

He was telling us this while standing in front of us, looking down on us. Richard stood up and asked to go somewhere private to discuss it. 'No. There is nothing more to discuss,' he said. His whole attitude came across as arrogant and dismissive. And then the bombshell: he was handing Lynn's case over to a psychiatrist.

I was angry and completely dismayed. I had expected him to come up with at least some kind of treatment plan. 'Why a psychiatrist? ME is *not* a mental illness! Lynn is *not* faking it!' I insisted.

'I am sorry but there is nothing further I can do. He may be able to help,' he said. And with that, we were dismissed.

With nowhere else to turn we had no choice but to accept it. A few days later we walked in to Lynn's room to find a man sitting on a chair beside her bed injecting her with something. 'What are you doing?' I asked sharply. It turned out this was the psychiatrist and he was slowly injecting her with a tranquilliser in a procedure known as an 'abreaction'. Abreaction is a term used by psychiatrists for the process of bringing repressed traumatic memories to the surface. Often hypnosis is used, but in this case, Lynn was being administered a drug. The theory was that if a patient is hiding some kind of trauma, they will tell everything when feeling the effects of the tranquilliser. In other words, it was a truth drug.

'You have not asked our permission to do this. She is only 14! She is a child,' I snapped.

'Well, she is under my care,' he replied while my cheeks grew redder and redder.

Fuming, I asked, 'What has she told you?'

'Nothing,' came the answer.

'That is because there isn't anything. There never has been any trauma. She is sick. Can't you people see that?'

Just when we'd thought things couldn't get any worse, we were being blamed for Lynn's condition. It made me so cross.

The next day we had a meeting with the psychiatrist and he spent an hour trying to tell us Lynn was suffering from 'hysteria'. He said hysteria could be so powerful it could make someone think they are paralysed. I am sure he believed that sex abuse or some other terrible thing had happened to her at home. Though he didn't put a specific accusation to us, we both became very defensive.

I tried to put my anger at the medical establishment to one side. It seemed to me that they were looking in all the wrong places for a cure for Lynn's illness – I knew that what she was experiencing didn't stem from psychological problems or repressed trauma. Once more I decided to search out some information for myself.

I had been frantically researching through ME Association files for something that might explain what was happening to Lynn. It was a struggle at first as I delved into theories packed with terms that I had never heard before. I was so worried and stressed it was difficult to concentrate but it got easier as I became used to the jargon. Every time I saw a mention anywhere of a scientific paper that looked interesting, I ordered it through Tunbridge Wells library and sat poring over it trying to understand.

I had read scores of papers before I came across one that gave me a eureka moment. The title was a mouthful – 'Evidence for the Impaired Activation of the Hypothalamic Pituitary Adrenal Axis in Chronic Fatigue Syndrome' – but the exciting thing was that the paper seemed to make sense of Lynn's symptoms.

I rushed home with it and showed it to Richard. He read it and was excited too. We were both so very desperate for a proper explanation of why Lynn was so stricken and felt convinced that Lynn's doctors would agree that this theory fitted the evidence. We made an appointment to see the psychiatrist at once.

'Please, will you look at this,' I said, handing the paper across the desk. 'Could it explain what is happening to my daughter?'

The brain is an incredible organ that allows us to move, eat, sleep, work and play. It also regulates the hormones and the chemicals that make everything in your body function properly. The part of the brain that controls the production of hormones is the pituitary gland. In healthy people, the pituitary gland receives messages from the hypothalamus – the part of the brain that controls the central nervous system – and releases hormones depending on the body's needs.

What the paper suggested was that in ME patients the hypothalamus misfires, sending the wrong messages to the pituitary gland, which in turn randomly sends out messages to the adrenal glands. The adrenals make adrenaline, the 'flight or fight' hormone, and also a similar hormone called cortisol. But, without receiving proper instructions, the adrenals can't do their job properly and don't produce enough cortisol.

Reading the paper convinced me that Lynn's body was getting a rush of cortisol, which gave her the fits, then the levels were dipping right down, which made her go unconscious.

The psychiatrist refused even to look at the paper. 'Look, the World Health Organisation classified ME as a neurological disease in 1969. *No way* is it hysteria. This may be the answer,' I insisted patiently.

But he would not be swayed. 'I really think the best route is for Lynn to have psychiatric treatment,' he said.

We were at once crestfallen and utterly frustrated. What use was it to treat someone who was gravely physically ill as if it was all in the mind? There *had* to be an alternative. We turned to our GP. Dr Woodgate said she did not believe Lynn was suffering from a psychiatric illness but she said a hospital paediatric ward would not take a child who was having noisy fits all the time whom they couldn't treat.

Then I ran into the woman I knew a little whose son had ME and she told me he had been treated at a special unit in Guy's Hospital in London, which had been very good and had helped him. It was on a psychiatric ward, but Guy's was one of the top hospitals in the country – surely any ward there must be good. We arranged to meet the consultant and he reassured us that he believed ME was a physical illness and offered to take Lynn in once a bed became available.

I longed to take her home but I was terrified. Despite my nursing experience, I didn't think I was capable of looking after her properly. I didn't know what to do to make her better and was so scared that she might actually die in my care. Lynn also dreaded going into a psychiatric hospital and so did we. Richard and I agonised over it but there were no other options on offer so we were forced to take the consultant's words on trust.

Dr Woodgate rang Eastbourne General and asked if Lynn could go there while she was waiting for the bed in Guy's, but the consultant said it wasn't possible.

Richard was furious. 'You *will* have to take her because I will put her in the car, she will go unconscious and I will drive her straight to Accident and Emergency,' he fumed. So Eastbourne agreed to take her.

Richard or I, or both of us, would visit Lynn every day. One day we arrived and saw immediately that she was upset. Her chin was dropped down towards her chest while her eyes peered anxiously upwards. It was the kind of expression someone puts on their face that says, '*I don't know how to tell you this.*'

'What's wrong?' I asked in alarm.

'Daddy', she whispered, 'I don't know if I can tell you what I've just heard.'

'What is it, sweetheart? You can tell me,' he said, gently.

'Some of the nurses were talking about me. They said that you were obviously sexually abusing me. That's why I am like this, they said. It was horrible.'

'Oh, for heaven's sake!' Richard exploded.

We were both outraged. As a policeman he had dealt with paedophiles and was absolutely disgusted that the nurses could associate him with something so vile. I was furious with them for insulting him like that when he had always been a wonderful father and we were going through enough torment without them adding to it. We were also appalled because it revealed that the medical staff at Eastbourne had the same basic attitude that we had met everywhere else – that because their tests did not reveal a medical cause, the illness must be psychological.

They didn't even consider that their tests were inadequate, or that their knowledge of the disease was deficient.

Our feeling that Lynn's illness must somehow be linked to her BCG vaccination was dismissed out of hand. It felt like anything we suggested was just being ignored.

We marched off to confront the ward sister who had the grace to apologise over the allegation but we were to meet this kind of suspicion again and again over the coming years.

After about three weeks in Eastbourne Lynn was stretchered into an ambulance and transferred to Guy's. Richard and I left the car at home and travelled to London with Lynn. We didn't exactly feel hopeful but had to hang on to some kind of belief that this would work because we had absolutely nowhere else to go.

At the desk we were given directions to the ward on the top floor. We went up in the lift, and found it was a secure, locked unit. Once we got inside we stopped dead, deeply shocked. The ward was full of noisy and disorderly children and many of them were running around untamed, banging or shouting.

They had told us that Lynn could keep away from the noise in a nice room of her own with a window and that she would have her own special nurse. Picking our way through the chaos we followed a nurse to Lynn's room and that was even worse. It was tiny, no bigger than a prison cell, with no window. It looked shoddily decorated and in desperate need of a paint job. The bed was shoved up against the wall and the whole place looked drab and didn't look clean. There was no bell to call for help.

Lynn was the only bedridden child on the ward. Already she was tormented by the noise and absolutely petrified. I sat on her bed feeling totally distraught. She clutched my hand and her big, pleading eyes were full of tears. 'Please don't leave me here,' she begged me in her tiny voice. 'I'm not mad. Truly, I'm not pretending. I can't stand this. Please, take me home.'

Desperate thoughts swirled in my head: *This is not right. This is an awful place. I can't leave her here.* But where were we to go? This was the end of the line. 'It won't be long. They are going to help you,' I reassured her with as much conviction as I could muster. Then came the moment when I had to say goodbye. It went against all my instincts as a mother to say the word. The heartrending scene will haunt me for the rest of my life.

Lynn wailed piteously and clung to me with all her remaining strength. I had to detach her hands from my arm and will myself to turn my back and walk away from her. Her desperate cries followed me as I stumbled, blinded by tears, from that horrible little room while a nurse murmured soothingly: 'She'll be fine, don't worry. We'll look after her.'

Outside, the ambulance crew who had brought her were waiting. Richard knew them and one of them came over to speak to us. We saw that he was crying. 'How can you possibly leave her here?' he said.

'Because we have nowhere else to go,' Richard replied wearily.

On the nightmare journey home that day, I was forced to stand on a crowded commuter train. Crushed beside the door, I felt as though my body needed to collapse there, on that spot, in a crumpled little heap. I was completely heartbroken. The only thing that kept me upright was that Lynn needed me. I could not disintegrate and leave her abandoned in that place. I had to summon all my reserves of total, physical determination to keep myself together.

The next day we found Lynn lying on a mattress on the floor of her room instead of in a bed. I grabbed a nurse. 'What's going on here? Why is she lying on a mattress?' I demanded.

'Oh, she threw herself out of bed,' she said.

'Why on earth would Lynn want to throw herself out of bed? She has never done it before,' I said.

'Well, she just did,' she replied, dismissively.

We insisted the bed was brought back but later it was taken away again and she was back on the mattress.

Every day we visited, Lynn was getting worse. I had to put my ear right up to her mouth to hear what she was saying as by now she had great difficulty getting any words out. Everything I heard caused me more anguish.

'They won't bring me a bedpan,' she whispered, obviously embarrassed and distressed. 'I knock and knock but nobody comes.'

It turned out they too were working on the theory she was pretending and believed that, if she really needed the loo, she would get up and walk. It was degrading and stressful and it caused her to become incontinent.

'The nurses are horrible,' she whispered. 'They pull me up roughly to make me sit up, then fling me back on the bed. Please, this is a place for mad people. Take me home, Mummy.'

I could not touch her wrists without her shaking and crying; they were black and blue. The staff told us she had banged them when she was fitting.

'They say you don't want me at home. That's why I am here. Is that true, Mummy?' she asked. 'They say I have to stay here until I do what I am told.'

Each word clawed at my heart. I dried her tears and kissed her. 'We want you at home more than anything in the world but we are not doctors,' I told her, struggling to hide my distress. 'These people are here to help you. They will make you better.'

A few days later we found the medical team standing round her bed with the consultant at her feet, going red in the face. Richard realised he could only see one of his hands. The other was under the bedclothes. 'What are you doing?' he snapped. The consultant had been squeezing Lynn's foot to check again whether she was pretending that she couldn't feel anything. 'Are you trying to make her feel pain?' Richard said. 'Because I tell you what, I wish you could.'

'The other children are nasty to me,' Lynn whispered to us one day. 'They all come round my door and swear at me. They throw balls of paper at me. I knock for a nurse but nobody comes. I am so frightened. I have horrible dreams.'

My heart lurched. The fact that her distress was coming out in nightmares convinced me that what was happening to her was really bad. She was being tormented during the day and tormented again during her sleep. She was having no peace when what she needed above all was rest. It was torture to me not to be able to be there to comfort her when she was having these dreams and suspecting that no one else was bothering to comfort her either.

She didn't appear to have been given adequate physical care. Her hair was very long and I usually combed it every day but I wasn't able to at Guy's because we were only allowed to visit for a short time and that time was too precious to spend on anything other than talking to Lynn. By the time she came home her hair was matted; it took me weeks of gentle teasing to get all the knots out.

The only thing that stopped us carrying her straight out of there was that they kept telling us they could make her better, that they had made others better. We felt we had to give it a try but it was soul destroying.

Each day we asked what plan they had formulated to treat her, but they seemed to give more attention to Richard and me than they did on Lynn. We were interviewed repeatedly by a team of three – the consultant in charge, the registrar and a senior nurse – while other staff watched us through a two-way mirror and recorded us. They asked us politely if we minded being recorded, reassuring us the whole time that they believed in ME. 'We have a plan,' they assured us. 'We just need to assess Lynn first to decide exactly what is the right plan for her.'

They asked about our relationship. Did Richard ever do anything nice for me, any surprises, things like that? I said, yes, he bought me flowers and did other nice things, what does that have to do with Lynn's illness? They wanted to know about Stephen and Lynn's childhood. Were there any problems in the family? Any traumas as they were growing up? It was obvious they thought we had done something to Lynn to make her ill or they would not have needed to ask all this.

They were especially hard on Richard. 'I can't work you out,' one of them said to him. 'You are going to be a tough one to crack.'

'I beg your pardon?' Richard said, startled.

The doctor went on: 'You are not telling us everything, are you?'

Richard couldn't believe it. He was a serving police officer and he felt that he was being questioned in a way similar to how he would interview a suspected violent criminal.

It was infuriating and frustrating but we answered their questions patiently, hoping to show them there wasn't any problem in the family so they would drop these irrelevant questions and start talking about what they were going to do for Lynn. 'There hasn't been any improvement. You keep saying you are going to help her and you haven't done it,' we pleaded.

They replied in what were supposed to be soothing tones, 'Just give us another couple of days and we will have the plan together. You have to give us time because if you take her out of here, you will lose your daughter. And you don't want that, do you? You want the best for her.'

So day after day we were struggling to go along with what they were saying, telling ourselves that we had to stick with it if they could really make her better.

But the stress that they put her under, physically and emotionally, amounted to torture. It almost destroyed her – and us. The guilt I feel over leaving Lynn there when she was begging us to take her home, telling us that she was terrified and that they were horrible to her, will haunt me for ever.

Every day at the end of visiting time, I had to drag myself out of that rotten place and leave Lynn behind when all I wanted to do was gather her into my arms and get her out of there. I had to summon all my strength to force my feet to walk through the door and away through the ward. And all the time her pleading eyes bore into my back and she was crying: 'Please, Mum. Please don't leave me. Please help me,' over and over again. It was horrific. Indescribably heartbreaking.

Richard and I came away from the hospital every day completely shell-shocked. We would get on the train at London Bridge like zombies and not speak to each other at all on the journey home. There were no words to describe what we were feeling.

Day and night my mind and stomach churned. Lynn was in Guy's, one of the best hospitals in the UK, yet it was apparent that they couldn't help her. Indeed her fits were getting worse. She had no control over any part of her body. All she could move was her little finger.

Once, when her whole body was seized by a terrifying, total spasm, we shouted in a panic for a nurse. She came and simply glanced at her. 'Oh yeah, she does that sometimes,' she said, casually.

'GET a doctor in here NOW,' I yelled.

She strolled off and came back a few minutes later. 'The doctor's busy,' she announced. Lynn was going blue.

I repeated, furiously, 'We want the doctor *now*, busy or not.'

At last the doctor came, took one look at Lynn and sprang into action. 'Get out, out,' she shouted to Richard and me. Nurses came at the run while we waited outside the room, trying to control our terror, not knowing if she would ever breathe again.

Ever since the consultant volunteered to take her into Guy's I'd been trying to convince myself this was the best place for Lynn. I was so desperate to see her well again. But my hope was disappearing.

'*I just can't let her stay here*,' I thought. But what was the alternative? I did not think my nursing training was adequate to care for her. I had only done a few injections, I had never inserted a feeding tube, I had never been in charge of a patient. The thought of it was overwhelming and I worried I'd make Lynn worse. I was in turmoil.

So I struggled to convince myself Lynn was in more capable hands than mine. '*They are the experts*,' I repeated to myself every day. But with each new day it became harder to believe as we found something new and worse had happened to her.

Two weeks after her admission, the registrar and head nurse asked us if they could use force on Lynn to make her do things. We didn't need to ask what they meant. By even asking such a question they made it blatantly clear that they did not believe ME to be a physical illness. With that question I realised finally that there was no medical plan to help her, there never had been. They wanted to force Lynn to walk, to eat, to talk. What they proposed amounted to torture in my opinion and they wanted us to give them permission to carry it out. Richard and I looked at each other in total disbelief. 'No, of course you can't use force,' we replied almost simultaneously.

This was the final straw. '*This isn't going to stop*,' I thought. We felt rising panic; we *had* to do something. I said to Richard: 'We can't leave her here another day. They are not going to make her better.' Home, no matter at what cost, no matter how incompetent I felt, home was better than this place that was totally destroying her body and mind.

So, after two weeks and two days of hell, we hired a private ambulance and arrived with it the next day without warning. When Lynn saw the paramedics walk in with the stretcher and we told her she was going home, I have never seen anybody look so relieved and happy. She had lost the ability to speak by then but her eyes and smile said it all.

We told the nurse in charge of the ward that we were taking Lynn away and asked her to sign her discharge and she did absolutely everything in her power to delay us until the consultant came. We suspected that the staff might try to detain Lynn under the Mental Health Act – what is known as 'sectioning' – in order to take her out of our care, which has happened to other children suffering from ME, and we were determined not to let that happen.

She said Lynn's nasogastric tube needed changing, as it hadn't been done for a few days. We reluctantly agreed to wait until that was done because we knew it could get blocked up. When she had finished, she tried some other delaying tactic but we just said, 'No. We are going now,' and we were out of the door.

CHAPTER SEVEN

A NEW LIFE
AT HOME

Back at our bungalow in Stonegate, the paramedics had to lift Lynn and carry her inside because the stretcher would not fit round the corners of the corridor to her bedroom. Once they had gone, we cried with relief and hugged each other. I looked at my darling daughter, lying pale and immobile on the bed, and my heart bled for what she had been through. There she was, a ghost of her former self, smiling at me through all her pain, her eyes saying, 'I'm so happy to be home.' She had lost her voice completely. I was never to hear my daughter speak again.

The last nine months had been so unimaginably awful that we felt like tiny bits of flotsam being tossed on an enormous stormy ocean. No words can describe the helplessness I had felt in the hands of those who had taken control of us while spouting the false hope that they could make Lynn better. Now it was just down to us.

I was utterly convinced we had done the right thing. But I had very little idea of what to do next. We had none of the equipment in the house that I would need to nurse

Lynn – no tubes, no bedpan, nothing to fix up her liquid food system. There was nothing for it but to improvise. Each of us was willing and determined to find a way to manage; anything was better than what went before.

Richard went outside searching for something to hang Lynn's liquid food from. 'What about this?' he said, coming back in from the garden brandishing the base and upright from the garden umbrella.

'What are you going to do with that?' I enquired.

'Just you wait and see.'

As Lynn watched in admiration, he fitted a clip that he used to attach handcuffs to his belt to a hook on the umbrella upright and, hey presto, we had an intravenous feeding stand that worked perfectly. One hurdle over, many more to come.

Before we took Lynn out of hospital, we had asked Dr Woodgate if she would support us. This was vital; someone as ill as Lynn could not be looked after at home without the backing of their GP. She gave it 100 per cent and it proved invaluable. Yet just two days after we got Lynn home the registrar at Guy's phoned Dr Woodgate to encourage us to send her back, saying they would keep her place open for two weeks. Dr Woodgate said that was not going to happen.

Throughout the following years, Dr Woodgate was wonderful. I could ring her any time and she was always there. She trusted me enough to explain things to me and we would work on problems together as a team. She made sure I had an understanding of everything so that I was able to deal with whatever I was faced with.

We somehow survived the first night and the next day I went to the Red Cross and got a bedpan. Then the district nurse came round with a collection of nasogastric tubes and connectors for the feeding bags and showed me how to use them. We pulled the curtains almost shut to shroud the room from the light that hurt Lynn and bought her a natural sheepskin to lie on as I knew that was the best thing to prevent bedsores in someone who is immobile in bed.

So the physical side of her care was soon set up but the trauma Lynn suffered as a result of her experience took much longer to abate. Every single night she had nightmares about being in hospital. She woke crying in terror. If a nurse or doctor came to the door, her whole body shook with fear. 'You're okay. This is someone we know. You are safe. I'm here with you,' I murmured soothingly. After a few months the nightmares no longer came every night but they recurred occasionally for years to come.

Another thing that caused us all untold distress was that she could not remember people, even those she loved the most in the world. After we got her home, I was the only person she always recognised because, I suppose, I was always with her. Often she did not know who Richard was when he came in from work. This completely broke his heart. Sometimes he came out of her room with tears and deep sadness in his eyes. But gradually he found a way to make it easier for Lynn by making light of it. 'Oh, it's your dad, you know it's me. Who else has a face like this?' he joked.

I gave up work to look after her. I saw my chief and most important role in life as caring for my children, in whatever way that turned out to be. 'You've given up your life for Lynn,' people said to me, but it never occurred to me to see it that way.

I still had a life and I could do anything I wanted with it, I had choice. I could go out and feel the sun on my face, I could meet and talk to people. Even the ordinary, everyday things like getting up and dressed, washing myself and eating my breakfast is precious when you are living with someone who can't do them. Yes, Lynn's illness turned our happy lives completely upside down and we all struggled to adapt to the terrible change that had overtaken us, but it was Lynn, not me, who had her life taken away; it was her who could do nothing but endure her dreadful suffering.

And with each passing day, I continued to hope and believe that she would get better. I hoped that whatever was the underlying cause of her sickness would go away, or be spent, and she would gradually regain her faculties and her strength.

The daily routine of caring for her was extremely time-consuming, like looking after a newborn baby. She had her medication every four hours during the day and I had to get the whole array of tablets out, crush them with a pestle and mortar, dissolve them in water, then sieve them, then push the resulting liquid through her nasogastric tube very slowly so she would not be sick. It was a very fine tube and if there was even the slightest lump, it would block. I would spend ages trying to clear it and if that didn't work, I had to take it out and Lynn and I together put a new one in. I was amazed at how coolly she did this – imagine having to slide a tube up your nose and down your throat into your stomach while lying flat. Sometimes it took hours. She did the hardest bit, round the corner of her nose, then I took over to push it down into her stomach. We were quite a team.

Then there was her hygiene regime to get through. Lynn's energy levels were so low that every little action I did with her left her completely worn out and she had to recover with a sleep. She was not up to having a complete bed bath all in one go so I washed her arms one day, one leg another day, the other the next, her torso the next day, and so on. Then I brushed her hair, did her teeth – she could do nothing for herself.

A hair wash was a rare and major event, involving both Richard and me, and had to be carried out with military precision. First I'd lift off the bedhead and covered the mattress with a plastic sheet. Then I'd fetch two bowls of warm water, a jug, shampoo and loads of towels and arrange them on a little table beside her bed.

Richard and I would lift Lynn up the bed, making sure to keep her flat so she didn't pass out, and lean her out over the side. Richard would then support her head while I shampooed and rinsed, running in and out of the bathroom at breakneck speed (to the sound of Lynn's giggles) to change the water before Richard's back gave up and Lynn's neck went into spasm. A quick lift back down the bed and then I'd leave her to rest for as long as necessary before combing out her hair. Job done.

Lynn never liked to be left alone so I would sit in her bedroom to keep her company, even if she was drifting in and out of sleep. She could not bear any light or even the slightest noise, like the rustling of pages, so I couldn't do anything, apart from sit there with my thoughts. I had never sat still in my life and I can tell you it is a very hard thing to learn to sit there in the dark and the silence, doing absolutely nothing for hours at a time. Difficult at first, but I got used to it.

Richard had to go from this hushed house to a busy, noisy police station where he had to be on the alert, ready to respond to whatever might be going on. The change for Steve was just as strange. Our house used to be busy with the children having their friends round, chattering, playing loud music and singing, tearing round the garden, laughing. Now his friends couldn't come and he could only listen to music through his headphones. We even watched TV with the sound turned down and subtitles. Our once lively home was silent.

My attention was almost totally taken up with Lynn. I remember when I was a child, on one or two occasions after my brother John had his accident, sometimes getting irritated. 'John, John, why does everything have to revolve around John?' I whined to my mother. But Steve never reacted like this. Instead he threw himself into studying hard for his A levels and ended up getting straight As. Occasionally Richard took him out for a pint and sometimes he went to his grandparents for the weekend for a break. And, of course, he could let his hair down when he went out with his friends in his old green Beetle car, fondly known as the 'Gilly-mobile'.

'I am sorry I don't have much time for you. I know it is hard for you,' I said to him one day.

'It's okay, Mum. I understand how things are. I am all right. I can cope,' he reassured me. I was incredibly proud and touched by how he dealt with the whole situation in such a mature way, looking at what it was doing to everybody in the family, not just himself. I think he just felt so awfully sorry for Lynn and frightened by what he saw happening to her.

When he got his exam results he celebrated with his friends and later with a family dinner and champagne toasts to a bright and happy future. Before we knew it, he was off to university, where he was able to enjoy a normal student life, making new friends, working hard and playing hard.

I was so pleased for Steve that he was moving forward with his plans and ambitions. There he was, out in the wide world, experiencing new things and meeting people. Poor Lynn was confined to her bed; her life had become limited by the four walls of her room. The contrast between my children couldn't be more apparent – or more difficult to come to terms with.

Lynn's response to her treatment at Guy's left her exhausted and she had lost control of her body. Slowly, with the aid of Dr Woodgate, we began to find medications that would ease the violent headaches, nausea and sore throats that she suffered constantly. And slowly she began to gain more control of her motor skills. She became continent again and we developed ways to get around all the difficulties we had to face just to get through the day.

When she was able to move her hands she began working out a communication system. It worked on a combination of Lynn making facial expressions and gestures and drawing letters on her hand and me or Richard or Steve guessing what she meant.

She had forgotten how to read and her memory was so bad that we could not teach her proper sign language. But she knew a small number of individual letters and used those to represent whole words. For instance, a T meant 'thank you', W was 'want' and holding up two fingers was 'to'. She pushed up the corners of her mouth with her fingers for 'happy' and pulled them down for 'sad'. 'Hot' was fanning herself with her hand. 'Sick' was a retching gesture. For 'I' she pointed to herself and if she wanted me to fetch something for her she would reach out and open and close her hand in a beckoning gesture. She spelt phonetically but not often with a clear letter. For instance, she traced a shallow curve on the edge of her hand for J meaning 'just'. Although, she couldn't write with a pen and paper, we managed to build up a system by her trying out letters on her hand and me guessing what word she meant and saying it back to her.

It was painfully slow and frustrating at first. When we were having a conversation, I could say a sentence in a few seconds but it could take her 15 minutes to reply, which was irritating for Lynn when she felt passionate about something and wanted to get it out quickly. And it was difficult for both of us if we were disagreeing about something.

Sometimes if I was especially tired I might be snappy, the way any two people who are close might be with one another on a bad day. Or I might insist on her doing something or taking some medicine and it would irritate her. 'I'm not a child any more, Mum,' she'd spell out painstakingly. 'Just because I'm ill it doesn't mean you can tell me what to do all the time. I have a mind of my own.'

Anyone else, if they are cross, can say their piece and walk away if they want to, but I had to stand there while she slowly wrote out what she was angry about. On top of that, I had to repeat out loud her cross words about me to make sure I got whatever she was saying right.

'It's all right for you,' she once protested, with me speaking her words. 'You can have a go at me but it takes me ages to tell you what I feel. By the time I have got it out, it's almost gone.' Sometimes that same frustration would dissipate the heat of the argument and we would end up laughing at ourselves – things that were very stressful could turn out to be funny.

When Steve left to go to university, we moved Lynn into his bedroom, which was bigger and overlooked the garden. We had French doors put in so that the paramedics could bring a stretcher in and we changed the decorations from blue to a paper sprinkled with pretty brightly coloured flowers on a white background.

All around the room were shelves that gradually grew to be completely crammed with soft toys, figurines, pictures, boxes of craft materials, make-up and jewellery cases. These were just a tiny fraction of the hundreds of presents people sent to her to prove to her that, though she was hidden away, she was not forgotten.

On one wall she had a big poster with the caption 'Step Into A Dream'. It was a picture of a window opening on to a beautiful scene of a tropical paradise beach with palm trees, blue sea lapping gently against a pristine white beach, and a clear blue sky. For her, this was the only window she could look through on to the kind of life she longed to step into.

Even more important to her was the huge fish tank, about four and a half feet long, that we kept on a stand about three feet away from the head end of her bed. We started off with a small tank and just a few fish but she loved it so much we graduated in stages to this whopper. In Lynn's permanently shrouded bedroom the glow from the bulb that warmed the water provided the only source of light.

Lynn could not go out into the world but in this way we brought a little drop of the living world to her. It was the only vigorous, active life she saw and the fish meant an enormous amount to her. She was absorbed for hours studying their behaviour and looking for any signs of illness or distress. She found it relaxing.

She searched through fish books and picked out ones she would like, which Richard scoured local fish shops to find. She got to know the fish as individuals and sometimes had to get rid of one. 'Can you take that one to the fish shop, Dad?' she would ask, pointing out the offender. 'He's bullying the others. I like peace in my fish tank.'

Lynn was never well enough to socialise. Seeing people even for a few minutes exhausted her so much she took days to recover. She would see family when they were here if she could, but even that was not always possible no matter how much she wanted it. The most upsetting thing was that she could not even see the old school friends she had been so close to, Laura, Michaela and Gemma.

I was delighted when one of them called round. 'Laura has come to see you. She wants to know how you are. Can you just say hello to her?' I asked her gently.

I felt my heart squeeze as she spelt out: 'I don't remember her. I can't talk to her. Tell her I'm sorry.'

The poor girl was embarrassed to be seen in her stricken state by her friend. 'I am very happy she came to see me,' she confided in me later. 'It means she has not forgotten me, doesn't it, Mum?' I was glad to see these girls growing up and getting on with their lives but it was unbearably sad for me that my girl was not doing the same.

Our lives had become highly restricted too. Richard and I no longer went out together; it was impossible to see friends and we only had family round on really special occasions. As time went on, we became increasingly concerned that Lynn could not be part of anything that happened outside the four walls of her room. We hated the thought of her being cut off and listening to us laughing about something and not knowing what it was. We wanted her to be able to share in what was going on.

'I've had an idea,' Richard announced one day. 'Why don't we rig up a video camera and sound system in the living room and connect it to her TV? When she is well enough, she can flip a switch and see us and hear what we are saying. Or she could have the picture without sound or vice versa. What do you think?'

I thought it was a brilliant plan and when Richard's police colleagues heard about it, they wanted to help. They organised a fundraising event that paid for everything needed to set it up. Lynn was delighted.

It worked well. If her grandparents were round for Sunday lunch they could sit at the table and wave to her. 'Hi Lynn, we are thinking of you,' they called out cheerily. She could follow my activities as I pottered about through the day and she could take an interest in who was coming to the door. A lot of the time she was asleep or too sick to be able to watch or listen, but the main thing was that she had the option. We did everything we could think of to bring life into her limited little world without making her sicker than she already was.

Billy was a police friend who was especially brilliant at raising money for us to buy things to make our lives easier. He had little lapel pins made in the shape of angel fish (Lynn had these pretty little fish in her tank and was especially fond of them) and we sold thousands of them. We raised enough money to buy a very specialised computer to try to help Lynn recognise letters and colours and all kinds of things. Billy also organised a do in Brighton with famous pop groups and celebrities, including Worlds Apart, the Average White Band, Let Loose, Milan and SSTAC. Other police colleagues had a hugely successful Golf Day and paid for an electronic bed, which meant we could easily keep testing if Lynn could be raised up from her horizontal position.

All these things brought something very special into Lynn's restricted life. They let her know that people cared about her; they loved her and they were willing to put in all this effort into trying to make her life a little better. In her lonely room, the warmth of that knowledge really did give her the courage to carry on fighting to get better.

CHAPTER EIGHT
SEARCHING FOR ANSWERS

The smooth-cheeked, white-haired doctor was totally confident of his opinion. 'I don't know what ME is but what I am absolutely certain is that it is not an organic illness,' he pronounced emphatically. 'The one absolutely clear-cut, clinical feature of ME is the personality of the people who develop it. Many of them have profound psychosexual difficulties with partner relationships and life in general. They are people who just aren't very happy with the life situation that they find themselves in.'

I felt like throwing the cup of coffee I was drinking at the TV screen.

Richard jumped up, arms outstretched in dismay. 'What's the matter with these people? How dare they insult Lynn and everyone like her with ME, who have happy family lives!' he shouted.

This doctor was talking in a TV documentary made for Channel 4's *Frontline* programme. He spoke with such confidence and authority that viewers might have been fooled into thinking there were no other explanations for

ME. I was furious, but not surprised by his apparent arrogance and absolute conviction in his own view only. We had come across so many like him ourselves. But it still hurt.

The documentary had been made by Dr Anne Macintyre who had herself developed ME seven years previously when she was working in a busy hospital and enjoying a full and active social life of going hill walking, climbing and sailing. She had nearly recovered when she made the programme but still had a lousy memory, became easily exhausted and sometimes fell over.

She had contacted us through Action for ME because we were on the register of people who were willing to talk to the media and we had agreed to take part in the programme. The crew had filmed Lynn and Dr Macintyre had interviewed Richard and me in the garden.

At that time, we were coping with a series of crises that led to Lynn being admitted to hospital with some dangerous infection or violent stomach upset on a horribly regular basis. She might be in for six weeks, back home for two, admitted again for four weeks, home for a month, back in for a fortnight. It felt like a continuous, relentless treadmill. Sometimes she was discharged, brought home by ambulance and had to turn round on the doorstep to go back in again.

Dr Macintyre was entirely sympathetic. She said in her introduction to the programme, 'Having ME like Lynn means you have to fight two things: the illness and the prejudice. Deep down the root of the problem lies with the medical profession itself and their inability to deal with things they don't understand.'

Her best example of this was the self-satisfied doctor (who did not know Dr Macintyre had ME). He described a case of a man who 'said that if he peeled the potatoes for dinner he was completely exhausted for several days.'

He claimed the man's experience was nothing to do with a dysfunction of his nervous system, but was actually all 'in the mind'. In her commentary Dr Macintyre said, 'Talking to Lynn's parents you realise how many doctors believe it is all "in the mind". And how desperate this makes people with ME feel.'

The scene switched to me and Richard in the garden. 'You get nurses who say to you "*I* know she can do that if she wants to,"' I said. '*How* do they know? How can we even begin to prove to them that Lynn is very ill? Probably in the whole history of medicine medics have been very slow to accept anything they can't see proof of. And they can see Lynn's ill but they can't do a test and have it in writing. We don't need Lynn to prove to *us* that she's ill. We know she's ill.'

It felt good that the prevailing scepticism was being challenged on prime-time television but we were still meeting it on a regular basis. At the Conquest Hospital in Hastings where Lynn was usually admitted, two of the consultants were wonderful but two others clearly believed it was 'in the mind'. One of these was an endocrinologist – a doctor who treats patients who have diseases affecting their glands and hormones. When we asked him his opinion of ME, he told us straight: 'ME does not exist.'

'So what is wrong with Lynn?' I enquired.

'Lynn Gilderdale syndrome,' he said.

My cheeks flamed red with anger. 'What is that supposed to mean?' I snapped.

'I don't know what it is,' he said. 'Whatever is wrong with her, it is how she is.'

What sort of explanation is that for anything? We wrote to the hospital and complained that time but we soon learnt that complaining gets you nowhere and drains you of energy in the process. We got used to taking all kinds of knocks and just carrying on.

Soon after we brought her home from Guy's I found Lynn lying on her side, doubled up in excruciating pain, clutching her stomach and crying. We had no option except to have her admitted to hospital. I did not know if I would be officially allowed to stay with her so I didn't even ask. There was no way I was going to leave her there on her own after the experiences we had been through. Whether the staff approved or not, I was going to be the 'overprotective mother'.

She was in for several weeks. I slept in a visitor's chair, which was upright with wooden arms. The nurses gave me a couple of blankets and a pillow and I found I could just curl up in it and go to sleep. I was lucky in that I could wake up whenever Lynn needed anything then when she settled I could go straight off to sleep again.

After her first few admissions the staff knew Lynn and tried to give her a side room whenever possible. It made things more bearable because there was less noise and light and it was more appropriate for a girl of her age.

Lynn was a self-conscious teenager of 15, then 16. Normally she would have been getting embarrassed about spots and first dates and silly fashion trends; instead she was getting embarrassed at having to use a bedpan behind a flimsy curtain with other patients either side of her.

On top of that, when she was in a main ward an elderly patient died in the bed next to her and was left there for several hours before she was moved. It grieved me to think how Lynn's peers were enjoying new and wonderful experiences in life while she was confronted by old age and death.

So it was a relief when she got a room to herself, and it also meant I could stretch out on the floor and get a better sleep instead of being propped up in the chair – what bliss. Not that I thought about looking after myself too much; Richard and I put every drop of our being into whatever was necessary to get through.

I remember sitting beside her bed at 7 a.m. one morning, eating a Mars bar, when a doctor, who had been marvellous with Lynn, came by. 'What are you eating that for?' he asked.

'It's good for energy,' I replied.

'You should be eating a proper breakfast,' he urged. But it didn't matter to me, I was just giving my body the energy it needed to keep going after being up all night. These were the sort of things you learnt to do.

Lynn's dreadful stomach pain was yet another unknown to add to all the others about ME. The doctors tried to control it at first with a variety of painkillers, eventually with morphine. They tested different strengths but nothing was working properly so a nurse who specialised in pain control came to see her.

She advised that the best thing to do was to have a continuous flow of morphine administered through a pump. This would avoid the problem of her being comfortable for a time after an injection but the pain returning gradually as the dose wore off. It sounded good.

The nurse calculated the dose of morphine from the amount of painkiller Lynn was already taking. It was quite a low dose to begin with but everyone becomes tolerant to morphine over time so the dose has to be increased to keep on top of the pain.

Lynn was always in hospital each time it was increased and I played no part in deciding on the dose except for one time when, instead of increasing it by the normal amount of 10 milligrams, they put it up by 30 milligrams in the space of 24 hours. 'That's a huge increase. It can't be right,' I protested.

The doctor insisted it was okay but Lynn herself began to worry about becoming increasingly tolerant and the dosage inexorably rising. 'It might stop working altogether unless I take a dangerous amount,' she said. So she decided to keep to a level that was moderate for her – though would have been extremely high for anyone not tolerant to it. The drug was pumped into her body 24 hours a day and then she'd have top-up injections for 'breakthrough' pain when it was particularly severe, which she administered herself.

In the first couple of years, the only treatment that helped Lynn at all was pain relief, a drug that stopped the blood clots she was getting and anti-sickness drugs, but she was still suffering from fits, spasms and frequent vomiting, which often made her feeding tube come out and left her dehydrated. The fits went on for hours – sometimes Richard and I would be up all night with her, taking it in turns.

It was a desperate way to live, with no improvement in sight. I thought there *must* be someone who could do something to help her so any brief spare moment I could snatch I used to search frantically for answers. I rang the ME Association and they put me in touch with Dr Alan Franklin, a consultant paediatrician who was the country's foremost expert on childhood ME.

Based in Essex, Dr Franklin travelled all over the country to visit families struggling to care for a child stricken with this soul-destroying and isolating condition. He came to see us and was our salvation. A smart, slim man with care and compassion in his eyes, he was the first consultant to make us feel not entirely alone.

He said he had seen lots of young people like Lynn and that ME was in fact the most common cause of children's long-term absence from school. 'She *will* get better,' he assured us. 'But you will need patience. It might take one, two or even five years, but one day she will be back on her feet.'

He advised Dr Woodgate to prescribe various drugs, including anti-convulsants, which at last controlled her horrible spasms and made an enormous difference to the quality of our lives. He made regular visits and knowing he was there to call on any time gave us great comfort and support.

Every time Lynn had any kind of investigation, we mentioned that her illness seemed to be connected to her BCG jab. But no one listened to us until a lovely doctor at the Conquest Hospital, Dr Dyson, offered to be her chief consultant. He read up on ME and became very knowledgeable.

He told us he had been doing research in Hong Kong on a condition called BCG-itis. This was a condition where a patient's immune system failed to deal with the live tuberculosis bacteria that was used in the jab. We were really excited when we heard this. We had had the batch of vaccinations that Lynn's jab came from investigated and that had shown there was nothing wrong with it. This led me to believe that the problem must lie with Lynn's immune system. Dr Dyson tried giving Lynn a combination of very harsh antibiotics that are used to treat TB. Over the next six months, Lynn improved a little – her energy levels were better and she had less sickness and pain. '*Great! Something's happening*,' I thought. But at the end of the course, she came to a standstill. Dr Dyson put her on them on two more occasions and each time there was a little improvement, then – nothing, apart from disappointment. It was the story of her life – hope constantly being battered down by reality.

Life that was so static for Lynn moved on for Steve. When he went off to university we missed him and loved it when holiday time came around and he was back with us. We almost burst with pride when he graduated with a first-class honours degree, despite all the worry over what we were going through at home. It was a joy to see him set off on his travels with his best friend, Dan, to countries far and wide; an even greater joy to see him come home safely after a few months as brown as a berry and ready to make his way in the world of work and responsibility.

Meanwhile Lynn's hospital admissions, which were especially frequent in winter when she was prone to many chest infections, were incredibly wearing. She tried her best to stay out of hospital but if she was vomiting, which she could do for weeks on end, she couldn't keep the nasogastric tube down and so was deprived of food. In hospital I was always humbled by her dignity and strength as she endured extraordinary things, awful indignities and painful procedures without complaining.

Once they tried to do a lumber puncture, which is when they put a big needle in your spine to extract fluid which they use to test for neurological disorders or infections like meningitis or spinal cord damage. Numbing the area doesn't work completely and people often cry out with the pain. 'I will curl you round to make it easy for the doctor,' I whispered to her as I held her legs up close to her chin.

I watched her wincing in agony as he stuck this huge needle five times into her back but she said nothing. 'We are nearly there. Just one more time,' the doctor said.

'Will you be able to cope with just one more? Because it is really important,' I asked her. Each time she nodded until it came to the sixth attempt. Then she shook her head: 'No, no more.'

Everything else they did to her, she just gritted her teeth and got through it because she believed that by doing so it would help her recover. 'I didn't go through all that not to get better,' she said to me.

Despite everything, Lynn was not miserable, she didn't complain or moan and she was never demanding. If Lynn wanted something but thought I was busy she would wait until I came to her room or would try to get it herself by using something to knock it towards her. Lynn was human, however, and sometimes she felt down. 'How can I be like this? What is going on? Am I ever going to get through this?' she would ask me.

'Of course you are. You are a fighter,' I said encouragingly.

In later years she wrote in her diary about how she deliberately '*put on my usual smiley face*' as though it was a mask hiding the pain behind it. She did that to help me and Richard cope. She knew it was a hard situation for everybody.

While coping with regular crises, we carried on searching for anything that might help. In 1994 Dr Woodgate referred Lynn to the National Hospital for Nervous Diseases for a full neurological assessment. She was wired up to various kinds of machinery for days while all kinds of tests and scans were carried out.

For one test there was a screen in her room that was connected to electrodes on her head. When she went into one of her spasms, Richard and I watched the screen go totally haywire. Yet when we got the results, the consultant said they showed everything was normal and what was going on onscreen was not significant. It was baffling. 'You seem to be doing all the right things,' he said. 'Go home and carry on.'

We had confidence in this man and a lot of respect for him. He had an excellent reputation and he took Lynn's illness seriously. He made us feel that if we carried on the same way, Lynn would get better eventually and it gave us a boost to be told we were doing the right thing. We clung on to little glimmers of hope like this. We had to; there were so few of them.

A speech therapist also did some tests and I found the results very interesting because they gave me an insight into the clever way Lynn was using what she did know to cover for what she didn't. The therapist put a page in front of her with words and pictures on it, including those of a toothbrush and a cup. She told Lynn to point at the cup, then at the word 'cup', then at the picture of the toothbrush and the word, both of which she did after slight hesitation. 'I thought you told me Lynn couldn't read?' the therapist said to me.

'Well, she can't,' I replied, puzzled. 'But she just did.'

I couldn't explain it. Afterwards I asked Lynn how come she was able to read the words.

'I didn't. I know the word "toothbrush" is a long word and "cup" is a short word, so I worked it out. I don't want to look silly, do I?' she said.

I almost chuckled inside. It was a glimpse of the old Lynn. She was still in there somewhere, using her intelligence to get round her difficulties and I realised that she was trying hard to make the best of her situation, dire though it was. A similar thing happened while we were travelling in an ambulance and a medic asked, 'Have you got any brothers and sisters?' She nodded. 'How many brothers?' She held up one finger. 'How many sisters?' Again, she held up one finger.

'Why did you do that?' I asked her later.

'I would look pretty silly if I did not know how many brothers and sisters I had, wouldn't I?' she said.

My heart sank. That was the hit-and-miss nature of the functioning of her brain. Sometimes information was there, sometimes not, sometimes she could think straight, sometimes not, and sometimes she would recognise her dad and sometimes not.

'*She doesn't deserve this,*' I kept thinking. '*Why does she have to be ill?*' I didn't resent being there, looking after her. I did resent, bitterly, her being ill. I didn't see why anybody should have to be that ill. I didn't think it was right. My Catholic faith died because of it; I couldn't believe in a God who would allow my darling daughter to suffer so unfairly.

It was now 1998 and Lynn had been ill for about six years when another major and disastrous change took place. She began to have hot flushes, extreme ones, in which her face turned bright red and she was drenched in sweat. She often knocked for me in the night and I had to go and change her pyjamas which were wringing wet.

Her hair started coming out and her periods became erratic, then stopped altogether. She was only 20, but it seemed to me that she was experiencing all the signs of menopause. I told myself this was only temporary. Lynn's dream of being a mum was so important to her, vital in fact, that I could not bear the thought that it was disappearing. She should see me going through the menopause long before it happened to her and even I was years away from it yet.

I thought that, once the messages started moving properly from her brain to her ovaries, she would start making oestrogen again and everything would get back to normal. At the time I was less worried about her fertility than about the effect her lack of oestrogen might have on her bone density, which was already reduced because of being bedridden.

The next time she was admitted to hospital, I mentioned the problem and an orthopaedic surgeon recommended she have a bone scan but he did nothing about her oestrogen level. This wasn't good enough. No one seemed to care that here was a beautiful young woman possibly losing the chance to be a mother. So I contacted a private endocrinologist through the ME Association and he told me to send a sample of Lynn's saliva by post for him to test.

Sure enough, the result showed her oestrogen level was low so I took it to Dr Woodgate who arranged blood tests. She then contacted an endocrinologist who had done research into low oestrogen in ME patients and he recommended a high dose of oestrogen coupled with some progestogen – in other words, Hormone Replacement Therapy.

'I hate taking this' she moaned. 'Does this mean I will never have a baby, Mum? I want to have a baby, more than anything. It is the only thing I want.'

I had to draw on all my reserves of strength not to dissolve into tears. 'There are lots of things going wrong in your body at the moment, I know,' I sympathised. 'But who's to say that, when you get better, all these things won't come right again?'

After about a year of slowly increasing the dosage her hot flushes were quite well controlled. She had the bone scan which revealed she had osteoporosis though I was not told at the time how much bone she had lost.

This episode set a pattern in my dealings with the NHS: I noticed a problem, no one listened, I arranged private tests, took the results to Dr Woodgate who got them confirmed by a specialist, then we could continue in the state system. It was expensive but it seemed to be the only way we could make any progress.

I was upset about Lynn's worries over her fertility, but I truly believed what I was telling her because nobody knew enough about ME to predict the course of the illness. And there were such strange things happening to Lynn on a daily basis that I felt that anything could happen, anything could change. If all the things going wrong originated from a problem in her brain, triggered by whatever had caused the ME, then when that got better I thought everything else might start to work again. I *had* to believe it – and she had to believe it too or her life would be hardly worth living.

I clung on to my hope and kept constantly busy, researching everything I could find. But it was very hard. All the time I was mourning for the loss of the lively, sparky girl she had been. Seeing teenage girls out with their mothers, perhaps strolling arm in arm window-shopping, tore my heart to ribbons. I did not dream of big achievements or exotic holidays; I just longed to do the normal day-to-day things in life with her.

It was difficult to hear the chatter of families in their gardens having a barbecue on a summer afternoon. I couldn't go to Eastbourne Beach where I had spent all those summer days watching Lynn so happy. I couldn't go out for a bike ride because Lynn couldn't do it. It upset me terribly seeing girls of Lynn's age giggling in groups together, having fun, flirting and discovering the world and their own place in it. It was so hard to face when Lynn was at home so ill. It caused me great anguish and heartache. The most important thing in life is just to be healthy. You don't realise it until you are not.

'*Why has this happened to her?*' I asked myself over and over again. '*Why Lynn? Why us? Why my family? Why does anybody have to suffer like this?*' But there was never an answer.

During the day, I struggled to hide my distress from Lynn. I could only release my utter devastation when I knew she was safely asleep. Then, alone in my bed in the dark and silence, I wept.

The terrible frustration I felt and my sadness for Lynn's illness and the sheer injustice of the medical profession in their misunderstanding of ME sometimes threatened to destroy me. It didn't because I looked at Lynn and thought, '*If you can do it, so can I.*' However hard it was for me, it was only a fraction of how bad it was for her; her courage and determination inspired and sustained me.

The thing about dealing with it is that you have to. You have no choice. Lynn would often say: 'People tell me I am brave. I am not brave. I have no choice. It's sink or swim. If you let it get to you, you can't cope.'

I carried on hoping despite growing evidence that Lynn was getting worse. One morning when she had been ill for seven years I could hardly wake her. She was sleeping for about 22 hours every day and she was more sick than ever. When she got any kind of infection, she started vomiting;

this time it went on for four or five weeks. She had to stay in hospital all the time, feeling totally lethargic, just lying in bed day after day, not able to do anything.

I knew something had changed. Something extra was wrong. Thinking it might be something to do with hormones, I called the private endocrinologist again and he did a 24-hour saliva test to measure the level of Lynn's cortisol. That is the hormone that enables your body to deal with physical and emotional stress and in normal people it is at its highest level in the morning when you have to get up and get going. Hers was extremely low.

Soon afterwards she was back in the Conquest because she was vomiting fresh blood – one of the side effects of the drugs she was taking for osteoporosis. I asked for her to have 24-hour cortisol tests there. These were conducted by the consultant endocrinologist who had once told us that ME did not exist.

Because of the battering they had taken, Lynn's veins were collapsing in a similar way to how a drug addict's might do. She was 21 and she had had blood taken from her so many times, sometimes two or three times a day, during her countless hospital admissions, plus hundreds of venflons, where they fix a needle in a vein to give intravenous fluids and medicines, that the doctors were now having terrible trouble extracting any blood for all the tests they had to do.

They put tubes in her neck and groin to try to get samples but they decided the best thing was to fit her with a Hickman line. This is a line permanently inserted into a major artery leading to the heart. It is more usually used to administer chemotherapy to cancer patients, which was profoundly depressing, but with it in place life got much easier because it meant I could give her intravenous drugs or fluids at home and her hospital admissions thankfully went down to about twice a year.

When the cortisol results came back they showed her level was so low that the consultant refused to believe them. He ordered for them to be done again. When the second results were the same he was finally forced to admit Lynn's adrenal glands, where the cortisol is produced, were not working properly. He put her on hydrocortisone, a steroid that had the side effects of making her face go puffy and her osteoporosis worse.

Lynn had grown into a beautiful young woman with large, dark eyes and creamy skin which she cared for with the very best products, often paid for by good old dad. She was proud of her looks and she loathed the puffiness. When she woke she would check her face in a little mirror she kept by her bed. It really annoyed her if it had blown up like a balloon. 'It's not fair, I can't even eat and look at me. My face is huge. How can that be?'

The cortisol test results dovetailed perfectly with the research which I had come across way back in 1992. The adrenal glands that produce cortisol are walnut-sized organs that sit on top of the kidneys. Scientists think that cortisol has hundreds of effects on the body, including controlling blood pressure and heart rate, the way the body uses food and the balance of salt and other chemicals in the blood.

The adrenal glands are stimulated to produce cortisol by a hormone produced by the pituitary gland. This bean-sized gland sits at the base of the brain and regulates growth and thyroid function and also the sex hormones, oestrogen and testosterone. It was all so scientific and complicated, but I was becoming a bit of a medical expert and once I'd got to grips with these new facts I was so excited. It all fitted in so perfectly with what was happening to Lynn.

To test the theory we needed an examination of Lynn's hypothalamus, the part of the brain that controls the pituitary, but the consultant said it was too dangerous for someone in Lynn's condition. In any case, at that time he refused to consider the theory. He insisted her adrenal failure was not connected to a problem in her brain.

Some years later, when Lynn was having a scan for something else, it revealed that her pituitary gland had shrivelled away almost to nothing, which can cause memory loss, fits, dizziness and hormone problems. This shrivelling – called 'empty sella syndrome' – is caused either by a tumour interfering with the production of hormones, or because messages are not getting through to it from the hypothalamus. We knew Lynn did not have a tumour so this was proof, at last, that she had dysfunction of the hypothalamus.

Then we had the satisfaction of seeing the consultant, who had fought the idea for so many years, finally accepting what I had said all along. He wrote a letter to Dr Woodgate confirming that the cause of Lynn's adrenal failure was because her pituitary gland had shrivelled away.

Getting this confirmation was a double-edged sword for us. When you know something is wrong and you finally get the proof of it, it's like '*Yes! Told* you.' At the same time, you so much don't want that thing to be wrong. So underneath the triumph, I was thinking, '*So what. What good does it do when there is no treatment on offer?*'

And it didn't explain what causes ME. All we know is that something causes the brain to malfunction, but we don't know what. Most doctors now think it is because a virus, maybe a common one like glandular fever, gets into the brain and causes neurological symptoms that affect all kinds of things in the body. In ME different things can be affected in different people, just to complicate things further.

One of the hardest things was seeing other ME sufferers recovering. I would always be so happy for them but each bit of good news made me think, '*Lynn's turn should come now.*' It was not that I begrudged them getting better, it was that my heart so yearned for the news to be the same for Lynn. At the same time, these cases proved it could happen; you could recover. So each time, I forced myself to find some comfort from them because they gave us the hope we needed to fight on. Because no matter how hard things got, that's what we had to do. We *had* to keep fighting.

CHAPTER NINE
LIVING WITH ME

'Okay, let's have a go at painting today,' I said brightly one afternoon. 'I have had an idea about how we might manage.' Lynn grinned. This was going to be our biggest challenge yet.

Lynn lived rather like Sleeping Beauty; it was as if we were eternally waiting for this curse that had blighted her to be lifted. In the meantime, we had to fill the days.

She was often too ill to do anything, or was in hospital, and what she could do lying flat on her back in the half-light was very limited. But on the days when she had enough energy we devised many ingenious and creative ways to stimulate her memory and pass the time.

I had rigged up a storage system for her craft materials from plastic containers. I had fixed them up inside with pieces of card to make sections to hold different items. I fitted the containers into a kind of frame that I propped up on pillows so that it was tipped up enough for her to see the contents without them all spilling out.

Nothing was straightforward but we found a way round most problems. If she couldn't tip something up far enough, she used a mirror to see inside. She also used the mirror to find things on her bedside table, which was crammed with all kinds of bits and pieces she kept there in case she needed them during the day. She grew adept at using something as a tool to pull the thing she wanted towards her.

We had done all kinds of things such as puzzles and making collages and cross-stitching, which was incredibly difficult because you need a lot of dexterity. It was time to try something new. I had bought the brushes and paint a while ago and waited for a day when she was feeling especially bright. This was it.

I fetched a big plastic sheet and spread it across her bed as she watched me, her eyes dancing in delight. Then I opened some pots of paint and put them in the plastic container and pinned a piece of paper to a board and propped them both up on pillows

'What shall I paint?' she said.

'Well, let's think. Look around your room and tell me what you can see clearly enough to copy.'

Lynn raised her hand and pointed to a shelf. 'I've got it,' she signed. 'You know how much I adore flowers. I'm going to paint that beautiful arrangement and they will live for ever.' She laughed as she said this, indicating that her reproduction might fall just a little short of the real thing.

When everything was in place I stood by the side of the bed holding what I thought would be the most likely thing to go flying – the water. Lynn started to paint, playfully waving the brush around flamboyantly, as though she was some great artist about to create a masterpiece.

Little speckles of paint found their way onto every nearby surface. I was thinking how wonderful it was that she was having one of her rare good days, when suddenly the cat jumped on the bed, landing on the tray of paints and catapulting the little pots into the air in every direction. Lynn and I and the bed and the room ended up resembling a paintballing venue. I couldn't believe it. As we took in the scene of devastation around us, we had a good laugh about it, but we had to admit to ourselves that painting had to go.

One thing Lynn really enjoyed doing, partly because it kept her connected to friends and family, was to make cards. I brought her catalogues and she chose materials like coloured sticky squares, little flowers and bits of ribbon and lace and ordered cards of different colours and sizes. She went to an awful lot of trouble thinking of a design and creating something beautiful by sticking on different things with double-sided tape. Each one could take many days because she could only work for short periods before feeling totally wasted.

She had a digital camera and a favourite pastime was taking pictures of old family photos and making them into something special. This gave her the idea of doing a beautiful thing for her grandfather's eightieth birthday. She sifted through all our photos and picked out ones that told the story of his life. There were pictures of him in his RAF uniform when he was a Lancaster bomber pilot during the war. Others showed him getting married, then with his children and grandchildren. Richard had arranged a trip for him to see one of the Lancasters that still flies and had taken lots of pictures so she added those too.

She photographed them, loaded them on the computer, printed them then painstakingly pasted them into an album in chronological order, with a little bit of help from me. The whole job took her about nine months. When she presented him with it, her grandfather was amazed at how she had managed to do it and he absolutely loved it.

The daily routine of care took up a lot of time but a significant part of every day was always devoted to Lynn's animals. From early on she had a hamster and because they don't live very long, she had five or six in the years she was ill. They lived in her room in an elaborate cage equipped with a wheel and long tubes they scurried through. It was on a table with wheels so I could take it out at night or if they got too noisy.

Lynn would get the hamster out and let it run from hand to hand which acted like physiotherapy for her. I did physio every day on her legs and back but she exercised her arms herself. I laid out a towel on her bed and she fed the hamsters by hand and trained most of them. It seemed like they sensed she was unwell – they never bit her, though one whom she nicknamed 'Psycho' wasn't adverse to sinking his long teeth into any hand other than Lynn's that happened to be in the vicinity. Mine, for instance.

Her fish had to be fed and the water changed once a week, which was quite an operation. Occasionally the plastic weeds had to be taken out and scrubbed so that provided quite a lot of activity in her room.

She loved her cats the best. Ollie, her favourite, who seemed to think that his one purpose on this earth was to be by Lynn's side, had followed on from Lucky. Then, because she was so vulnerable to infections, we got a couple of cats of a breed which lives indoors so they couldn't bring in any bugs from outside. Named Willow and Shadow, they were very handsome with blue eyes and long hair. She loved to stroke them and comb their silky fur.

Lynn saw more of her animals than she did of any humans, apart from me, Richard, Steve and her two nurses. If people came she tried to look her best, smiled and answered questions but just a ten-minute visit would take so much energy out of her that it left her wiped out. Animals, in contrast, did not demand anything from her, indeed, they gave their energy to her. And they gave her joy. They were very good for her to have around.

She had the big computer which Richard's police friends had raised the money to buy but it was not easy for her to use it on her own because she could not raise her head from the pillow even a couple of inches without passing out. So we got her a very small computer that she could hold in one hand and keep on the table by her bed. That was good because she could use it whenever she felt well enough but it was difficult to see and didn't have a stand.

Finally we found the perfect compromise – a notebook-sized computer, about six inches by four, which could be propped up on a stand.

If she was not too sick she worked on trying to get her recognition of letters back by copying words from a book on to her computer. She kept it up laboriously for years even though she could never remember the letters the next day.

We were always looking for ways of dealing with every-day things that other people take for granted. For instance, when Lynn needed her eyes tested the optician came to the house but Lynn couldn't speak or recognise letters. So I made a card with all the letters of the alphabet on it and held it beside her. He then pointed to a letter on his board and she showed me which one she thought it was and I would tell the optician.

After we had appeared on the TV documentary a lot of people who were in a similar position contacted me asking for advice. The result was that I got more involved with Action for ME and later The 25% ME Group, which represents the quarter of ME sufferers who are very seriously affected, like Lynn.

Lynn welcomed being involved in the documentary because she wanted to show people the true meaning of ME and that she was not lying or pretending. She continued to let the media come to see her whenever she felt up to it. She even became the 'face' of The 25% ME Group when they had a big push to publicise ME Awareness Week. Large posters with a photograph of Lynn in bed were pasted on hoardings all around the country. Her picture also headed The 25% ME Group's web page with a write up about her for people to send to their local media and doctors.

Mothers often rang me and said their daughter or son was having fits like Lynn. 'I am terrified. I don't know where to turn. The doctors aren't doing anything,' they told me, sounding desperate. 'That used to happen to Lynn but it doesn't any more,' I reassured them. 'There is medication they can have. Yes, they are frightening, but they are not lethal.'

Lynn felt that she was helping and it was good for me too to bring something positive out of our awful experience. But she got to the point where she got tired of the media and began to say no to things. Richard grew sick of it as well. They both felt, 'We can't do it any more.'

The problem was, it never seemed to do any good. Stories appeared in newspapers or TV and nothing happened. Lynn didn't want them coming and talking to her, or she didn't want to listen to me going through the story all over again. Yet she wanted me to continue to do it, so long as I did it where she couldn't hear it, because she wanted me to keep working on making people realise that ME is a real illness.

Lynn thought deeply about things, probably because of her enforced solitude. She considered carefully about the consequence of actions. Before her old school friend, Michaela, went to New Zealand to work as a doctor she came to say goodbye but Lynn, as ever, was too unwell for visitors. 'Would you not like to see her even if it makes you feel worse?' I pleaded. 'You can manage it when you have to see a nurse or something.'

'Of course I would *like* to see her but it's not about *like*,' she explained. 'What do you think it will be like, me lying here, unable to speak, unable to remember her, probably bursting into tears. How do you think that would make Michaela feel, never mind me?' She was right, she was always right. We had this ongoing joke between her, Richard and me about Lynn *always* being right.

Instead she asked me to take a photo as a reminder that she once had friends and that they still cared. Lynn's memory loss meant she was robbed even of the memories of the happy life she had led before ME. That was very sad but perhaps it was in some ways a blessing because if she had remembered every single day of all those years in that room, how would she have survived for as long as she did?

Lynn was remarkable in that for the great majority of her 17 years of illness she was mostly cheerful and resilient, loving, generous and thoughtful of other people. But she did have her bad times, especially around Christmas and her birthdays, which she grew to loathe because they meant another year had passed without anything changing for her.

Her first significant birthday came four years after she fell ill when she turned 18. I was determined to make it special. She couldn't have a party so instead we decorated her room with streamers and balloons. Richard rang up

Southern Radio and asked for a request for Lynn, telling them a bit about her. The female presenter picked the most appropriate song you could imagine, '(Something Inside) So Strong', written and recorded by Labi Siffre. The song was about how anybody can achieve anything, no matter what is thrown at them and it became our anthem.

We were always finding ways around our situations. That same birthday, even though Lynn couldn't eat anything, I got it into my head that she must have an eighteenth birthday cake. An idea came to me. I got an old biscuit tin and chose 18 little presents to go in it. There was a silver bracelet and five other pieces of jewellery, some nail varnish – she loved doing her nails – face cream, make-up, just small things. I wrapped them all individually, arranged them inside, then I covered the tin with icing and put 18 candles on it.

We sang 'Happy Birthday' as I carried it in to her room. She didn't have the strength to blow the candles out on her own so Richard and I leant down by the bed and helped her while making a wish, each of us knowing what the other had wished for. 'It's very nice, Mum. You have a piece. You know I can't,' she said, obviously believing it was really a cake. Then I revealed the secret within.

She was delighted to find that her coming-of-age cake was something she could enjoy after all. She opened one or two presents but then was worn out and left the rest for other days. Though that was a lovely day and afterwards she thanked us for making it so special, times like these, so very hard for Lynn, were extremely difficult for Richard and me too.

To see our beautiful, vibrant daughter reduced to this pathetic little celebration in a darkened room when all her friends were going to university or on gap years, getting jobs, finding boyfriends and making exciting plans for their future, tore us apart.

Lynn spent many of her birthdays in hospital, and quite a few Christmases too, with me sleeping in a chair beside her. When she got to 21 and had been dreadfully ill for seven years, she felt totally desolate and gave in to a rare bout of self-pity. 'When is it going to be my turn? How long am I going to be like this?' she asked me plaintively.

I was at a loss as to how to cheer her. Then a friend of mine remembered the case of Craig Shergold. He was a nine-year-old who had suffered from a brain tumour back in the '80s, and his family circulated a chain letter asking people to send him cards. So many thousands – eventually millions – arrived that he got into the *Guinness Book of Records*.

It was a phenomenal story at the time and the publicity led to a wealthy American paying for Craig to have a life-saving operation. My friend thought that sending a message out over the Internet for people to send cards to Lynn might also have a double effect – cheer her up and gain publicity for ME.

To our astonishment, thousands of cards arrived. I had to collect them from the post office in sack loads. On Lynn's birthday we lugged them into her room and she was completely amazed and extremely touched. It gave her a huge boost – and us too – to think that total strangers would care enough to buy a card, think of a message to write and post it.

It made her feel she was not totally cut off from the world. She could only open a few cards at a time so they kept her going for weeks. She didn't always remember what had happened either, which made it a delight all over again when I explained.

So many painful indications of time passing came and went, and they never got any easier to bear. The first time one of her friends passed her driving test and drove round to our house, Lynn said, 'I should be doing that.' Then a friend got engaged, 'I should be doing that,' she said again; friends got married, had babies, 'I should be doing that.'

Her lovely friend, Laura, sent an invitation to her wedding. 'I know that as you are at the moment, you can't come,' she wrote. 'But I would really love you to be there and I am hoping for a miracle so you can.' Lynn was deeply touched. 'It is lovely of Laura to take so much trouble to express her feelings,' she spelt out to me. I knew it would have been so much easier for Laura, in the midst of the preparations for her wedding day, to forget about Lynn and say nothing.

Gemma sent presents and newsy cards and Michaela also stayed in touch with Lynn, writing long letters from New Zealand all about the adventures she was having.

Again, Lynn really appreciated her not taking the easy way out but she was always tearful after I had read the letters to her as she yearned, so much, to have adventures of her own.

There were no words adequately comforting – hugs worked best, and comedy. But even Richard sometimes just couldn't do his usual funny-make-everyone-laugh routine and had to walk out of her room so she wouldn't see his tears. We tried our best not to get upset in front of her. Tears from us would have made it so much harder for her. If we cried every time we wanted to, our tears would never stop. We had to look to the future, keep believing that Lynn would be well again. It was that that kept all of us going, but it didn't stop the pain.

When Lynn was 22, Steve got married – another bitter-sweet day for me, feeling so happy for him while Lynn's absence from the occasion cut me to the quick.

His bride was Marcela, a stunningly beautiful girl from Chile whom he had known for a couple of years. They decided to get married in our local church, St Peter's, so they could involve Lynn as much as possible and she did her best to get into the spirit of things.

The process of getting her ready had to be spaced out because it exhausted her so much. So her hair was done three days before the ceremony, her nails two days before, and so on. She had ordered a special outfit from a catalogue that had a loose, long, cream jacket, and on the morning of the wedding I changed her into that and helped her with her make-up. Marcela got dressed at our house and pirouetted around Lynn's room looking totally gorgeous in her finery.

At the service they used a mobile phone so Lynn could hear the whole thing, then the new Mr and Mrs Gilderdale came back home to see her before going off to the reception. Obviously she was upset she couldn't be with them but she was happy about all the effort that was put in at least to make her part of it.

Lynn's favourite nurse, Julie, volunteered to spend the day with her so that I could be at the wedding. Until then I had never been out for more than a couple of hours and I was nervous about leaving her for the whole day. She was nervous too in case something happened. I coped by popping back twice when her important medicines had to be given and I left the reception early, at about 8 p.m.

Sadly, Stephen and Marcela's marriage didn't work out. I think she missed Chile and her family and she wanted him to move there but it was not an option for him. He had secured a very good job and there were few opportunities for him there. A while after the split, he met Sarah, equally beautiful, who is from Belgium. Having learnt Spanish when he was with Marcela, he now started working on his French.

They have been together nine years now and are planning to marry in the summer of 2011. When they had a baby son, Steve rang Lynn first to tell her, before he told anyone else. She banged on her table and I came running to find her face transfigured with joy even though tears were running down her cheeks. 'I have got a nephew,' she told me with flying hands. It was so lovely to see her crying for joy for once rather than in pain.

She couldn't wait for them to bring little Liam to show her. She absolutely loved babies. I arranged cushions around her so that he could lie beside her safely and when Sarah laid him down beside her, she gazed at him adoringly, playing with his tiny fingers. She was so very happy to see him and she put so much energy into looking her best and smiling.

Afterwards she was completely exhausted and a little weepy. 'I am sorry. I am only sad because I want a baby too, so very much,' she signed to me, as big, fat tears splashed onto her pillow.

'It will happen one day, you'll see,' I comforted her, stroking her hair. 'You will get better and your body will start working again. Then you will be able to have your own adorable baby to love, just like Liam.'

And I truly believed my words. One day my daughter would have all the things she dreamt of and all the things I dreamt for her, too. She'd be a mummy. But we just had to find out how to make that happen first.

CHAPTER TEN

A SAD PARTING

I knew I had to speak to Lynn. I had been tossing and turning in my bed at night for weeks trying to find the courage. I didn't want to do it because I knew it would hurt her and, God knows, she had enough misery in her life without me adding to it. I kept putting it off, waiting for a day when she was not so tired, not so sick.

One morning she woke to one of her better days with enough energy to do one of her favourite activities, using a rubber stamp to make designs on cards. This had to be it. I washed her as usual and when I had finished brushing her lovely dark hair, I sat down beside her bed, took a deep breath and said, 'Lynn, there is something I have to tell you.'

Her eyes immediately looked anxious and locked on to mine. I continued, as gently as I could. 'You know your dad and I have not been getting on recently? Well, I am so very sorry but I really feel that we can't go on like this any more and we will have to split. I am going to ask him to move out.'

She shook her head, tears filling her eyes, deep sadness casting a shadow across her pale and beautiful face. It was so very hard. Her whole world consisted of the four walls of her room and me and her dad and here I was, knocking away one of the main props of her existence.

Lynn loved Richard very much and he was utterly devoted to her but my relationship with him had hit rock bottom and the atmosphere in the house had been awful for months. I said to Lynn, 'We are arguing all the time. It is not good for us and it is not good for you.'

Signing the letters on her hand – an agonisingly slow way of communicating when she felt passionately about something – Lynn urged, 'No! You must not split up! You can work it out. Talk to each other. Go to counselling.'

But I knew we had come to the end. The daily emotional battle between Richard and me was draining the vital energy I needed for looking after Lynn and I honestly felt that separation was the only solution.

Full of misery and emotion myself at the time, I did not see clearly how we had got to that point but, looking back, I now realise that I had become obsessed with the mystery that was ME. I felt compelled to find the maddeningly elusive answer that would give my daughter her life back.

Since conventional medicine could do nothing for Lynn, I sought help from all kinds of alternative therapies: aromatherapy, reflexology, flower remedies, evening primrose oil, faith healing, vitamins and minerals – you name it. Any time I saw something on a website or read about a treatment in a magazine or health journal or was told about a friend of a friend who had benefitted from such and such, I discussed it with Lynn: 'Shall we have a go with that?' But we learnt to be cautious; some remedies were like poison to her.

The therapists were often supremely confident. One day I called up a homeopath. 'Oh yes, I know about ME,' she said. 'I have helped a lot of people. I am sure I will find just the thing for Lynn.'

She came and asked a lot of questions. 'Now, I want you to try this,' she said, writing out the name of a potion. The first time she took it, Lynn was violently sick. And she carried on being sick for weeks, which meant she couldn't have her feeding tube in and she ended up in hospital being fed intravenously. So we were not too impressed with homeopathy.

One chap told us that water under the ground and energies in the house affected things in the body. He examined the arrangements in our house with an authoritative air. 'You should not have a TV,' he announced, to my bemusement. 'It conducts negative energy which is very bad for Lynn.'

Proceeding to the bedroom, he enquired: 'Do any of your mattresses have wire springs?' Another source of 'negative energy', apparently. He also advised us to change all the furniture round to take advantage of 'positive energy'. It sounded a bit too far-fetched so we didn't do it. But it was probably the only thing we didn't try.

Lynn and I liked the sound of an American treatment where they put you on a big revolving table with magnets all around which are supposed to put energy into you. We talked it over for a while but eventually faced up to the reality that she was too ill to travel to the US.

I was not sure how many of these therapists really understood ME but I couldn't stop trying everything. One day I read in a magazine about a herbalist who had been successful with sore throats. Lynn's throat had looked lumpy, bumpy and red since the beginning of her illness and felt continually raw, like it was lined with broken glass, so I was always looking for something that would soothe it.

I got to the end of the article and noticed that the man lived not far from us, in Tunbridge Wells, so I gave him a ring and invited him round. He examined Lynn's throat and asked the usual raft of questions. Then he turned to me and said gently, 'I won't mislead you. I am not going to attempt to cure Lynn. Her illness is so complex and I would not be so presumptuous.'

I didn't expect him to be able to cure her, and I appreciated his honesty, yet I couldn't help feeling a twinge of disappointment. Each time we tried something new Lynn and I both tried not to expect a miracle but we couldn't help building up our hopes. Only hope makes you willing to bear the emotional and financial cost – and all these treatments cost a lot.

'What I will do is have a go at treating her throat,' he went on. 'I am afraid the mixture I will make up will be really horrible but you will have to persist with it to get results.'

True to his word, the mixture was absolutely vile. But the herbalist's humble manner had inspired us with confidence and I persisted in getting it down Lynn's tube. After about two months her throat was less sore and in six months all the lumps and bumps had gone. This was the only alternative therapy that had any success and it was the only one of Lynn's symptoms that had improved since Dr Alan Franklin controlled her spasms.

As well as trying all these treatments, every time I stumbled upon news of a research project, I read all I could on it and got hold of the doctor in charge to ask if it could help Lynn. I talked to a doctor at the Middlesex Hospital in London who had found that ME patients had reduced blood flow to the brain. I contacted a gene research project in Scotland and I sent a sample of her blood to another in New Zealand. They discovered her sample had a large number of misshapen cells, which apparently could have affected the flow of blood to her brain. A clinic in Holland was injecting patients with stem cells and announcing big improvements in people with multiple sclerosis. We talked it over and Lynn thought it was something she would like to try so I started seeing how we could get her there.

The treatment cost £10,000 and the only way she could travel to Holland was by air ambulance, costing a further £20,000. 'Shall we go for it?' I said to Richard. 'We will have to remortgage the house,' he said.

Just as we were making the arrangements, it was revealed that the clinic was a big con. Of course I was relieved we had found out in time before putting Lynn through so much pain and disruption and to save us wasting all that money, but that feeling was outweighed by the frustration that another little glimmer of hope had been snuffed out.

While I was obsessively eating, sleeping, talking, dreaming ME, it was not the same for Richard. It *could* not be the same for him because he had to keep going to the police station and behaving normally around people who had never heard of ME. Though he did as much as he could at home, he got to the stage where he really needed, for his own wellbeing, to get away from the situation for a while and do some ordinary things.

I would not do them. I had lost all balance in my life. I was totally submerged in ME and that was the way I wanted it because I was determined to spend every breath I had looking for answers. The result was there was no room left for my relationship with Richard and no way of us doing something together which would have lightened our load for a little while.

I remember him saying to me one day when we had a nurse coming in. 'Shall we go swimming at the pool?' he suggested.

'Swimming?' I replied, incredulously.

'Yes, swimming,' he said patiently. 'We like swimming.'

I reeled. 'I could not go *swimming*,' I scoffed.

I couldn't face doing something that Lynn had enjoyed so much before she was trapped in bed. The memories of her streaking joyfully through the water would have been too painful for me to bear. And I made Richard feel bad for suggesting it.

Perhaps we could have worked things out between us if, when Richard said, 'You are obsessed with ME,' I had responded with, 'Yes, I know. What can we do about it?' But instead of talking things over properly, we bickered constantly over every stupid little thing.

Richard started working longer shifts and I nagged him about it, which just made things worse because the more you nag, the more someone wants to get away. This had been going on for months by the time I finally spoke to Lynn, but I'd tried my best to hide it from her. And now seeing the complete horror spread across her face, I felt so guilty.

She was angry with me as well as extremely upset. 'I don't want Dad to go,' she sobbed. I was desperate to make her see things my way.

'I cannot go on like this, the emotional drain is too much,' I explained. 'The choices are that Dad leaves or I leave. I'm sorry to be so blunt but you know me. I don't want to put you through this but I really can't keep going as things are. Please try to understand'.

When Richard came home, I knew I had to speak to him straight away, before he saw how distraught Lynn was. 'Please, sit down. I have something I have to say,' I said. I took a deep breath. 'We can't go on living like this. We are arguing all the time. It's not good for you or me or Lynn. I am sorry but I want a separation and one of us will have to leave.'

He didn't disagree that our relationship had hit rock bottom but he didn't want to leave the home that he loved and that we had worked so hard to build up together. Most of all, he hated the thought of leaving Lynn.

'I could move out and you could stay with Lynn and get nurses in to look after her,' I suggested. But I knew as I said it that it wasn't going to happen.

Our local Primary Care Trust had already agreed to pay for more nursing care, even nurses 24 hours a day if I wanted it, so I could have gone out more; even going back to work would have been possible. But I was the person who knew best how to lift Lynn and attend to her needs without causing her any more pain. I was the one who understood everything she wanted to communicate in our special sign language. I saw it as my job to make her life as easy as it could be; I could not walk away and leave her in the hands of strangers.

Neither Richard nor Lynn accepted it at first but I stuck to my decision. Our marriage had been very good for a long time and had withstood a huge amount of stress but now it was dead.

After a little while Richard found a house not far away and moved out, which I am sure was very lonely and difficult for him at first. 'How am I going to see my dad?' Lynn asked me. 'I absolutely promise that, no matter what is going on between us, I will never stop your father coming to see you as much as he wants to,' I reassured her.

I made every effort to stick to my promise, though it made going through the process of separation and divorce really stressful. Usually a warring couple can keep away from each other for a while but, no matter how badly we were getting on, Richard had to come to the house to see Lynn.

She and I started falling out too, having a go at each other on a daily basis, sparked off by any silly little thing. 'What's wrong with you?' she might sign if I came in with a gloomy face.

'There's nothing wrong with me,' I'd snap back.

'There's no need to speak to me like that,' she'd retort.

Lynn could never be horrible but she could be unpleasant on rare occasions. I could be unpleasant as well. Locked together as we were in the house, we made little niggly remarks to irritate each other. We were both struggling to adjust to a huge change – Lynn had to come to terms with her dad not being at home, and I had to cope with doing everything on my own.

A lot of the problems were caused by the logistics of Richard visiting. If he said he was coming at a particular time then rang up half an hour before and changed it, I got annoyed because I had made plans for what I was doing while he was with Lynn.

'I've gone to the trouble of changing the time the nurse is coming, the least he can do is be here,' I'd fume.

Lynn would leap to his defence. 'It's not Dad's fault. He's got to work,' she'd point out. She hated me criticising him so that often led to an argument.

The difficulty was that a lot of people, including Richard at this time, thought that because I was here constantly, I would not have any particular timetable so it didn't matter if they changed their plans. But that wasn't the case. Because Lynn had so many needs I had to plan every day meticulously and adjust it according to how she was. There was always a certain amount to do for her care and I had to work it in around other things. For instance, if someone was coming I had to maybe do her medications before and wash her after the visit. If nobody was coming, Lynn and I worked things in through the day.

There were lots of bust-ups during the first nine months after the split, but we ironed out the problems once Richard fully grasped how important it was for me to be able to count on him coming when he said he would, and I understood that sometimes there were valid reasons why he could not stick to the arrangement. Basically, we realised we had to respect each other.

To reduce the tension I made up my mind to try not to argue with Richard and I usually slipped out for a while when he came to visit. Slowly Lynn accepted that the marriage had gone. 'I hated it when you were rowing so much,' she confided in me one day. 'I knew something had to be done. But I still wish my dad was here. I miss him so much.'

She was an adult woman of 24 when Richard moved out and, though she had been ill for ten years, shut away in her silent and shrouded room and cut off from normal life, she had somehow developed an emotional maturity which gave her great insight and understanding of the feelings of others. Once she had come to terms with the reality, she was able to help me.

Sometimes, when I complained angrily about Richard doing this or that, she said: 'Yes, I can see what is annoying you, but look at it from this point of view…' and she would put things in a way that made me stop and think and realise I had to try a bit harder. She helped us to be civil to each other.

And despite the stress, Lynn and I had a lot of fun as well. On better days, we continued to find things to laugh and joke about. I might read her something funny out of the paper or tell her about somebody I'd met out shopping who had said something amusing.

Whatever else was going on, if Lynn had to go into hospital, Richard and I were still both there for her, working closely together as a team. Things gradually settled down between us until we were getting on well again and I realised with relief that we could be friends. About four years after our divorce, he met Jeanette and they got married.

Lynn had yearned for us to get back together but she could see her dad was happy with Jeanette so she was happy for him. She wanted to get them something special for a present. Lynn's memory was patchy, but this was when she had regained some ability to read and write and she spent ages looking at catalogues of crystal glasses to choose just the right set. She also wanted to surprise them on their wedding day because she couldn't be there in person.

She asked Richard where the reception was going to be, looked it up on the Internet, found the email address, contacted them and explained her situation. She told the function manager in her email that a telegram would be arriving from her and asked him to give it to the best man to read out. Then she found a telegram company and wrote a lovely message wishing her dad and Jeanette happiness and saying she was sorry she couldn't be there.

She set it all up perfectly – she would always go that little bit further, thinking up ideas and doing whatever she could manage from her room to show how much she cared. She liked making people feel special.

Lynn once said to Richard, long before the split, 'I am sorry for ruining your life, Daddy, and ruining Mummy's life.' But I did not see it that way. Lynn *was* my life.

I eventually started ballroom dancing in the evenings and occasionally I went away for a couple of days either to see Steve and Sarah who had gone to live in Belgium, or over to Ireland for a family celebration. I let my hair down on those occasions and partied the night away in the old-fashioned Irish way.

Richard would come to stay while I was away and Lynn adored having him all to herself. When he was there he would clean out the fish tank, rearrange her plants, sometimes watch something on TV with her or point things out in a magazine or just sit on the edge of her bed and talk. It was like a little holiday for her when he was there.

Her dad remained very important to Lynn and she was very important to him. He used to phone her every day, usually several times and he said that colleagues at work were amazed at how he could carry on conversations lasting half an hour with her even though she couldn't speak.

They worked out a code where she tapped on the phone for 'yes' and stayed silent for 'no'. She could make noises too like clicking her tongue or a sharp intake of breath, which helped him guess her answers. 'What have you been doing today? Making a card for a friend?' he might ask. Silence, so that wasn't right. 'Watching TV?' A knock – yes.

'Anything good?' – knock. 'What were you watching? One of the soaps?' If she gave an intake of breath, it meant he was getting close, and he would go on guessing, drawing her out, until he got it right. They managed brilliantly.

But I never stayed away for long – I had no desire to. After a couple of nights I always wanted to get back because I had no wish to be anywhere except at home with Lynn so long as she was unable to be anywhere except at home in bed.

I never stopped looking for a cure for ME and following up every bit of scientific research that crossed my path. I came to realise that one of the major problems for people trying to do research into the disease is that they first have to find a way of making sure that the subjects taking part in any clinical trial really do have ME because sufferers are often lumped together, under the umbrella term of 'Chronic

Fatigue Syndrome', with people who are actually suffering from extreme stress or depression.

The conditions share many symptoms, such as acute tiredness and aching limbs, but people with ME have an increasingly recognised set of other symptoms as well. And one crucial difference between the two groups is that with ME, sufferers get worse after physical exercise, whereas those with depression generally feel better.

It didn't take me long to work out that the first and absolutely essential thing that has to be done is to develop an accurate diagnostic test for ME so that sufferers can be properly identified and then research can go forward on treatments. But I know it will cost millions. And until ME emerges fully from the ignorant belief that it's a psychological disorder, that funding will be hard to come by.

CHAPTER ELEVEN

FINDING FRIENDS

One day Lynn knocked on her table – bang, bang, bang – which was her signal for me to go to her urgently. I jumped up and dashed to her room, scared there was something wrong, to find her grinning like a Cheshire cat. She was holding a book and pointing to a page. 'That word is…' and she spelt it out on her hand triumphantly. She was 27 years old and it was the first time she had recognised a word for nearly 13 years.

I was absolutely thrilled. It meant her memory was coming back, and if that could recover, I told myself excitedly, why shouldn't all her other functions recover too? It was a reason to hope, a rare occurrence, and I leapt on it with a desperate hunger. The next day the word had gone again but I did not let that get me downhearted. It was a beginning and over the following months, slowly she recognised more and more and began to read again.

To help her memory, I made some cards with things written on them that she needed to know. I had them laminated so they would not get tatty with all the handling they got. She kept them on the big table beside her bed so that when she woke in the mornings she could look at the list to remind herself.

At first I wrote just one or two things on them like 'Ollie is my cat'. Later I made the list longer with things like: 'Mum and Dad aren't together any more', 'Steve's baby is called Liam', 'ME is the name of my illness'.

Gradually over the next couple of years her memory improved and she was able to read everything and use the computer to connect to the Internet and send emails. That opened up her world considerably. For a start she could shop online – and she loved shopping. At first she ordered clothes that she thought she would wear one day. She believed just as strongly as I did that she would get better eventually and enjoyed picking out dresses, blouses, skirts and jumpers, often in her favourite colours of lilac and purple.

On a more practical note she also searched for pyjamas that would cater for her tubes and physical restrictions while looking fashionable. She never got to wear the clothes – for 16 years she only wore pyjamas because if I dressed her in proper clothes it stole precious energy from something else.

While her memory was returning, her noise sensitivity was lessening and she began to be able to tolerate listening to music on earphones. Her love of all music was reignited and she bought herself CDs over the Internet. She also ordered books, though they were left unread. There just wasn't enough time between her regular bouts of sickness to do everything she wanted to do. And what she wanted to do most was to make cards or presents for her friends or family or find something special for them.

She began reaching out to people – she joined ME groups over the Internet but also made contact with people who were not ill through cat groups, craft groups and Facebook. She made friends with people of all ages, some of them in America, and a select few became very special to her. Her very best friend, Laura, who was also extremely ill with ME, could swallow and speak, but she was bedridden at home and too ill to see anybody. They were both limited in what they could write but the two of them just connected.

When Lynn first started emailing she told me what she wanted to say, then I wrote it out on a piece of paper and she copied it into the computer. She wanted to tell her friends, 'I typed this.' Her ability to spell never came back completely but she put words together phonetically. It's basically the language young people use to text each other but possible for us oldies to understand too.

Lynn became an extremely good writer. Her ability to construct sentences and connect with people through her words was astounding. I was amazed that someone who had missed out on education and who had been removed from society for all those years could access and process information the way she did.

She listened to people's problems and sensitively suggested solutions. Wisdom born from suffering is something you have to see to believe. From her quiet, shrouded room she reached out like an experienced agony aunt. It used to worry me because some of the situations she was hearing about were very, very sad. Many of the people she talked to had ME or were terminally ill with other conditions.

She often spoke to me about her friends' problems. One day she asked me if I knew anything about a particularly sad and complicated situation. 'What advice do you think I should give?' she said.

'I don't know if you should be taking all this on,' I said. 'Isn't it too much of a strain when you are so ill yourself?'

She thought about it for a bit then shook her head. 'Even though it upsets me to read what they are going through, it helps me to be able to feel that I am doing something for them,' she said.

It brought it home to me that Lynn needed to be caring as well as to be cared for. Though she was disabled and sick, she was still Lynn and she was a mature woman. She worried about me and Richard and she gave advice to us and Stephen as well as to her friends. When the GP came she often told her if I'd been ill or not sleeping or not eating properly. 'Oh, be quiet,' I tutted. But Dr Woodgate encouraged her to talk. 'She is looking after you and that helps her too,' she explained to me later. 'It is important for her to have a role in the family so that it's not always you doing the caring and worrying.'

Everyone who knew Lynn before her illness remembered her as the 14-year-old child she had been then and tended to forget that she had grown up in between. I was guilty myself of forgetting that she was nearly 30. But people she met over the Internet treated her like the young adult she was and as a person separate from us. 'Communicating with people outside has changed my life,' she confided to me. 'It has made a huge difference to getting through the day.'

Another thing that was vitally important about her Internet friends was that this was the first time since she was 14 that she had had any privacy. In every single aspect of her life she had to get somebody to help her. '*My mum even has to wipe my bum,*' she once wrote. '*It's okay when you're a baby, but you don't want it when you're an adult.*'

Now she loved having secrets. 'Everything until now has had to go through you, Mum. This is private,' she said. 'I want you to promise never to look at the messages on my computer or on my phone. Never, whatever happens.' I promised her I wouldn't and I never did, not even when she was asleep. I respected her wishes. I was delighted that she was having a life of her own and making relationships that were not filtered through me.

We had now been developing the vocabulary of our unique sign language for over a decade and we could talk about everything under the sun. Lynn took a lot of interest in what was going on in the world and if she couldn't sleep she would sometimes watch the 24-hour news.

At first she could only remember things for about three hours after she had heard it and she couldn't find the words to relate them to me. But she gradually improved and by the time she was 29, when I went into her room in the morning she would tell me the latest – bird flu epidemic, mud slides in faraway places or changes in the government's health policy. I would sit on the edge of her bed and delight in her ability to remember it all.

She had missed so many world events – the fall of the Berlin Wall, Nelson Mandela's release, Princess Diana's death. But what hurt her far more was that she missed her own life. Her friends were doing all the things she wanted to, getting married, having children – and she still couldn't do any of it.

Every day we tried to have a laugh and a joke and Lynn was amazingly resilient. But she was not superwoman and as the years rolled on with no sign of change for her, no progress being made towards the life as a mother that she so desperately wanted, sometimes she felt down. 'Mum, I am so fed up,' she complained to me. 'Why has this happened to me? How can so many things be broken? Do you think I will *ever* get better?'

My heart contracted with sorrow and pain. Why had it happened to her? Why had it happened to my family? It was so unfair. She, I, Richard, Steve, none of us had done anything to deserve this. We were not saints but I could not find any explanation for why cruel fate had singled out my lovely daughter for this torment.

I could not afford to give way to bitterness or despair or any of the negative emotions lurking in the background. In order to get through every day, I *had* to push them firmly away and keep believing and I *had* to keep Lynn on the path of hope. I carried on reading stories to her of other people who had got better on this therapy or that pill even when she wearied of hearing them. 'How is that going to help?' she would ask me. 'What will it do for *me*?'

And while I searched and searched ever more desperately for a treatment or a cure, new torments befell her all the time, always made worse by being met by disbelief. One day when I was going to wash her, she indicated: 'My back is itching. Can you see what it is?' I rolled her over, pulled up her pyjama top and saw a rather nasty, red circular sore that was weeping and bleeding. 'How horrible,' she moaned.

Lynn had really beautiful skin, pale and almost translucent, and she was immensely proud of it because it was the one thing that had not been affected by her illness. She took care of it with very expensive, top-quality creams from Clarins or Clinique which were specially formulated for sensitive skin.

She absolutely loathed breaking out in these itchy sores. We tried all sorts of medicated creams as more of them appeared all over her neck, face, arms and legs, but nothing seemed to help. At the time she was also having bowel problems and a bad reaction to her liquid food and was becoming nutritionally deficient. She was desperate to avoid going into hospital but then she developed a bout of severe stomach pain and sickness and there was no alternative to taking her into the Conquest Hospital.

As soon as he saw her, the consultant – who was one who had previously made it very clear to us that he did not believe in ME – took far more interest in the sores on her skin than the pain in her stomach. 'What are these?' he asked suspiciously.

'It's some kind of eczema,' I said. 'Dr Woodgate has been treating it at home for a couple of months.'

Then he called in a dermatologist and, without consulting Lynn, me or Richard, the two of them then decided to bring in a psychiatrist. I happened to overhear a nurse talking to the psychiatrist's secretary to arrange this meeting and I went mad. I demanded to see the consultant but was told he was not in the hospital. I rang Richard and he came immediately.

Despite requesting a meeting several times, it was four days before the consultant casually appeared in Lynn's room while on his ward round. 'Why are you bringing in a psychiatrist? What are you suggesting?' I asked him straight out.

'When you see a rash like that it makes you wonder about the whole illness. The rash does not fit any pattern,' he replied.

'It's obvious you are influenced by not believing in ME,' I pointed out.

'It's difficult when you can't find physical reasons for symptoms,' he countered. 'Lynn's case is complicated.' After some more debate Lynn signed to me that she no longer wished to be treated by him. I conveyed her message to him and he left.

Later that day Richard and I were sitting with Lynn when the dermatologist came into the room. 'We will go to another room to discuss this,' he announced, with a sideways glance at my daughter.

'No, we won't,' I snapped. 'Lynn is an adult. She has the right to be involved in every aspect of her own care.'

He absolutely refused to speak in front of her so Richard and I, both fuming, had to give in and go with him to the consultant's room. 'We want to bring in a psychiatrist because we believe Lynn's skin problem is dermatitis artefacta,' he told us. 'That means her sores are self-inflicted – she is doing it to herself.'

I was completely dumbfounded. 'Why are you saying this?' I demanded. 'What on earth do you think she is using to damage her own skin?'

'Well, she has got all these creams, hasn't she?' he said. 'She must be mixing them up and rubbing them in circles to cause a reaction.'

'That's absolute rubbish!' Richard burst out.

I was so annoyed, I felt like screaming at him. Somehow I managed to control my voice. 'These are very expensive creams,' I said, coldly. 'They don't cause a reaction no matter how much you mix them.'

'How do you know she is not getting out of bed at night and getting her hands on other things?' he said.

'She's paralysed! She *can't* get out of bed,' I cried. I could not believe my ears – after all these years doctors were *still* questioning whether Lynn was genuinely ill. 'How the hell do you think she reaches to the middle of her back to make sores when she can't move? She is itchy and uncomfortable and absolutely hates having these sores. Why do you think she would cause them herself?'

'To get attention,' he suggested.

Fury coursed through my veins. 'She has been ill for weeks at home while we did everything possible to avoid coming here,' I pointed out icily. 'She is frequently in hospital. She is sick and tired of attention! She doesn't need it. She has got enough things wrong with her to be in hospital constantly without damaging her lovely skin. And she does not want to see a psychiatrist. She had enough of that in the past.'

We suggested that if he was still suspicious he should carry out patch tests with anything that Lynn had access to. He refused. 'Negative results would not prove innocence,' he insisted. We told him we did not accept his diagnosis, that he was wrong and that we would be discharging Lynn the next day.

Some months later Steve was leafing through a cat magazine that I had been given by an elderly neighbour and he saw an article that said some cat conditions can be transferred to people who have suppressed immune systems. I thought back to when Lynn's skin problem began and remembered that her cat was being treated at the time, also for a skin condition. '*She is always stroking the cat,*' I thought. '*I wonder…*' There was a picture in the magazine of one transferrable condition – round red sores just like Lynn had. Ringworm.

I phoned the vet and he confirmed that he had been treating Lynn's cat for ringworm at that time. Richard and I demanded a meeting with the hospital's medical director to make a complaint. We showed him the article and told him what the vet had said. He agreed that ringworm was the likely explanation for Lynn's skin condition.

'Can you please take the diagnosis of dermatitis artefacta out of her notes?' I requested.

The director shook his head. 'No, I am sorry, we can't change it because that was the doctors' opinion at the time. But we can put a note in saying that at a later stage evidence came up to show that it was something else.'

I was not satisfied. I could just imagine people who don't believe in ME pointing to this diagnosis and saying: 'Look – Lynn Gilderdale self-harmed.' But there was nothing I could do. My only revenge was to blank the arrogant consultant. I saw him once coming towards me along a long empty corridor. He gave me a big smile but I walked straight past, looking the other way. It was very unlike me to behave rudely but I just could not bring myself to pass the time of day with him. And we put on Lynn's notes that she never wanted to be treated by him ever again.

Lynn grew to detest hospitals over the years. They stabilised her in the numerous crises she suffered but they had nothing to offer to treat her underlying illness and this scepticism, these veiled accusations, made us all angry and despairing.

She was better off at home where I did my best to keep her spirits up because every instinct told me that only hope would pull her through. I kept my eyes fixed on a sunny tomorrow and painted pictures of it for her to cling to. 'When the virus has burnt itself out and you are better, even if you can't walk straight away, you will be able to go for rehabilitation and they will help you get mobile,' I told her. 'Even if you have to use a wheelchair, you can have your independence. You can get your own place, maybe not far from here, and I will pop in all the time to make sure you are managing. It will be okay. You will have a life one day, you'll see. You have a future.'

Lynn listened and smiled, but she didn't reply. I just hoped that she believed in a life after ME as firmly as I did.

CHAPTER TWELVE
DISASTER
IN HOSPITAL

Lynn was now 28 years old and as she had been ill for half her life. Every day I watched my daughter closely and I knew intimately every nuance of expression on her face, every movement of her hands. I knew exactly how much energy she had, I knew when she was cheerful, when she was hopeful, when she was philosophical, when she was sad.

I was sitting beside her bed in the Conquest Hospital in Hastings. She was admitted as she had to have her Hickman line moved from one side of her chest to the other. Hickman lines are usually only left in place for a short time but Lynn's had been in place for seven years and it had perished.

As I watched her face, there was an expression I did not recognise. All I knew was that it made me anxious. 'What's the matter?' I asked, gingerly. Her large dark eyes locked on to mine, desperately trying to convey the message. 'There is something wrong,' I said sharply to the doctor.

'Oh no,' he said airily. 'Everything's fine.'

Everybody had been feeling as good as we ever did that morning. I had just come back from a rare weekend away in Ireland, where I had been to a big fancy dress party in Dublin for my niece's fortieth birthday and had a great time. Lynn had helped me choose my outfit: a 1920s flapper-style dress complete with headband, long gloves and a cigarette holder. We had pored over catalogues together and she had picked out a few that I ordered on trial and when they arrived, I did a little fashion parade for her. She really liked one and I liked it too so I ordered that – she loved to be part of everything that was going on.

I had had fun telling her all about the party and how good the dress had looked and the news of the rest of the family, and she was happy that she had had her dad looking after her for the weekend. Her general mood was the same as it had been all the years of her illness: believing she would one day get better and hoping that something would come along to help her.

Though the procedure to change the Hickman line was relatively straightforward, she was a bit apprehensive about it because she was having it under local anaesthetic. She was worried that she might be able to feel something and be unable to tell anyone. We were warned that there was a small risk of a pneumothorax, where the line punctures the lung. But as Lynn had had a Hickman line fitted successfully before, and we had the same surgeon, we were pretty confident all would be well.

So when we got to the hospital, I went to find the consultant who was doing the operation. 'Can I come into the theatre with Lynn because she cannot speak and she may need me to interpret what she needs?' I enquired. 'I promise I will keep out of your way.'

He wasn't very keen but agreed to allow me in and Lynn was obviously relieved that I would be there to 'translate'. Richard was there too but he had to wait outside the operating theatre.

The perished Hickman Line was removed from the left side of Lynn's chest by another doctor in the morning. Now it was afternoon and all that was needed was for the consultant to put the new one in on the right-hand side. There was a big blue sterile area over Lynn and some sort of machinery down the middle of the trolley which meant he could not see her face. I stood on the other side of it and watched her for signs of distress.

Everything was fine at first. As the consultant pushed the new line in, the nurse said encouragingly, 'Well done, that's the worst bit over.' Lynn smiled as if to say, 'That's good,' but the next moment her face contorted and she started trying to tell me something. She couldn't use her hands to write out the words because her right one was pinned under the sterile area and because of the angle she was lying at, she couldn't use her left one freely, either. As I struggled to get what she was trying to say, my heart raced with anxiety.

'Is it pain?' I asked, but she always did a sharp intake of breath for pain. She shook her head and pulled the same face again. 'There's something wrong,' I kept repeating, ever more urgently, to the consultant. 'I don't know what it is, but something is *definitely* wrong.'

Whatever I said made no difference to him. 'Don't worry,' he said airily. 'I've nearly finished.'

Lynn was growing more and more distressed and suddenly I realised she was indicating she couldn't breathe. Again I told him, even more forcefully, 'There is something very wrong.' I couldn't see the consultant properly because of all the machinery and he wasn't making any effort to communicate with me or to look at Lynn's face.

I turned round in desperation to the nurses. They looked as unconcerned as the consultant. Nobody was taking any notice of me. I was badly frightened, and now I was getting thoroughly angry. Why wouldn't they *listen* to me? 'Look at Lynn's face!' I cried to the nurses. 'There is something terribly wrong here.'

The consultant just raised his hands in the air and said, 'Look, no hands! It's all done. I'm not touching her.' He presumably thought Lynn, or I, was just making an unnecessary fuss.

'But she can't breathe!' I burst out.

Lynn was now fighting desperately for breath. I was about to march round the trolley to drag him physically to look at her panic-stricken face when he checked the monitor and then the Hickman line and realised with a start that the possible problem highlighted to us before the operation, had happened.

'It's a pneumothorax,' he said – in other words, he had punctured Lynn's lung. 'Get oxygen straight away.'

Now at last the nurses raced to get what was needed to help Lynn breathe. Young doctors clustered round to watch with keen interest as the consultant quickly took the Hickman line out again.

Once the panic had died down I sat by Lynn's bedside and took her hand in mine. 'I'm so very sorry,' I told her. I felt anguished with guilt: before the procedure I had assured her that I would be there to see she was okay, but I had failed in two ways. She was not okay, and it had taken me too much precious time firstly to understand her distress and what she was trying to say and secondly to force the consultant to respond.

I was dismayed that, on top of everything she had to put up with on a daily basis, she had now been made a lot worse by someone who was supposed to help her. Dismay turned to anger because the consultant didn't seem overly concerned. 'Oh, she'll be all right,' he said. 'She's on oxygen now and she will have a drain for the lung.'

He walked out of the operating theatre and spotted Richard who had been getting twitchy because things had gone on for so long. 'She's got a punctured lung,' the consultant informed him, and walked off, leaving Richard standing there, gaping after him in shock.

Staff pushed Lynn into a bay then took ages locating an available bed on a ward for her. 'Which consultant should she be under?' they kept muttering until Richard got mad. 'I don't care who she should be under,' he shouted. 'You have done this to her so now you had better find her somewhere to go pretty sharpish.'

Eventually she was admitted to a side room on a ward and I stayed with her, sleeping in a chair or bedding down on the floor. She was in terrible pain despite being given extra morphine and was having great difficulty breathing, even with the oxygen.

Over the next seven days the pain increased and I repeatedly asked for something to help her. Eventually they did an ultrasound scan that revealed what they thought was old, thick fluid and that her lung was still not inflated. They decided to 'aspirate' the lung, which meant inserting a needle and drawing out whatever is there – in this case blood. 'It is nothing to worry about,' the doctor who had taken over her care told us. 'She'll feel better after this.'

She didn't. Her pain got worse and worse. When I lifted her on her right side, or when I rolled her off the bedpan on the right, her face screwed up in agony and she was fighting for every breath. She looked at me pleadingly, with tears in her eyes, and signed, 'It hurts so much.'

Yet again, I kept telling the doctors and nurses, 'There is something wrong.' And yet again they repeatedly insisted, 'No, there isn't.' They made me feel I was being a nuisance, like they thought I was an overanxious mother. Finally, after I had pestered and pestered, growing increasingly worried and insistent, a doctor told me on a Thursday evening that they would do a CT scan on the following Monday.

That night, Lynn had a dreadful time. She was exhausted and distressed by the effort to breathe. I watched her chest struggling to rise, I heard the rattling in her throat and saw the panic in her eyes. Every few minutes I strode out of her room down to the nurses' station and demanded, 'Please get the doctor on call down. Something awful is happening to Lynn.'

Three times I had the doctor on call summoned who said she was okay; everyone was getting irritated with me. At last I persuaded them to do something and they arranged an X-ray: they said it showed there was nothing wrong. I felt like I was going mad. Lynn was sobbing because being moved on to a trolley for the X-ray had increased her agony and she was gasping for breath and panicking because she couldn't get any air in, yet everyone was treating her as if she was just making a fuss or hyperventilating. They could see what I could see: she was flinching in pain and fighting to breathe but because their equipment indicated no problem, they concluded it was self-induced. There was no kindness, no concern.

About an hour later I could stand it no longer. Because Lynn had been through so much, we rarely panicked about anything but I was seriously panicking now. '*Why will nobody see there is something dreadfully wrong? Why will nobody do anything?*' I asked myself, my heart thumping. I was convinced that if she did not get help soon, she would die. I ran to the nurses' station again. 'Really, something needs to be done,' I pleaded. 'You *can't* leave her like this a moment longer.'

The chief nursing sister came along, peered at Lynn and stroked her hand. 'Now just calm down, dear. You'll be okay, there is nothing wrong,' she soothed.

'*Oh my God. What use is that?*' I thought. 'She *is* calm!' I burst out, furiously. 'She is distressed because she can't breathe.' I felt utterly helpless, angry and dreadfully afraid.

I was left alone with Lynn again to watch her getting worse by the minute all through the night. When morning eventually came I stood looking out of the door of her room, which was next to the nurses' station, feeling overwhelmed by hopeless despair. What could I do now? Who could I turn to for help?

As I stood there in the doorway, my mind racing, desperately seeking some solution, a glimmer of hope appeared. I spotted a consultant who had treated her kindly in the past, standing by the nurses' station with his team of doctors.

I dashed up to him. '*Please,* can you come and see Lynn,' I begged. 'I know you are not her consultant this time but she is in terrible distress. She can't breathe.'

He immediately came along to her room, took one look at her and ordered: 'I want a CT scan done. Immediately.'

She was rushed off for the scan while the consultant studied the X-rays. He noticed something everyone else had missed and that the scan confirmed – Lynn was bleeding into her chest cavity and her lungs were awash with blood. One lung had already completely collapsed and the other was in the process of being flattened by the large volume of blood in her chest.

After Richard and I had waited an agonisingly long time, the consultant sought us out. 'I need to speak to both of you, but not in front of Lynn,' he said. We could see by his face that he was worried. He took us into his room and explained what had happened. 'This is very serious. We can't deal with it here,' he said. 'Lynn needs to have assisted breathing. She has to go on a life-support machine and she may need surgery to open up her chest to stop the bleeding. I am ringing round the intensive care units in London to find her a bed.'

I was stunned. I couldn't believe it. For ten whole days we had been telling the doctors and nurses that something was going wrong but no one had listened and now she was fighting for her life. But I was too exhausted for anger. All I thought of was whether Lynn was going to die.

Richard and I raced down the corridor with her as she was wheeled to the Conquest's intensive care unit (ICU), then Richard phoned Steve, who was in the UK for business, to tell him what had happened. 'It's not looking good,' he said. Steve immediately rushed to the station to catch a train from London to Hastings. He was desperate to get to the hospital before Lynn was put under anaesthetic in case she never woke up again.

When we were allowed in the ICU, Lynn was still just conscious. Her eyes above the oxygen mask sought us out and she beckoned for us to come near. We leant over her. She was so weak and pale and racked with pain, it broke my heart.

Summoning all her remaining strength, and fixing us with great determination in her eyes, she slowly and very deliberately wrote on her hand: 'Please don't let me die.' For 'die' she made a gesture of drawing her hand across her neck. I guessed: 'Die?' She nodded and repeated, 'I don't want to die.'

I smoothed back the hair from her forehead. 'You're not going to die,' I whispered. 'They are going to sort you out. That's what this is for.'

Then she looked at both of us with so much love in her face and drew on her hand: 'Goodbye. I love you.'

The next minute she was put under general anaesthetic and a team of doctors and nurses went through the horrible process of pushing a huge tube down her throat and connecting it to the life-support machine that pumped air through it into her lungs to keep her alive.

When it was done, Richard and I stood by the bed of our unconscious child, feeling helpless and numb, waiting in anxious torment as the medics continued the miraculous work of saving our daughter's life. There were tubes going in and tubes going out, bloods being taken and medications being given. All the while the steady puff of the life-support machine resounded in the room. And still we waited.

It was evening before they managed to find a bed for her in King's College Hospital in London. Lynn was stretchered down the corridors and loaded in an ambulance accompanied by a crash team. Steve, Richard and I watched it roaring off at speed with blue lights flashing and sirens blaring. We went home to collect some things we needed to stay with her then drove in miserable silence to London, not knowing if she would be dead or alive when we arrived.

We got there at about 10 p.m. and were directed to the intensive care unit. It was a large ward, painted white and dimly lit with little lights of different colours glowing and winking from the state-of-the-art machinery clustered around each bed. I remember thinking it looked like the inside of a spaceship. The nurses moved silently about their work; there was just the sound of the life-support machine puffing air into Lynn's lungs and other machines whirring and beeping by other patients' beds.

It was very upsetting to see Lynn hooked up to all these tubes and wires but at least she was stable. Everything possible was being done for her. We retreated to the visitors' waiting room where we stretched out on the long seats and fell into exhausted sleep.

Over three litres of blood was drawn off Lynn's lungs and she spent two weeks on the life-support machine. She was gradually weaned off it and went from intensive care to high dependency and was then transferred back to the Conquest, where she still had to use a special machine to help her breathing. She was in hospital for over three months altogether – including over Christmas – and she needed oxygen for a long time after she came home.

We were upset that the consultant who had attempted to insert the Hickman line did not seek us out afterwards to ask us how she was or to say, 'I am sorry she had to go through so much.' He could have shown us just that little bit of human kindness.

We made a complaint, not about the procedure going wrong, but about his attitude and the answer came back that he hadn't realised Lynn had become so ill. He also said that he had apologised at the time, but I cannot remember hearing him. We replied, 'If you puncture the lung of somebody who is severely ill, you would expect them to be badly affected. So the least you can do is enquire.'

We were appalled by the apparent lack of concern and disgusted that it had taken too long to draw everyone's attention properly to Lynn's distress, but we didn't pursue the complaint. We didn't have the energy. We had taken so many knocks that we had no reserves left and we relied on the medics so heavily that we couldn't afford to be at war.

I was used to arguing with doctors to stand up for Lynn. There were times when I felt so angry that I wanted to grab them and shake them to make them see what was right in front of their eyes, but I learnt early on that if I let rip I was treated as an overprotective, neurotic mother.

I learnt to hold back my anger and frustration and talk to them in a measured way, requesting calmly that they do whatever was needed. I had become knowledgeable about what that might be so if, for example, they pronounced that Lynn was hyperventilating. I'd reply, 'That is not the case. I would appreciate it if you would do a perfusion scan.'

If they insisted there was nothing wrong, I'd enquire, 'Have you treated people with severe ME before? Have you encountered this problem in the past?' The answer would usually be, 'No but...' So then I'd press on: 'We insist on this test being carried out.' If a doctor continued to refuse treatment I'd tell him or her, 'Lynn does not want to see you any more. Can she see somebody else, please?'

I hated the way most of the medical profession treated Lynn, the additional unnecessary pain they caused her by their scepticism in her illness. There were a few wonderful exceptions and it was their care and belief that kept us going, but that didn't stop me from being angry with the medical establishment as a whole. However, anger was useless, futile, and I had to channel it elsewhere, into research, and looking after my daughter. Little did I know that I was soon going to have to call on all my reserves of strength and energy to face Lynn's decision – a decision that would change all of our lives for ever.

CHAPTER THIRTEEN

YOU CAN'T
FIX ME

Sitting down next to Lynn's bed, I smiled brightly. 'Well, which one do you want to do first?' I asked. I was setting things up for her to make some birthday cards. I had got her craft box out with the sequins and stars and bits of lace she liked to stick on them and had propped it up in the special frame.

I was looking forward to a cosy time doing one of our favourite activities. But instead of answering me, Lynn turned to me with a serious look on her face, lifted her hands and signed, 'I want to talk to you about something.'

My heart skipped a beat. 'I really can't go on,' she spelt out. 'I am too broken. You can't fix me any more. We have to do something.'

I closed my eyes as desolation washed over me. She had been gently leading up to this for some time, saying quite regularly that she was fed up with her life. Over the past few weeks I had found her quietly crying at some point most days, which was very unlike her. Through all her years of suffering, Lynn rarely indulged in self-pity.

I took a deep breath. 'I understand the way you feel. It is a rotten life. I am so sorry for you,' I said, softly. 'But you don't know what is going to happen tomorrow. You can never tell what is round the corner. There is a lot of research going on which may find a cure. And look how much more you can do now than you could six months ago. Your memory is so much better – why shouldn't other things start improving as well?'

Lynn looked deep into my eyes. 'Yes, but you have been saying that, and I have been believing it, for how long?' she asked gently. 'I am tired, Mum. I just can't keep doing it any more.'

I *did* understand. Completely. Who would want to live a life like hers? I knew that this was something she had been going over in her own mind for months, maybe years, before she had spoken about it and that it had taken great courage to tell me. And I knew what she meant when she said, 'We have to do something.' But how could I bear it? It would mean that I would lose her.

At the same time she had been so emphatic during that terrible time in hospital when she begged me just before she went on the life-support machine: 'Please don't let me die.' So I did not believe she really wanted to die. But she was losing hope, that was clear. And I could not let that happen.

My mind raced. 'What about trying some antidepressants? They might help,' I suggested.

'I am not depressed. I am unhappy with the quality of my life. I don't want to go on like this,' she persisted.

I tried again. 'But maybe if you got the right pills it would put a sort of cloud over everything and help you deal with it,' I said.

Lynn looked at me pleadingly, willing me to understand. 'Mum, can't you see? I have been dealing with it. I just can't do it any more.'

As she signed frantically, my heart squeezed painfully and I desperately searched my mind for words that might bring her comfort and the will to battle on.

'Being depressed is nothing to be ashamed of,' I told her. 'It doesn't mean your illness is psychological. You have every right to be depressed with what you have to put up with. You haven't had it before but I really think you are suffering from depression now and if a drug can help you not feel so sad all the time, it will be worth it.'

I argued for as long as I could but she remained adamant she would not take any antidepressants. I was forced to accept that it was her decision to make. By the end of the conversation she was exhausted and I felt drained. I sat beside her bed for a while in silence, holding her hand, trying to push thoughts of her despair and what it boded for the future from my head and wishing with all my heart that I could find something more to say to restore her hope and strength.

Part of what was affecting Lynn's mood was that she was putting on weight even though she was only taking in 400 calories a day in liquid nourishment. She looked in her hand mirror, saw that her face had grown puffy and she really hated it. 'I can't even eat and I am getting fatter all the time. How can that happen?' she complained.

Without hope that her torture would end, I knew that Lynn's life would be literally unbearable. None of the scores of medical people we had seen over the years had given her that hope. I was the only one who could do it. I plunged into a hectic flurry of activity contacting stem cell researchers, nutritionists, hormone specialists, doctors of all description asking for advice, tests, anything that might help.

I tried to carry on as normal with Lynn but she would not let the subject rest. Almost every day she somehow brought it into the conversation. 'I have had enough. I don't want to go on like this,' she'd say with gentle but determined persistence. 'You *have* to admit it, Mum, come on. We *have* to talk about this.'

Though it made my soul sick to recognise it, I realised what she was doing: she wanted both Richard and me to face up to the fact that it was only a matter of time before she died, and to come to terms with it. More and more things were going wrong in her body. A kidney condition, liver dysfunction and heart problems had been added to her other afflictions. It seemed that all her organs were slowly giving up, just like her spirit.

The turning point had been that terrible time in hospital when she had to be kept alive by machines. It hardened her former dislike of hospitals into an implacable determination to keep out of their hands. 'I never, ever want to go into hospital again,' she insisted. 'They are more likely to kill me than cure me.'

We all knew that every winter she developed severe infections that only responded to intravenous antibiotics that could not be administered at home. So if she refused to go into hospital and an infection raged unchecked, her chance of survival would be low. This was the reality she wanted us to face. She was asking the impossible; we could never do it.

When she tried to talk to Richard about it, he just couldn't stand it. 'Look Dad, we have to talk about this, it's not going to go away,' she cajoled him. She tried to explain to him how she felt about being 'too broken'. But each time she began, he soon broke down in tears. 'I can't talk about this. I am sorry,' he confessed. It was harder for him because, while Lynn and I were together all the time and she was softly but insistently raising the subject with me every day, his time with her was much more intense. Every time he visited she wanted to discuss this awful, awful thing. It was just too upsetting for him.

As for me, I was hearing what she was saying, and understanding it in my head, but I was a long way from accepting it in my heart. Lynn, however, was unwavering. And having made the decision she wanted everyone she cared about to be forewarned so she started writing a long letter for the friends she had made over the Internet.

Lynn was 29 years old and had been stricken with ME for more than 15 years when she started on this letter in early 2007. She didn't show it to me, but she talked it over with me because she was worried about the effect it might have on her friends.

'I've been thinking about this for a long time and I know I don't want it to be a terrible shock for my friends when I go but I don't know how to tell them. What do you think I should say?' she asked me.

I was so torn. She was my beloved daughter, I would do anything in my power to help her do anything she wanted, but it hurt so much to help her say that she didn't want to live any more. But this was not about me. I had to do what no mother should be asked to do and advise her as best I could. 'I think it is probably a good idea to warn them,' I said. 'Perhaps you could tell them you have had enough but because your friends are ill themselves you have to be careful. Hearing of your plans and feeling so sad about you could make them worse.'

'Yes, that's what worries me. I will have to think a lot about how I word it,' she said.

After that she mentioned it occasionally. 'I am still writing. It's a very hard thing to write,' she would say and I would murmur words of sympathy.

Around the time that Lynn was thinking about her letter to her friends, she developed severe pain around her kidneys. She was referred to a specialist at Eastbourne General Hospital who diagnosed kidney stones and she went in to have them treated with lipotripsy, which is where they blast them with rays. It was agonising and she had it done twice but it still didn't work properly. The sediment from the stones usually comes away when the patient gets up and walks around but as Lynn was bedridden that didn't happen.

After the lipotripsy failed to treat her kidney stones, she had to go into Eastbourne Hospital to have them removed under general anaesthetic. I went with her in the ambulance and saw her settled in a pleasant room and prepared to spend the night with her before she went to theatre in the morning. Richard arrived after his shift to spend the evening with us.

We were sitting talking when Lynn knocked on her bedside table to get our attention. We looked across at her and she beckoned us over. I saw she had tears in her eyes but also a look of fixed determination on her face. A lump of alarm rose in my throat.

'I want to talk to you, seriously,' she signed to us. 'If anything goes wrong tomorrow, I do not want to be resuscitated. I do not want to be kept alive on machines. You must let me go peacefully.'

I had been hearing Lynn say this sort of thing for weeks, so though tears filled my eyes, I did not break down. But Richard, heartbroken, burst into sobs. 'Please, no. Don't say that,' he cried.

'I am so sorry, Dad,' she signed with trembling hands. 'I love you both. I don't want to leave you. If there was a better choice I would take it. But I am too broken. You can't fix me any more.'

My big Irish family and the reason I wanted lots of children of my own.

Young and in love – Richard and me in 1973.

Big brother Steve, almost four, proudly holding his baby sister Lynn.

The photo from a holiday in Portugal where Lynn was snapped having a sulk – parents can be so annoying!

Lynn, three, Richard, and Steve, six, having fun in the sun in the South of France.

Lynn, aged seven, smiling shyly for the camera, with those cute freckles that I loved and she hated.

Enjoying a sunny afternoon at home with auntie Rosie and cousin Nathan.

Perfect poise. My little ballet dancer was so happy to be a winner.

Lynn (centre) as the proud captain of her school netball team.

Isn't this fun? The born entertainer (left) waiting in the wings at one of her school plays.

Even homework didn't wipe the smile of Lynn's lovely face.

Lynn, aged 12, holding on tight as she learns a new water sport with her brave brother.

This is one of my all time favourite photos. It is so special to me and somehow captures the depth of Lynn. It was taken shortly before she fell ill.

A snapshot of the rest of Lynn's life. A cuddle from Ollie would help and the only place he ever wanted to be was in her arms.

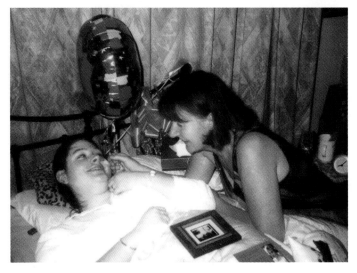

Lynn's 21st birthday. We were determined to celebrate and Lynn smiled and made the best of the day.

Steve visiting Lynn in hospital. They used to go on adventures together, but eventually Lynn had to let Steve explore the world without her.

Lynn, aged 22, with her dad. He was her friend, her confidante and always there for her.

Shrouded in darkness. Lynn spent most of her life behind closed curtains, even when her much-loved grandparents came to visit.

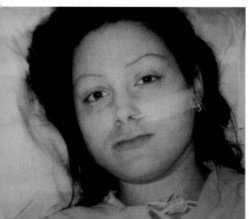

This was taken for one of the articles Lynn did to raise awareness. You can see her fish tank in the background – a little drop of the ocean.

Lynn couldn't always hide her pain behind a smile. This was taken a year before she died and her eyes tell you all you need to know.

My world collapses. Just hours after saying goodbye to Lynn, the police guard our bungalow while I was being questioned on suspicion of murder.

Coming out of court the day Richard gave evidence at my trial. It was so painful going over everything again and again.

Being interviewed by Jeremy Vine for *Panorama*. I felt I needed to speak out about just how bad ME can be.

The verdict finally arrives. Steve (centre) spoke to the press on my behalf. We were all feeling immense relief, but it was overshadowed by exhaustion and grief.

The spot on Eastbourne Beach where we scattered Lynn's ashes. She wanted to be 'let go' in a place where we were all happy once and this is it.

This picture symbolises how I'll always feel about Lynn. Our heads were together here, but our hearts will be together for ever.

'Are you sure?' Richard pleaded. 'Are you absolutely certain this is what you want?'

It was agonising. I could see how much she hated hurting him like this. But though the tears trickled down her cheeks, she didn't waver.

'I understand,' he whispered finally, wrapping her in a tight hug and burying his face in her hair. 'But what would I do without my best mate?'

For a little while the three of us wept silently as we each faced the bleak reality that we could be parted for ever. Then Lynn pulled her hands free again. 'Promise you will tell the doctors?' she signed, looking into our eyes in turn.

We nodded, with heavy hearts.

Thankfully nothing did go wrong under the anaesthetic and I felt like we had had a reprieve, another chance to find some answers. After the operation Lynn was transferred to the Conquest Hospital, where she had to be slid across from a trolley on to a table for a special scan.

I said to the nurses, 'You must be extremely careful because she has severe osteoporosis.'

They probably didn't realise the extent of her bone loss, and nor did we at that stage, but after the scan she was in excruciating pain in her back whenever I moved her. An examination revealed she had lots of old micro-fractures and a new injury – one of her vertebrae had been broken when she had been lifted on to the table. She had not been dropped or anything. This had happened just because she had been moved. It was worrying and we thought we had better find out what was going on so arranged for her to have a private bone scan done at Pembury Hospital. The result was profoundly shocking – she had lost 50 per cent of her bone density.

She was totally distraught. I remember coming home in the ambulance with her, my heart aching as I could do nothing to stem the tears streaming continually down her face. She knew she had osteoporosis but she had been taking calcium and a special IV drug to counter the bone loss that she was experiencing, and so she didn't expect it to be that bad. My poor child had bones in a worse condition than many women of 90. I didn't know what to say.

'How am I ever going to sit up?' she asked me plaintively. 'Will my back be strong enough to hold me up? Will my bones just crumble if I try?'

I searched my brain for words to comfort her. 'When you get better nobody would expect you to sit completely upright straight away. We will lift you a little at a time and see how you feel,' I soothed. Then I remembered something I had read. 'There is a new treatment for osteoporosis,' I told her. 'You can have liquid cement injected into your bones to strengthen them. We could look at whether that would work. It is available in this country.'

I still clung to the belief that she was going to get better because, for every problem she had, there always seemed to be something that could potentially solve it, like the liquid cement. I felt that if we could look at one problem at a time, work through them and eliminate them one by one, then Lynn could get to the point where she could do *something* other than lie in a darkened room. I told myself that even if she never walked again, she could still have some quality of life.

'You know that is not right. I am too broken,' she repeated whenever I came up with these arguments. And the more she looked things up herself on the Internet, the more she realised just how many things were wrong with her and what the long-term implications were.

Between her bouts of infection or vomiting, Lynn's demeanour was usually happy. Sometimes I knew it was strained and that she was 'putting on her fake happy face', as she called it, for my benefit. But at times the mask slipped completely and every day I would find her crying at some point.

One evening a few months after she started writing the letter to her friends, Richard was with her while I was on a rare night out. He was in the living room when Lynn banged on her table and he went to her bedroom to see what she wanted. As he walked in she held up the syringe that was usually connected to the slow-release pump that delivered morphine into her thigh over a 24-hour period. It was empty.

'What have you done?' he cried. She showed him that she had injected the morphine into the Hickman line going into her chest. I had recharged the syringe in the morning so only half the daily dosage was left but it was still enough to kill an ordinary adult.

She was crying. 'I hate my life. I want to die. I can't take any more. I just want to go. Please, please, let me go,' she sobbed.

'No, you mustn't. Not this way,' he pleaded. He held her and stroked her hair as she drifted off to sleep.

Richard judged that she had not taken enough to threaten her life so he didn't call an ambulance. When I came home he met me at the door and held his finger to his lips. 'Shush, Lynn's sleeping. We've got a serious problem,' he whispered. He looked worried and strained and I was alarmed. 'She's taken an overdose but it didn't work,' he said. 'She's all right.'

His words, 'She's taken an overdose,' hit me like a thunderbolt and my stomach lurched. Despite the numerous times she had talked about how she wanted to die, I refused to believe it would become a reality. It wasn't that I didn't take her seriously, I did. I guess I was hoping that some miracle would happen to make her change her mind.

When Richard finished telling me the details and describing how distraught Lynn was, my mind went into overdrive. 'What are we going to do?' I asked. 'What if she does it again? I can't watch her every minute of the day. We can't remove her syringe driver; she couldn't cope with the pain without the morphine. I'll have to ask Dr Woodgate to come to see her tomorrow. Are you sure she's okay?'

'Yes, her breathing is fine, she's just sleeping,' Richard said. 'We'll talk to her tomorrow and work out what to do from there. There's nothing more we can do tonight.'

She slept a long time but when she finally woke the next day I told her I was going to call the GP. 'Please don't do that, Mum,' she begged. 'She might make me go into a psychiatric hospital.'

I knew how terrified she was of this prospect but I couldn't stand by and do nothing. 'I must call her to check you over but if I don't tell her about what happened last night, will you *promise* never to do anything like it again?' I asked.

'I promise,' she pledged.

So I told the GP that we were worried Lynn was getting depressed. She came, asked a few questions, then said to her: 'I am going to prescribe antidepressants. Don't feel bad about taking them. You are suffering from a reactive depression to your situation. It is not depression that is making you ill – I understand that and so does everyone else.'

Lynn began taking an antidepressant called Sertraline. It stopped her crying every day but after a few months she got a serious infection that caused violent vomiting. This meant that all her food and drugs had to be given intravenously because the nasogastric tube would not stay in place. Every time she was sick, out it came. Sertraline could not be injected into a vein, so she had to come off it suddenly and as a result had very bad withdrawal symptoms. When she came home I gradually restarted her on all her medications but she refused the antidepressant. 'I know it stopped me crying but it didn't make me think or feel any different,' she told me.

A couple of months after this, on 20 September 2007, my darling daughter turned 30 years old. She told us, more forcefully than ever before, that she did not want to celebrate her birthday. She hated all her birthdays. And I knew that 30 was very important in the whole way she thought about things. She once told me that she had said to herself that if she was not better by the time she was 30, she could not go on because her dream of having a baby would be gone for ever.

'Even if the ME went away it would then take me, how long, to get strong enough to be able to sit up, let alone go out?' she reasoned sadly. 'I would need months, maybe years of rehabilitation. And would my periods ever come back? Would my bones be strong enough to carry a pregnancy? Even if I managed to get fit enough, I would then have to find the right man. Where would I start? It all takes time. It is just too late for me now.'

Once again I grappled for the right words to say to her, to find a way of reassuring her. 'There are lots of ways of having a baby even if you can't give birth to your own. You could adopt. Or use a surrogate mother,' I suggested.

'I know, Mum, but I have always longed for a baby of my own,' she replied plaintively.

I felt so sorry for her. I couldn't bear to see her giving up on her dream and it caused me such anguish that I couldn't fix it for her. 'I understand why you feel that way, but once you have a little baby you will love it just as much as any baby of your own,' I urged her. 'When you care for a baby, love grows inevitably and a bond will be forged between you. Please believe this.'

She would not be persuaded. 'It would not be the same,' she answered.

However bad she felt about her birthday, other people were not going to let it go unmarked, including me. Several bouquets of flowers arrived and she had loads of cards and presents. The latest craze at the time was balloons shaped as different characters. Her room was stuffed with pirates and personalities, cats, dogs and frogs from friends and family. To my delight, they made her laugh.

Richard came and we spent a quiet day with Lynn helping her open her cards and presents and reading messages from people who loved and thought about her. By early evening she was worn out and wanted to sleep. As we said goodnight, she said, 'It was a lovely day. I wasn't looking forward to my birthday but thank you for everything you did.'

Lynn always said thank you. It comforted me, even though I knew that she was just making the best of things. Even though we had tried to make her day special, I knew that it wasn't enough. She might have thanked us – that was the type of girl she was – but it didn't mean she had changed her mind…

CHAPTER FOURTEEN

DO NOT RESUSCITATE

'Please, Mum, can you ask Dr Dyson to come to see me?' Lynn asked. My heart sank. I thought I knew what she wanted to say to him, but I didn't want to think about it.

It was two months after her thirtieth birthday and Lynn was back in the Conquest Hospital as an emergency admission for a severe bout of vomiting and diarrhoea. She always got infections like this in the winter. Tony Dyson was her favourite consultant and one of the very few doctors she trusted. He took her seriously and had become very knowledgeable about ME over the years. Just as importantly, he unfailingly treated her with kindness and affection.

He came along with the ward sister to the side room she had been given off a general ward and greeted her in his usual jokey way: 'Hello again, old thing. How are you doing?' He said hello to Richard and me and I am sure he could tell from our tense, miserable faces that something important was about to happen. 'So, what's all this about?' he said.

'Lynn has been talking something over with us and now she wants to tell you,' I said.

Using her sign language, and with Dyson watching intently, Lynn pointed to herself for 'I,' drew a 'W' on her hand for 'want' and then 'DNR' – do not resuscitate. He looked at her with infinite compassion and gently began to ask her questions. He could understand quite a lot of her signs, others I translated for him, and sometimes all she needed to do was nod or shake her head.

'Is it just because of the way you are feeling right now after being so extra poorly and with the pain of your back fracture?' he asked. 'Would you be content to go back to how you were before this most recent episode or do you feel like this all the time?'

I could see from her trembling hands that Lynn was nervous about how this doctor who had always done his best for her would react to what she was saying. But she also got that familiar determined look on her face; she would not be talked round. 'All the time. I have felt like it for a long time,' she signed.

'Why do you feel this way?' he continued.

'I can't do any of the things I want to do. I do not want to live like this any more. I am sick of this life,' she replied.

'I completely understand why you have come to this when you have so much to put up with,' he said. 'What if something did happen to you and we resuscitated you and you survived but in an even worse state than you are now? How would you feel about that?'

Lynn shook her head vigorously to indicate that she couldn't cope with it at all.

Dr Dyson sighed. For a long time they just looked into each other's eyes, hers pleading for acceptance and understanding, his full of compassion and sadness, while Richard and I looked on miserably, wishing with every fibre of our beings that this was not happening.

Blinking away tears, Dr Dyson eventually patted her hand. 'Okay,' he said and immediately got up and left the room.

Lynn turned to us with a smile. 'He really gets it,' she signed to us. 'He is so lovely. I always knew he had a soft spot for me.'

We nodded, too upset to trust ourselves to speak.

In a few minutes Dr Dyson returned with a DNR form. 'This is what you need,' he said to Lynn. 'It gives the instructions you want to your medical team. Are you absolutely certain this is what you want?'

Lynn nodded vigorously, eager to get on with it, and indicated to Richard and me to sit on either side of the bed to help her.

Feeling utterly sick at heart, I sat beside her and took the paper in a shaking hand. Dr Dyson pointed to where Lynn's signature had to go and handed her a pen. Though she could type words on her computer, she couldn't write so she looked towards Richard pleadingly. With tears in his eyes, he closed his hand around hers and guided her to make a wobbly 'L'.

It was sheer agony for me to have to hold the piece of paper for the daughter I loved so much to sign her life away and to watch her pathetic struggle to make her mark. Then Richard and I had to sign the form too. Afterwards Richard wanted a bit of time with Lynn because he was due to go to work and I stumbled almost blindly away from her room. I had to get outside.

It was a nice bright, crisp day and there was a large lake in the grounds of the hospital. I wandered around it, staring at the water and the ducks without seeing them, feeling more desolate than I had ever done in my life.

The thoughts chased each other round and round my head. '*This is it. She is serious. She wants to die.*' I wept inside. '*She wants to leave this world and it could happen any day.*' It would be within six months, maybe sooner because winter was closing in. '*Only six more months with my precious girl.*' How could I bear it? As I walked I let my tears fall freely, giving in to all the pain and heartbreak where no one could see.

A terrible battle was raging inside me. Logically I knew that I had to face up to the real possibility that she was going to go. But as a mother it was quite another thing actually to accept it. To accept that my beloved daughter was soon to die meant that I would be forced to extinguish the hope that she would one day recover and rise up from her bed and have a life of some kind. A life with experiences and relationships. I had clung to that hope for so long and had fought for so tenaciously that it was impossible to let it go.

My heart was telling me that to let go of that dream would kill something inside me. If Lynn died, part of me would too. Yet my brain was telling me that Lynn was an adult with the right to make her own choices. And I must respect and support my intelligent daughter in whatever decisions she made over her life.

Dr Dyson had said to us after she signed the form, 'It is very important for someone in Lynn's situation, who has no control over her life, to be allowed to have some control. To be allowed to have a choice.' Bleak though it was, this was the only choice she had – to live or to die. So now my duty as a mother was to start trying to compel myself to follow what I *knew* in my brain instead of what I *felt* in my heart.

I longed to carry on the same way I had always done, searching for treatments to relieve her symptoms until the magic cure came along. But I knew I couldn't argue with Lynn and nor could Richard. She wasn't mad. She wasn't depressed. And it was not a whim. She had obviously given it a long and thoughtful consideration and she didn't want to live because she really hated her life.

We understood absolutely how and why she had got to that point. So many times we had said to each other: 'How on earth does she put up with it all?'

I stopped walking round the lake and gazed at the rippling water, thinking of all the awful procedures she had gone through in hospital and how between admissions there was never any let up for her. Despite being on a high daily dose of morphine, she was still in pain every single minute of her life. She had spasms, sickness and everything else to contend with.

I thought of my brother, John, and of how he coped with life as someone who is terribly disabled and severely limited in what he can do. Having lived with him and lived with Lynn, I knew there was a huge difference in the way they experienced life.

John never has any pain and is rarely sick. On a day-to-day basis he feels well in himself, he has no nausea, no headaches, no spasms, no muscle aches, no light and sound sensitivity. It means he can go about, meet people, enjoy the beauties of nature. He can take pleasure in life.

If only Lynn felt like that, I told myself, I could have thrown everything into rehabilitating her enough to get her out in a wheelchair one day, even if she remained paralysed. But every single day Lynn felt how you or I might do if we had flu, nausea and diarrhoea, on top of a bad headache, a sore throat and more, much more, all rolled into one and multiplied by ten. Lynn had been feeling as grotty as that every day for 17 years. I knew it was not disability she found impossible to bear, it was being so ill. And it going on for ever and ever with no end in sight.

After more than an hour of wandering round the lake I was exhausted by the mental struggle and turned back inside. I found Lynn looking content except for an obvious anxiety about me. 'Please understand,' she signed. 'Don't be sad.'

I sat beside her and took her hand. 'I do understand,' I sniffed. 'But you can't stop me being sad.'

While I was feeling cut to ribbons inside, Lynn was calmer and more cheerful after signing the DNR. 'That was a big step for me, Mum. I have been thinking and worrying about it for a long time,' she confided. 'I feel much lighter and happier now.'

Ever since the punctured lung disaster, Lynn had been saying she didn't want to go back into hospital, no matter how ill she was. After she signed the DNR, she was even more determined. One day, not long after she came home, Richard was in her room chatting to her and I was in the living room when Dr Woodgate phoned.

We were discussing the results of some blood tests Lynn had done for her hormone levels and the doctor wanted her to go to a London neurological hospital to have further investigations. Lynn could hear the conversation over the intercom and sent Richard out to speak to me. 'Lynn wants you to say that she doesn't want to go to hospital,' he informed me.

Putting my hand over the phone for a moment, I whispered, 'I can't say that.'

Suddenly I heard a loud bang, bang, bang from Lynn's room. Richard went back in and found Lynn really angry. 'No more, no more. I am not going in. I won't go in. You tell Mum to tell the doctor that I am *never* going into any hospital again,' she signed furiously.

And so I told Dr Woodgate what she had said. There were a number of occasions like that which showed that Lynn had really made up her mind about not going back to hospital. She would rather stay at home and die.

I assumed that is what would happen – an emergency would arise and she would refuse the treatment necessary to save her life. She kept saying, 'We *have* to talk about this…it would be easier if we talk about it.' I guess it was her way of trying to get me to come to terms with losing her.

One day in December 2007, I discovered her thinking had gone much further. As I was tidying up her room she signed, 'I have found a place that will help me die. I want to go there.'

Unknown to me, she had been researching on the Internet and had come across Dignitas, a clinic in Zurich, Switzerland, which helps people to end their lives.

'I emailed them and they have replied with their brochure in English. Please, will you read it, Mum, and tell me what you think?' she asked.

This was another step along the road she was travelling. It meant she was not just going to wait to die naturally; she was actively seeking ways to end her life. My heart sank but I could not refuse the appeal in her eyes. 'Okay,' I sighed, and she forwarded it to my laptop. Later on I read it and I told her I had but I didn't do anything about it at first.

Dignitas was founded in 1998 by Ludwig Minelli, a lawyer and former journalist, after Swiss law made assisting a suicide legal within certain safeguards. Its slogan is: 'To live with dignity, to die with dignity', and it claims to be non-profit-making. It has now assisted in around 900 suicides, more than 100 of them from Britain.

In the brochure that Lynn sent me, I learnt that a doctor interviews a would-be suicide at least twice to satisfy himself that they are mentally fit to make this choice. Then they are moved into the 'death room' and a video is made of them making their wishes clear which is later shown to the coroner. They say goodbye to their loved ones then, when they are completely ready, they receive death in the form of tablets of sodium pentobarbital, a barbiturate which slows the activity of the brain and heart down to a stop if the dose is strong enough.

I saw pictures of the clinic, where the death rooms were plain anonymous apartments, and felt chilled. I've since seen some more homely looking rooms but I would have to be desperate to end my life there and I didn't want that for Lynn either.

I put it to the back of my mind and did nothing but Lynn did not forget about it. A few months passed, then another email arrived in my inbox. *'Please will you print out the Dignitas membership form and send it off for me?'* Lynn had written. It was not obligatory to become a member but Lynn wanted to so she would get all the information.

I had nothing against Dignitas. After reading the stories of some of the people who went there, I thought it was probably a good thing that, if someone is desperate to die, at least there is somewhere for them to go. But I couldn't face the idea of Lynn spending her last moments in an anonymous room far away from everything she knew and everyone she loved.

On a practical level, it would have been incredibly difficult to get her to Zurich. The only way was by air ambulance, and how could I face making the necessary arrangements to transport my only daughter to her death? In addition, people had to swallow the drug, and Lynn could not swallow so she could not administer it to herself – how would that fit in with the law?

Worse than that though was the thought of her ending her life in those cold and unfamiliar surroundings, far away from her home which was the only place she felt safe in the world. 'It would be awful for you to go to a strange country, to a grim block of flats and a little impersonal room with none of your own things around you,' I said. 'I don't want you to have to go somewhere like that. Do you really want to go there?'

'Yes, absolutely, I do,' she insisted. 'Please just tell me how you are going to arrange for me to get there.'

'Well, let's get all the information and see,' I sighed. I sent off the form and had some correspondence with them.

'Are you absolutely sure this is what you want to do?' I asked her over and over again in the following weeks. 'You can change your mind any time about this or the DNR. Don't feel you have to stick with it. If you feel you *can* go on, just say so.' But she never wavered.

'All right,' I finally agreed. 'I will take you. I hate the idea but somehow I will find a way.'

For Richard, the thought of taking Lynn to the clinic was completely unbearable. He could not contemplate such a thing but, no matter how horrible it was to me, I could not refuse to help her.

I could not say to her: 'You should never, ever think of taking your own life. You don't have the right – God gave you life and only He can take it away.'

This is what I had been brought up to believe, as a Catholic, but I had lost my faith.

And I respected Lynn's wishes. I had no right, nobody had any right, to tell her that she should go on when her situation was intolerable. It was her right to decide because she was the one who was living this life.

These thoughts went round my head all through the day, every day, as I cared for Lynn, crushed up her pills and put them down her tube and tried to think of things to keep her cheerful. They did not keep me awake at night though because I was always so sleep deprived. I usually went to bed at about 12.30 or 1 a.m. and was up between 6 and 7 a.m. and sometimes I was up in the night as well. I was so tired that, no matter how much emotional trauma I was going through, when I went to bed, I slept.

But as soon as my eyes opened in the morning, it came into my head straight away. Although I knew it wasn't what Lynn wanted, I continued to explore every single avenue I could think of to help her. I told myself, '*Somebody* must be able to help her. *Somebody*, somewhere in this world, must be able to put together all the pieces of the jigsaw that are already there and find a cure for this rotten, horrible illness.'

Even while I was filling in the Dignitas forms, I could not truly accept that it meant the end. In my heart of hearts, I did not really believe that it was going to happen. I thought that, if we could put it off, and put it off, *something* would come up and she would change her mind.

I knew she needed an escape route, at least in theory, and I felt I was keeping her going by going along with it. Painful though the process was, if it helped her carry on even for a few more months, it was worth it. So at every step I agreed to help, without fully facing the reality of what that actually meant.

CHAPTER FIFTEEN
LYNN'S WISHES

The Do Not Resuscitate form that Lynn, Richard and I had signed in the hospital was only valid for that specific admission. To make her wishes known to all doctors in all circumstances, a solicitor had to draw up a legal document called an Advanced Directive – better known as a 'Living Will' – which could be officially lodged in her medical records.

'Now, Mum, you really have to see a solicitor and do this for me,' Lynn said as soon as she got home from her latest trip to hospital. 'It's urgent now. You can't keep putting it off.'

I steeled myself to do as she wished. First I told Dr Woodgate, who knew already that Lynn was losing hope and was very understanding. Then I called a solicitor. She told me that Lynn should decide what she did and did not want to be treated for and to write it down as clearly as possible. For instance, would she want pain relief or help to breathe if she was conscious? At the same time the solicitor said it would be a good idea if Lynn drew up a 'Letter of Wishes' to set out anything else she would like to happen after she had gone.

Lynn started on it straight away. It took her ages to do, lying flat as she typed it into her small handheld computer. She talked to me about what she was thinking of putting in it. It was so awful to have this conversation, yet I wanted to help her as I had always helped her. Richard could not bear to discuss it, which made it even more important that I somehow found the strength.

Then eventually, four months after she had told Dr Dyson, an email from her appeared in my inbox. Subject: '*My first list ov wishes*'. She had warned me this was coming but still my heart gave a horrible lurch when I saw it there among messages from various ME groups and advertising spam. I sat and stared at it, my finger hovering over the mouse but not clicking it, feeling sick.

Finally, after sitting dazed in front of the computer for ages, I forced myself to open it.

Mum,

Here is my list ov wishes. Its not really finished yet – its only a first kopy. I really need mor time 2 think about sum things, sutch as wer I wont 2 be buryed, or if I wont 2 be cremated (burnt). I no that dad dusnt wont 2 discus things 2 do with this, but I wont 2 giv him 1 mor charnce (sp) 2 hav a say in wer/if I'm buryed. If he wont tork then it'll make it eesyer (sp) 4 me in a way. Id lik 2 giv it 1 mor try tho, if that's okay.

Rite...

My hand went to my mouth as I read her email. She always was a compassionate person, and even when writing about her final wishes, she knew and understood how Richard felt. Yet even so, there was a steely determination in her words.

1. Buryed or cremated.

As u no, iv always wonted 2 b buryed. However, as u ritely sed, if u mov bak 2 wer u kame from (witch is likely) then u wont b able 2 visit me (not that I see y u would wont 2;). If dad dusnt wont 2 b part ov th desiding, then I ges I could b buryed with yor family. OR, I'm stil thinking about being cremated so u could take me 2 sumwer that we wer al happy together...Iv just got 2 get over th yukkynes ov th thort ov being burnt ;)

So I stil havnt really desided on that 1 yet, sorry.

Number 2 on my list wos 'funeral'. This wil obviously take time 2 plan and I don't think thers a rush 2 do it rite NOW with my wil – is there.

3. Hoo/wer gets wot.

(I'm not entirely shor how mutch I hav so I Kant say 4 shor how mutch I wont 2 go 2 eetch person yet, sorry).

I would lik 1 thowsand pownds 2 go 2 ME Research in my name. Mum is 2 decide esaktly wen/wer it gos 2.

Jewellery – family AR 2 take wotever they lik, including mum, dad and my brother, Steve. Th rest, mum is 2 decide esaktly wer it gos, but its 2 go 2 good/deserving homes (ME Or not), eether sold or givn as gifts.

Brother, Steve – any jewellery, any fotos, any electrical items...anything he wonts, really.

Al my bits and bobs, including craft items, soft toys, books, makeup, klothes, ornaments, music, movies kan go 2 good homes (soft toys mayb go 2 a hospital, craft stuf go 2 ME), or 2 b sold 2 giv money 2 ME Research. Mum is 2 organise and decide wot 2 do with al ov this.

Fotos AR al 2 be kept, not destroyed. Memories AR precious. Family AR 2 divide these up between them.

After everything has been settled, everything has been given 2 th peeple I described above, and everything has been sold or given away, then wots left is 2 b devided up between mum and dad, th same amount eetch (sp).

The permanent knots in my stomach worsened. My lovely daughter was putting her affairs in order, making sure that her material possessions went to whoever wanted or needed them most. Although I was in charge of distributing some of her things, she was trying to make it easier for me to deal with when the time came. It may have seemed surprisingly stoical and practical, but it was an immensely considerate thing for her to do.

4. Wot I do/don't wont 2 be treated 4.

This is difficult. Thers so many different situations that COULD happen, but i'l try my best 2 rite down wot my wishes AR...

My mayn wish, is that I'm not 2 be brort bak 2 life if I ever collapse – my hart is not 2 b started up and I'm not 2 b forsed 2 breath agen.

I DO NOT WONT 2 BE KEPT ALIVE ON MASHINES.

If I am obviously suffering, say I kant breath and I'm wide awake and aware ov wots happening, then I DO wont help 2 breath – but ONLY if I'm aware ov wots going on. If I'm aware ov wots going on it should b MY decision about wether or not I'm treated. If I'm unable 2 decide 4 myself then th decision is my parents.

If I hav a ordinary infection, I DO wont antibiotics.

If I hav a life thretning infection I do NOT wont treatment, UNLESS I am wide awake and am obviously suffering, in witch kase I DO wont treatment. Agen, if I'm aware ov wots going on it should b MY decision about wether or not I'm treated – if I'm unable 2 decide 4 myself then th decision is my parents.

If I get a nasty lump (wots that ilnes kalled), I do NOT wont treatment 4 this.

Baysicaly, th mayn thing is this: if I'm suffering, I wont treatment. If I'm not aware ov wots going on, then I do NOT wont treatment. And if I'm ever not able 2 make th decision 4 myself then it gos 2 my parents 2 decide 4 me.

NO 1 SHOULD BE ABLE 2 PUT ME IN A MENTAL HOME.

Mum, I Kant really think ov anything els, kan u. Hav I forgotton sumthing obvious.

By now tears were streaming uncontrollably down my face. There was absolutely no question that she had thought everything through and was trying to plan for every contingency, from everyday infections right through to cancer. At the age of 30, when most young women are working hard, having children, planning their lives ahead, my poor Lynn was thinking about how she should die.

5. Guidance 4 attorneys.

Mum is 2 be in charge ov giving away/selling al my bits and bobs, as described above and is 2 decide wer/hoo any resulting money is 2 go 2.

MY BODY IS 2 GO 2 ME RESEARCH.

IF im cremated, id lik mum, dad and my brother, steve, 2 go 2 a spot wer we al used 2 b happy together and let me go ther.

Mum is 2 look after th kittens, willow and shadow. But if she kant 4 any reason, then id lik dad 2 take them – i realy dont wont them 2 just be given away, if posible. Hooever has them must remember that they arnt 2 go owtside at al.

My fish – unles any1 in th family is willing 2 take them on, they wil hav 2 b given away, unfortunately.

Al my very personal things lik any paper diarys (from any age), or obviously private documents/ notes that ar saved on2 th storage kards in my computers or fones, please do NOT read. I no that sum peeple lik 2 read thru peeples diarys wen they dye, but i realy would prefer if mine wer kept private...u could even bury them with me so that my secrets go with me ;)

Iv discussed my wishes about not being brort bak 2 life with Mum and dad a lot and they ar very klear on wot i do and dont wont. If im ever unable 2 make my own desisions, I trust my parents 2 make th rite choise 4 ME, and not 4 THEM.

Mum, hav i been klear enuf. Is ther anything else iv forgotton. I kant think ov anything else rite now so i'l send this 2 u just as a first kopy. Please do let me no wot u think and tel me if i should ad in or take away anything.

Hope this isn't silly, I realy wosnt shor wot u wonted.

Thanks 4 reading – i hope its not TO upsetting 4 u.

Luv,

L.

I don't know how long I sat there trying to stop the endless flood of pain and grief that washed over me. Eventually I managed to pull myself together and went to her room. I must have looked ashen. 'Have you read it?' she asked.

'Oh Lynn', I sighed. 'Are you *absolutely* sure this is what you want? A cure could be found tomorrow. Anything could be round the corner.'

Lynn looked full of pity for my suffering, but her resolve was not shaken. 'It will be too late for me,' she said.

'But death is the end of everything. You have wonderful nephews that you love – don't you want to see them growing up?' By this time Steve and Sarah had had another baby boy, Ethan, a brother for Liam, and Lynn adored them both.

She winced and a faraway look came into her eyes as she pictured the lovely children. 'Oh Mum, I would love to,' she signed while looking at me with eyes that begged me to accept her wishes. 'But I can't stay. I just can't. It is already too late – I am too broken,' she insisted.

I had spent all the years of her illness frantically searching for a cure, reading any relevant paper produced anywhere in the world, so I knew she was right to say that at that moment there was no treatment. But who knew what was round the corner? What about the advances in stem cell research? I believed scientists might come up with something, the next day, the next week, the next year. Lynn might have lost all hope but I had hope enough for the two of us. But even I could see that hope wasn't enough any more.

Somehow, I found the strength to talk the letter of wishes over with her and help her refine it. I wrote it out again, correcting all the spellings, then I had to take it along to the solicitor. That was one of the hardest things I have ever done in my life.

Making it all legal was so final; it was forcing me to recognise that this was really happening, she was really going to go one day, perhaps very soon. And I, the mother who had brought her into this world, was helping her prepare to leave it. It was like I was carrying her death warrant in my hands. It ripped me apart.

My hands trembled violently as I handed the document to the solicitor who was very gentle and professional. I asked her if she needed to come to see Lynn once she had drawn up the Advanced Directive. 'No. You need to get your GP and another witness to read it out to Lynn to make sure she understands and agrees with everything that is in there,' she said. 'They must both sign it in her presence and then you send it back to me.'

I phoned Dr Woodgate and arranged for her to come and also asked Julie, Lynn's favourite nurse, to be there. Listening to the doctor reading aloud the details of what should happen to the little things that made up her sadly restricted life – her cats, her photos, her diaries – broke even more of my already tattered and shattered heart.

But once it was over, Lynn was obviously contented and relieved. 'I am happy it is done. I feel a huge weight has been taken away,' she told me afterwards, searching my face anxiously for signs of distress. 'I know this is terribly hard for you and Dad. I know you don't want me to go. I am very sorry for hurting you. But I need to trust you to do what is best for me, not for you. Can I do that?' I nodded miserably.

Among the agonising conversations we had in those distressing days were discussions over what should happen to her body. 'Please let my body go to ME research,' she begged me. 'I truly believe that a lot of answers will be found in my body and I desperately want to help anyone else who suffers from this horrendous condition. Promise me you will make sure this happens.'

Again I felt pulled – no, that's not strong enough – hauled in two opposite directions. I wanted to keep her with me, keep her safe, keep her whole, but I also wanted to help her fulfil her vitally important wish, even if it meant having to arrange for her body to be used for scientific research. Oh, but how could I bear it?

As I struggled to cope with the emotions that were churning me up every day, the only scenarios that I could see in the future were Lynn catching some infection and refusing treatment, or somehow being transported to the

Dignitas clinic. Since she was helpless, it never occurred to me that she would look for another way out.

When we talked about Dignitas, she said she was worried about what could happen to me if I took her there. It was against the law in Britain to help someone to die, even if they were doing it abroad. In theory, you could be charged with aiding and abetting a suicide, which carries a maximum jail sentence of 14 years, but several people had taken their loved ones to Dignitas and nobody had actually been prosecuted.

At the time the law was being challenged by the case of Debbie Purdy, which Lynn and I followed closely. Ms Purdy, who suffers from multiple sclerosis and uses a wheelchair, argued that the Director of Public Prosecutions (DPP) was infringing her human rights by refusing to clarify the circumstances in which he would enforce the Suicide Act of 1961 and prosecute someone. She said that if her husband, Omar Puente, could be prosecuted for pushing her to the plane to go to Dignitas, she would have to go there earlier while she was still able to travel without him, which could force her into deciding to die sooner than would be absolutely necessary.

Her case began in the High Court on 2 October 2008, before Lord Justice Scott Baker and Mr Justice Aikens. The DPP said that she could not be given any assurance that her husband would not be prosecuted because the law was clear that assisting suicide is an offence. She lost her case but announced she was taking the fight on to the Court of Appeal.

For me and Lynn, these things became part of daily conversation, but it was still almost impossible to discuss any of it with Richard. He and I sometimes wanted to talk about it away from Lynn but it was difficult because she could hear everything said in the house over the intercom system. We could switch it off but she didn't like that. She would go 'bang, bang, bang' and, when one of us went into her room, she would give us one of her looks. 'I don't like you talking about me,' she complained. 'Tell me to my face if there is something you want to say.'

A few times Richard paused on the doorstep at the end of a visit and we managed a hurried conversation. 'You realise she really means this. She has thought about it for a long time; it is not a whim or a phase,' I said on one of these occasions.

'I know,' he said, sadly. 'What can we do?'

'I don't know. I just wish I could make her feel there is something to hang on for.'

We would do anything on earth to help Lynn. We would willingly swap places with her, if only we could. But we couldn't. We felt helpless.

We did not talk about the legal implications. I did not know if Richard would go with us to Dignitas or not, if it came to it. Lynn would obviously want her dad there but she didn't want to get him into trouble and it was even more complicated because he worked for the Police so there were a lot of implications if he deliberately broke the law.

I didn't know if I would be prosecuted, even though others had not been. Quite honestly, it wasn't my greatest concern. I had to respect Lynn's wishes, whatever they were. She had been through so much; it was her right to choose. But I didn't want to put any pressure on Richard. He knew what Lynn wanted and it was for him to decide. I thought that, if there was going to be trouble, it was better if only one of us got involved rather than both.

Richard and I realised we had to prepare the rest of the family. He gently told his elderly parents that Lynn had made an Advanced Directive. He explained that she was weary of the daily struggle with sickness and pain and that she had lost hope. They responded with silence and sadness in their eyes. They could find no words to express the deep sorrow they felt at hearing that their beloved granddaughter might leave this world before them; something they did not want to contemplate.

My family and close friends all responded in a similar way. Not one of them condemned Lynn's decision. Each and every one could understand and sympathise with her terrible plight.

I decided to go to Belgium to speak to Steve and Sarah in person. In the afternoon when Sarah had put the children down for a nap, the three of us sat at the garden table on their patio and I took a deep breath. 'Do you know how serious Lynn is about wanting to die?' I asked them.

Steve looked at me pityingly. 'Yes, she told me last time I was home. I know she really means it and I understand,' he said.

Sarah leant forward. 'Please ask Lynn to give us some warning, if she can,' she said. 'Please tell her to let us have a chance to say a last goodbye to her.'

I nodded and took out a copy of Lynn's Advanced Directive to show them. 'She could get a serious infection at any time and refuse treatment, so we don't know when it will happen,' I explained. 'I am afraid you have to treat every time you see her as if it were your last goodbye.'

I told the family that Lynn had researched Dignitas and wanted to go but what I didn't say was that I was going to arrange it and go with her. Because of the law, talking like that would have involved them and potentially exposed them to prosecution too. It meant I was alone with my dilemma.

Though we both felt completely desolate, Richard and I respected and admired Lynn for how she was handling everything. It takes a remarkable person to put up with what she had all those years and to face up to death the way she did.

Many people who are dying refuse to accept it. They are not able to face the reality and don't want to talk about it or make any plans even though that would make life easier for their loved ones.

Lynn was the opposite – she looked death in the face, even welcomed it. Death was not the enemy. It was nothing to be frightened of, it was something that was going to give her peace. Staying as she was for a normal life span was much more frightening.

We had spoken about this before, when we both believed she was going to recover. 'You're going to get through this,' I had said to her. 'It would be different if you thought this was going to go on for sixty years or something. That would be impossible to stand, but you are going to get better.'

I said those words never imagining that I would find myself in the situation where the choice would be a reality. That had been my feeling – that a lifetime ill like that was too much to bear. But now I wanted her to bear it. I desperately wanted her to stay with me.

CHAPTER SIXTEEN

IN HOSPITAL AGAIN

Lynn was getting terrible pain in her muscles and an excruciating stomachache. I suspected the level of potassium in her blood had dropped dangerously low – it had happened before and the effect could be really horrible.

I took a blood test and dropped it round the surgery for sending off to the Conquest for analysis. Late that same evening I took a call from a doctor at the hospital. 'Miss Gilderdale must be admitted *immediately*,' he insisted. 'Her potassium is at a very serious level.'

I went into Lynn's room and told her what had happened. 'I will *not* go to hospital!' she declared.

I was shocked. I knew she urgently needed to be given potassium intravenously and I was not allowed to do it because it had to be monitored carefully – too much or too little could be fatal. '*Please*, you must go into hospital,' I pleaded.

Potassium is a very important mineral that is found inside all the cells of the human body and plays a role in contracting the muscles, transmitting nerve signals and making the heart work properly, among other things. If it reached too low a level – something called severe hyop-kalaemia – she could have a heart attack. The tests had shown that Lynn's potassium level was dangerously low.

By this point, Lynn had been talking about wanting to die for well over a year and maybe she thought this was her time. But it would never be the right time for me. I could not stop fighting to keep her with me.

I sat beside her bed, trying to marshal my arguments. 'I know you want to go but this is not the way,' I pleaded. 'You could be in terrible, terrible pain. Remember when you had very low potassium before and your arms went all twisted and you suffered absolute agony? It could get much worse than that. And you don't know how long it will take. Please, just go to hospital for a little while until it stabilises so you will be comfortable.'

I didn't think I could stand watching her go through such suffering. And I justified my begging her to change her mind by telling myself that she put in her Advanced Directive that she didn't want to die in pain. Richard was terribly distressed to see her doubled up with pain and added his voice to mine but it took us nearly a week of gentle cajoling to persuade her.

She kept holding out while she got more and more sick. But eventually, maybe because she hated to see me and her father so worried and stressed, she reluctantly agreed to go into the Conquest. After assessment she was wheeled into a busy general ward. This had sometimes happened before when a side room was not available, but she had always been moved when one became vacant because everyone knew she needed to be kept away from light and noise, as the bustle of a main ward caused her even more pain. Plus she invariably picked up bugs in hospital. Her immune system was so vulnerable, whatever was there, she contracted. She'd already had MRSA twice. And a side room was much better for me because I could lie down to sleep on the floor whereas in the main ward I had to make do with a hard chair.

I was dismayed when I saw the bed she had been assigned in the crowded ward. Lynn, loathing the fact she had to be there in the first place, was cross and so was Richard. 'Is there any chance that she can be moved into a side room in a day or two?' he asked the ward sister.

'No, I am sorry. Protocol has changed. She will have to stay in the main ward,' she replied.

Yet again, it seemed that Lynn's miserable life was being made to feel worse by her experiences in hospital and only made her more determined to end it all.

There was a tummy bug going round the ward and, inevitably, she picked it up straight away. But while most people fought it off and were okay in a few days, Lynn became horribly ill and stayed that way for months.

Bright lights glared down at her for 16 hours a day so she had to wear dark glasses all the time. Mobile phones were allowed in the ward and in the next bed was a young South African woman who talked loudly on hers almost constantly. It nearly drove Lynn crazy.

Also right opposite Lynn – and the beds were only a few feet apart – there was a woman who had very bad diarrhoea. She had the commode at the end of her bed and she got on to it several times a day, with her back facing Lynn. She never pulled the curtain round. Then she got up and left it open and did not ring for a nurse to take it away.

So there was this awful stench when Lynn was feeling so sick all the time, and the noise and the lights…sometimes all she could do was lie on her side sobbing quietly because it was all too much for her. Richard sought out the sister and pleaded again, 'Lynn is not doing well here, she needs to be in a side room.' The answer again was: 'No.' And again I felt utterly helpless, unable to protect her from this torment the way I could do when I cared for her at home.

Every day she said, 'I am not staying any longer,' but her potassium level was still too low. 'Even if it doesn't go up, I am getting out of here,' she insisted. Richard and I had to plead with her to endure it just a little longer. When her level was up to just below the safe range, she demanded we take her home.

'I am never, ever going into hospital again, whatever happens to me,' Lynn said adamantly when she was back in her bedroom. 'Every time I go in it gets worse. If nothing else kills me, they will.'

She had been admitted to hospital about 60 times since she fell ill. There was no question from now on that this horrible experience would be her last-ever admission.

She was still terribly ill when she got home. For the next six weeks she was on the bedpan for about 12 hours a day. I thought she must have something more serious than a normal stomach bug, so I sent off a test to the hospital. It came back showing negative for bacteria in the bowel.

I was sure that could not be right. How could there be nothing wrong when she was in such a state? So I had a test done privately. It detected four major bacteria in Lynn's bowel. One of them was MRSA, one of them was of a kind you can usually only pick up in the Far East and the other two were so serious they had to be treated with strong doses of antibiotics.

She was prescribed antibiotics and the problem eased off a bit but when she stopped them, it flared up again. I sent off another test to the hospital, it came back negative. I thought, '*It can't be negative.*' So I had another private test done which showed that she still had these four bugs.

She had all these things happen to her in a short space of time – the punctured lung, the broken vertebra and all these bugs. That was on top of everything that had gone before. Everything conspired against her.

She had no more fight left in her. It was so sad because she deserved to get better *because* she had fought so hard and put up with so much. And she deserved respect and good care and belief and kindness.

She never fully recovered from the bugs she picked up in hospital. Dr Woodgate advised that she needed to be readmitted for intravenous antibiotics but Lynn totally refused to go. For the last six months of her life she was often on the bedpan for six hours at a stretch, and that is lying down. I slept in snatches during the day as well as the night.

Yet Lynn wasn't miserable. She was fed up with it and some days she was tearful for a while but then she would perk up and be joking with me or telling me about her friends. It wasn't like depression that takes you over and you lose interest in everything. She was still interested in the world. She still enjoyed listening to music, watching TV, seeing her nan and grandpa, having a joke with her dad. She just couldn't endure her life the way it was.

Sometimes I talked about a plan for the following year and she gave me a look that said, 'Well, you know that is not going to happen.' In August she emailed me a list of her friends' birthdays up until 15 October, then adding, *'And then there ar a few kards after that, but obviously I don't no if I'l stil b "'arownd" then, so wont list them now.'*

Making these friends over the Internet had added so much to her life but she was sad that she couldn't meet them, see them or hear them. So as her birthday approached in September, I got an idea. I emailed them and asked if they would record messages on CDs or videos so Lynn could hear or even see them. It was like an up-to-date version of her twenty-first birthday card appeal. Quite a few of them responded. She was sent cards with recorded messages on them, she had CDs, messages on the answering machine and the computer. She was thrilled and it really made it a special birthday for her.

I felt proud of her when I saw these messages flooding in. *I* knew how lovely she was but she had had so little opportunity to make an impression on the world. When she did, I saw it was a good and lasting one, and it acted as a balm to my ravaged heart.

CHAPTER SEVENTEEN

KEEPING HER GOING

As Lynn now refused to go into hospital ever again, I couldn't help but think that we would soon be losing her. All that was left was to try to make her see how much we loved her and wanted her to stay with us. And to try to think of things that might make her want to hang on long enough for something to come along to help her.

Every day I racked my brains for things for her to look forward to or goals to achieve, trying out new medicines, making a card for somebody's birthday coming up, Steve and Sarah coming to stay with the babies. Anything to keep her going on for a few more weeks or months.

After Lynn had done the Advanced Directive and felt she had her escape route guaranteed, her mood lightened and she was more willing to join in with my various schemes. One day she said to me: 'You know what I would really like before I go?'

'No. What would you really like before you go?' I smiled, sadly.

'I would like to go on a really nice holiday. Somewhere out of this room. Somewhere really special.'

'Well, that's going to be a bit tricky, isn't it?' I said.

We had a bit of a laugh about it but I was hugely heartened that she had enough spirit left to have conceived a dream, even if it was with the proviso 'before I go'. She loved the poster on her wall of a window opening out on to a tropical paradise. I knew she lay in her darkened room imagining the feel of the sand between her toes and the sun on her face and the freedom of running and laughing under a clear blue sky.

'I tell you what, there are places that are especially adapted for holidays for disabled people. I think some of them take people on stretchers. People on stretchers go to Lourdes, for instance. What do you think of that?' I said.

'Yes, let's try to find somewhere. But not Lourdes. I want to be by the sea,' she said.

Feeling much more cheered, I immediately started researching, keeping Lynn up to date on my progress. I thought what could work best might be a cruise – we could get on the ship at Southampton so we would not have to fly anywhere and I knew some cruise companies were quite accommodating for disabled people.

Of course, very few people went cruising on a stretcher but after searching around for a while and making lots of phone calls, I found a company which said they could do it. They were extremely nice and went to a lot of trouble;

they even measured the width of the cabin doors and corridors to make sure a stretcher would fit through them.

They asked the medical staff on board if they would be prepared to have someone as ill as Lynn and they said, yes, so long as I came along to look after her. We were elated and were getting quite excited – it seemed Lynn might actually go somewhere that was not her room or a hospital ward for the first time in 16 years.

It was to be a cruise through the Mediterranean and we leafed through the brochure chatting about the beautiful and interesting places it would call in at. 'Even if it kills me, I am going to do it,' Lynn joked. 'It would be so great to live in the lap of luxury while seeing all these different places, even if only through a cabin window.'

The only thing left to do was to get insurance as the company would not let us travel without it. They gave me the name of three insurance companies that specialised in people who were unwell. I contacted all three and had to list everything Lynn was suffering from. When they heard it all, they each said no.

I had really begun to believe that we would go so I was bitterly disappointed. And I couldn't bear the thought of seeing Lynn's face when I broke the news. 'I am sorry. We can't go,' I forced myself to tell her.

She looked philosophical. She always took such knocks with quiet dignity. 'Oh, that is such a shame. I really thought that we might make it. But thanks for trying, Mum,' she said.

*

As time went on, the more she said she could not stay here any more. She said something about it every day, and the more she spoke about it, the harder it was for me to find things to keep her looking forward. Whereas at one time smaller, short-term goals would work, I was now frantically searching for things that would be attractive enough to make her fight on, even for another two weeks.

I threw myself once more into contacting any doctor or therapist who I thought might offer even the slightest glimmer of hope. Once again we had a succession of practitioners coming and assessing Lynn to see if there was anything they could do, trusting that they would come up with something, anything to keep her going.

For a year we had a huge battle with her thyroid gland, which had become underactive and wasn't producing enough of the hormone thyroxine that regulates the body's metabolism. She had badly wanted treatment for that because she felt it would help her weight, which was creeping up steadily and making her very despondent.

I arranged for a nutritionist to come down from London. 'Wait until he comes to assess you,' I urged her, clutching at another reason for her to linger. 'Just see what he has to say. You never know, he might come up with something.' The nutritionist did lots of different tests and talked about supporting her whole system as well as tackling her weight gain. He identified quite a few things, including problems with her immune system, liver, bowel and further hormonal deficiencies. He made recommendations to

Dr Woodgate that he hoped would help alleviate some of the symptoms.

Meanwhile trying to get the right treatment for her thyroid also took over a year. She started off on synthetic thyroid but she had read good reports of a natural alternative, called Armour Thyroid and she desperately wanted to try it because she thought it would make a big difference to her weight. I tried everything to get a doctor to prescribe it. We had contact with three of them and there was always something to wait for – the initial appointment, waiting for test results, waiting for the consultant to write.

All the time I was saying, 'Just wait for this because you might feel a lot better if you get it.' It was one more lifeline for me to cling to in the hope it would keep Lynn going.

Each doctor refused to prescribe it until I contacted Dr Andrew Wright, a GP based in Bolton who specialises in ME. He had been treating Lynn since 1999. He was extremely kind and travelled all the way from the northwest, a ten-hour round trip, to visit. He prescribed the natural thyroid for her.

Richard and I were both building Lynn up about it because it was something she really thought would help her weight problem, and we were building our own hopes up too. I read avidly everything about thyroid function on the Internet and leapt on any positive account of this treatment. We had so little else to hang on to. Flying in the face of all my experience so far, I told myself that this *could* really help.

When I went to pick it up from the surgery, I was so pleased. '*I've finally got it, after all this time, she's going to be so happy,*' I thought. I brought it home and took it in to Lynn's room with an encouraging smile. 'Look, here it is, I've got it at last,' I said.

She looked at me sadly and signed on her hand: 'Thank you, Mum, for everything, for all your efforts, but it's too late. It's not going to work now. I am too far gone.'

CHAPTER EIGHTEEN
LYNN'S MESSAGES OF LOVE

My birthday is in September and as my fifty-fourth approached in 2008 I thought Lynn had a special gleam in her eye. Usually she chose a present for me and also got Richard to order flowers but she loved going that extra mile for people and this year she seemed excited. I was wondering if she was planning something extra special, though I had no idea what it could be.

On the morning of my birthday I went into her room as usual to do her medicines. She greeted me with a huge smile. 'I can't wait to give you your birthday surprise, Mum, but I guess I will just have to,' she said gleefully.

She was teasing me with a big cheeky grin on her face because we had always had a tradition that cards and presents were hidden until everyone had done the routine tasks of getting washed and dressed. Having to wait so patiently used to drive the children mad when they were small. So now Lynn was having a bit of fun with me, getting her own back, but I could see she was really pleased with whatever it was she had planned.

It was 11 a.m. by the time all the chores were done and I sat down on her bed ready for my surprise. She produced a card from under her pillow and handed it to me, her eyes dancing with delight. 'Happy birthday, Mum,' she signed.

As I pulled the card out of the envelope I saw it had pictures of herself on the front – one of her with long blonde hair and freckles across her nose, smiling shyly, aged about seven, one of her in a leotard holding her ballet trophy and one more recent of her, a beautiful young woman lying in bed. '*Happy Birthday To A Very Special Mum…*' it said and inside was the most beautiful message in the world.

My Wishes For You
I wish for you…all the love in the world.
I wish for you…freedom to do whatever you want and
to go wherever you want.
I wish for you…happiness.
I wish for you…long, lazy days.
I wish for you…someone to share your life with.
I wish for you…lots of time to yourself to do whatever
you want to do.
I wish for you…to have someone to spoil you, take you
out and treat you as well as you deserve.
I wish for you…to travel to beautiful hot places and
discover lots of new things.

I wish for you…to have your biggest desire come true –
for me to get better.
I wish for you…to have your life back.
I wish for you…to have ALL your dreams come true,
for ever and ever.
To Mum…MAY ALL YOUR WISHES COME TRUE

I want you to know how much I love you and appreci-
ate everything you do for me. I can never give you as
much as you've given me, but I do try to show you how
much I care. So, I hope you never feel unloved, unap-
preciated or uncared for. Because you are NONE of
those things.
All my love for ever, Lynn xxx

As I read, I could not hold back the tears. I felt completely choked up, not just at the wonderful words but because my lovely girl had been unable to remember how to read and write for all these years and now she was capable of thinking up this beautiful message and putting it together via an Internet site while lying flat and silent in her darkened room.

'This is incredible. Thank you so much,' I said as I hugged her and kissed her gently.

She was delighted that it had worked so well and that I loved it so much. But it broke my heart too because I knew she wanted these good things for herself, and I wanted them for her, oh so much. Realising she couldn't have them, she wished them for me. She could be happy if I was happy, but I did not want to be happy and free while she was still stricken.

I thought back to the times she had said to me: 'I am sorry I have spoilt your life,' and I replied fervently: 'You haven't spoilt my life. You are ill; it is the illness that has ruined your life and done this to mine, it is certainly not you. Don't feel guilty. It is my choice to look after you as long as you need me and as soon as you are better, I'll be off doing my own thing.' I did not want her to feel she was a burden to me but that was not the only reason I said it – I meant it – what made me unhappy was Lynn's situation, not mine.

Earlier that same year, on 2 March, she had given me another moving and beautiful card for Mother's Day. It had a photograph of our two heads together, surrounded by a pattern of flowers on the front and this message inside:

Mum,

My wish for you this mother's day is really 1 for the both of us and it's very simple…I wish we can spend some *nice* time together just doing whatever we want and enjoying each other's company – that's all (well, apart from the other, obvious wish that is!).

Thank you for all you do…I can never thank you enough for everything you've given up for me. I love you lots.

All my love, Lynn xxx

She was always thanking me for what I did for her. She didn't resent it or take it for granted as some highly dependent people do. She was sweet and grateful and loving.

All this time, she was still struggling with her Internet letter to her friends. When she finished it some time in the middle of 2008, it took her ages to post it on the website. 'I have to get the guts to send this,' she kept saying. 'People are going to think all kinds of things about me. Some people are going to hate me for it and think I am a quitter.'

I was sure they would not think that and I told her so but still she hesitated. Sadly, I knew it was not because her resolve was wavering but because she was so thoughtful and concerned about upsetting people. I don't know what prompted her in the end, but one night in November 2008, she finally clicked on 'send'.

When I went into her room in the morning, I could see she was perturbed. 'I have sent it,' she told me straight away. 'It was a hard thing to do. I hope people don't hate me for it.'

Within hours replies came flooding in, all of them positive, all of them saying they could understand. She was deeply moved and heartened. Though she still hadn't shown me her letter, she wanted to share some of these replies with me so forwarded them, with this introduction:

Monday 24 November 2008 05:59

Mum, Here ar sum mor messages from people that hav read my diary (think that's every1 now). Agen, they ar so luvly they made me kry. I do hav special friends, don't I...I may not hav had a lucky life in sum ways, but in another way, I'm actually EKSTREMELY (sp) lucky – I hav been given AMAZ-ING family, friends and pets, and I'l always b grate-ful 4 that, if nothing else...Its u that's kept me going 4 so long and hav given me th strength 2 keep fiting wen I felt lik giving up. I'm just sorry it kant keep me going 4ever...

Anyway, hav a read. Luv, L. Thank u 4 looking after me yesterday wen I wos so poorly. Think 2day's going 2 b better. Hope so.

As I read through the replies, we cried over them together. Her friends told her how much she had helped them through difficult times, how sad they were at her decision and how they would really miss her.

Some of those who were seriously ill said, '*I am not as sick as you but I sometimes wonder how I am going to go on. I don't know how you have battled on for so long.*' They said: '*I admire you. I don't think less of you for taking this brave decision.*'

I felt the same way. No matter how much I longed for this not to be happening, I admired her courage, her dignity and her fortitude. Lynn and I discussed many things that no mother should ever have to talk about with their beloved child, like what I should do if she was in terrible pain or if she got a bout of sickness and could not keep her feeding tube down.

At the time of her Advanced Directive she said she did not want to die of starvation or dehydration as she thought that would be a horrible death, but after her last, appalling, hospital admission, she said: 'No matter how much I am suffering, I am NOT going into hospital.' I tried not to think about what that might mean.

We never discussed how I was going to cope without her; it would have been too upsetting. I desperately wanted her to stay but I wanted her to want it for herself, not to save me from heartbreak. And we never discussed her taking an overdose – I believed her when she promised me she would never do anything behind my back again.

I dreaded her potassium levels plunging again because that meant she would be in terrible pain and I didn't know if I could bear to watch her go through agony. Or I thought that perhaps she would get an infection but with very careful nursing care, I could save her to live on a few more months while I searched for a cure. Realistically, however, I knew that any serious infection would mean she'd need to go to hospital for intravenous antibiotics, which I was not allowed to administer at home, and without them she could die.

Every day I wearily played out these different scenarios in my head, the multiple ways that death might take her.

My imagination tortured and drained me but Lynn had developed a serenity that came from the knowledge that her escape route had been set up and the belief that she would soon be travelling along it.

In the meantime, we were getting ready for Christmas. 'Just hang on and we will make it a really special Christmas this year,' I said. 'Steve and Sarah and the children are coming. Won't it be lovely to see the boys opening their presents?'

She looked at me a little exasperated at my relentless harping on about things to look forward to. 'It will be really hard for me,' she pointed out.

I was deflated. 'Yes, I know it will. I understand. But because we don't know what's going to happen in the next few months, let's make it especially memorable for everyone. Will you try?'

She sighed. 'Okay, Mum. I will try, for you,' she promised.

I was so pleased she had agreed – we'd found yet another thing for her to look forward to. We started our preparations in October, looking in catalogues and on the Internet to choose presents for her friends and the family then wrapping them and writing cards. It took a long time because she could only do two or three a day before becoming exhausted. While she was busy and interested, I secretly hoped, she would not think about dying.

It was never far from her mind, however. 'I want this to be a special time for us, Mum,' she told me one day. 'I want us to spend as much time together as we can and to make it as nice as we can.'

I felt the same way and we drew even closer together. As the days grew shorter and the threat of a winter infection grew closer, I couldn't help thinking sometimes: '*This is the last time we will do this,*' but I tried to push the thought away.

We had ordered about 30 presents and she wrapped them in Christmas paper and went to a lot of trouble sticking on flowers and ribbons. Then I covered them in brown paper and wrote the addresses and they were all piled up in the hall, waiting to be posted off. But if we spoke about presents for her she said she didn't want anything. It would be a waste of money, she said, because she would not be around long enough to use it.

I was going to ignore her wishes and buy her a new camera. I had already bought her smaller things like iPhone covers, jewellery and a 'Loving Thoughts' poem that you can get in card shops for different family members. It was a moving one called 'To My Daughter', which I put in a frame. '*Who knows how long she would be around anyway,*' I thought, defiantly. '*Who knows what's round the corner that might save her?*' If my love and care could do it, she would stay with me for as long as it took.

And if I could make Christmas special enough, she would *want* to stay, I thought. I would make sure that there was a huge warm ocean of love in the house from Richard and her grandparents and Steve and Sarah and their two gorgeous little boys and from me that would wash around her so that she could not bear to strike out into the unknown.

CHAPTER NINETEEN

SAYING GOODBYE

The persistent knock, knock, knock, broke through my dreams. I struggled to open my eyes and glanced at the bedside clock. It was 1.45 a.m. I groaned. I had only been in bed about an hour and a quarter and was not too pleased that Lynn was waking me so soon by knocking on the intercom.

I sank back on the pillow, trying to gather some strength. The knocking came again, more urgently, and I jumped out of bed and ran along the corridor to her room. 'What's going on? I've only been in bed an hour,' I snapped tetchily.

Then I saw that her big dark hazel eyes were looking at me imploringly and were filled with tears. Silently, she lifted up a large syringe. It was the one I had filled up just before I went to bed with her 24-hour supply of morphine and had attached to the pump that fed it slowly into her thigh. It was almost empty.

'Oh, Lynn,' I cried. I felt like I had been kicked in the chest and my knees almost buckled. I knew instantly what had happened. Despite her promise to me and her dad never to try to end her life in secret again, she had injected the syringe of morphine down her Hickman line, sending a massive overdose straight into her bloodstream. '*This is bad*,' I thought fearfully. '*This is really bad.*'

I grabbed a little square coffee table that was near her bed, put it down beside her and sat down heavily, trying to contain my rising panic. 'What is going on?' I asked her gently. 'What has happened? Why have you done this?'

There wasn't much light – the hall light was on as it always was and there was a small lamp on the floor behind her door. Even in the dimness I could see she was crying quietly, fat tears running down her face. She signed on her hand, 'I can't take any more. I can't go on.'

I took her hand and held it between my own, fear turning me cold. 'Oh, but why now?' I cried as my own tears spilt over. 'This is not the right time. Please, Lynn, not now with Christmas coming. With Steve and Sarah coming over and bringing the boys. It really isn't the right time.'

Lynn looked so lovely, lying there in a pair of white pyjamas that were fresh on that day, her lustrous dark hair spread around her on the pillow. She was young, too young to die. But that determined look was there in her eyes. 'There will never be a right time. I am sorry,' she signed.

My heart was thumping so hard, I feared it might burst and my mind was a maelstrom of questions. '*What am I going to do here? What can I say?*' I asked myself. To her I burst out, 'But you promised! You agreed. We said we

243

would have a really special Christmas. And everybody wants to see you. Nanna and Grandpa will be here. Everyone who loves you wants to remember a lovely time together. You *can't* go now.'

There was a soft bubbling from the fish tank but otherwise my voice was the only sound in the room. Lynn's trembling hands started to move again as she tried to make me accept that this meant the death of all my hopes. 'I can't put up with it any longer. I can't stay, not even for one more day. I need to go. I have to go.'

She was crying but not in a hysterical way. I was forced to acknowledge that beneath the tears she was completely determined. I felt almost suffocated by a wave of the profoundest sadness. After all our years of struggle, the struggle that should have been rewarded, if there was any justice in the universe, with Lynn's recovery, this was the end.

The date was 3 December 2008. I don't know why she chose that day; I don't think she had planned it precisely. The day before had been more hectic than normal but otherwise nothing out of the ordinary. I had not spent a lot of time with Lynn because a nurse had come in and I had gone out to do some shopping.

In the few days before there had been people calling and the phone ringing a lot as I finalised the Christmas arrangements and we had been busy with the presents and cards. I was very tired and Lynn was quite poorly. Her pain was worse and she was completely exhausted from trying to do the extra work needed to wrap the presents. But exhaustion and pain were part of the pattern of her life. So after I had done her bits and pieces and said, 'Goodnight, I love you,' and left her to sleep just after midnight, I had had no reason to suspect she would do this.

Perhaps she had spent the hour after I had gone to bed thinking everything through before detaching the syringe from her pump, reattaching it to her Hickman line and pushing the plunger to send the morphine flooding down into a vein next to her heart.

The last time she had attempted suicide, she did not have a full syringe. She must have thought that this time the whole 24-hour dose of 210 milligrams would have an instant effect. A dosage of 20 or 30 milligrams could be enough to kill any normal adult but Lynn had been on the drug so long that her body was extremely tolerant to it.

I am sure she wanted to manage without involving me because she was afraid of getting me into trouble. Because of the law forbidding anyone to help with a suicide, she was trying to leave this world alone, without even saying good-bye to me. That hurt, but I knew she had done it out of love. My only crumb of comfort in the bleakness was that the overdose had not had the effect she wanted and she had been forced to call me.

I was sitting awkwardly and uncomfortably on the little coffee table, but I didn't notice. I didn't even think of wiping away my tears as I continued to beg her to wait a little longer, to hang on to see the family, to get through Christmas… Lynn listened, her eyes full of compassion for my heartbreak, and repeated her answer calmly. 'I can't stay. I have had enough. I am so sorry, but I need to go.'

After a little while she made it clear she had a plea of her own. There was something she wanted me to do. 'I have taken all this morphine already, but it is not enough. Please, Mum, you must get me some more,' she indicated.

Her request hit me like a thunderbolt. In all our discussions, all the times I had imagined how her end might come and how I might manage it, I had never thought of this. That I might have to do anything other than nurse her. What was I to do? I needed time. I had to think.

I suddenly realised I was frozen. I kept Lynn's room particularly cold because she always felt hot and my teeth were chattering as I sat there in my light sleeveless nightie. 'Just wait while I go to put on some clothes. I'll be back in a minute,' I said.

As I walked through the house from her bedroom to mine, my heart was racing and my mind was in turmoil. What could I say to her to convince her that this was not the time, that she had to hang on a bit longer? I wanted to scream and shout to the heavens: 'This is not how it was supposed to be! Bloody, bloody disease!'

I thought back over all the things she had put up with in her 17 long years of illness: people disbelieving, doctors sticking huge needles into her spine, contracting MRSA and the excruciating pain she experienced then. I thought of all the times we had nearly lost her and how amazingly brave she had been in the face of everything she had to endure.

All these images of her jostled in my brain and from the whirlwind one thought began to emerge clearer than the rest: my beautiful, feisty daughter had taught me how to be strong. And now, when she needed me more than she had ever done, I could not let her down.

'*If she can be strong and stay calm, as she has the whole way through, I can't make it harder for her by going to pieces,*' I told myself. '*But I am not going to let her go. I am going to fight to persuade her to stay.*'

I threw on some trousers, a jumper and some socks and went back into her room determined to try harder to convince her. Her eyes went straight to my hands with a hopeful look, then she turned away, disappointed, when she saw I had not brought more syringes.

I switched on the light in the fish tank so we could see each other a bit better and took up my position again on the little coffee table. 'Honestly, Lynn, I understand how you feel,' I said earnestly. 'I know you feel you have put up with so much for so long and there is no hope left, but can't you change your mind? I don't want you to go. Can't you stay a little while longer and wait for nature to take its course?'

Lynn shook her head firmly. 'Please, Mum, please help me, you know I can't go on. Please get me some more,' she begged.

We pleaded with each other, over and over, me begging her to stay, her urging me to help her. 'I can't go and get it myself. I can't do anything. You are the only one who can help me. Please help me,' she said.

She was very clear in her mind, and unwavering. 'We have talked about this many times. I am sorry but I am not going to change my mind,' she said.

I thought about how the subject had come up more and more frequently. Even though we carried on doing all the normal things and often laughed and joked together, she always said at some point during the day, 'Mum, you know I don't want to be here any more. I have tried long enough. I am never going to get better. I'm too broken. I am so tired of it all. I have to go.'

In my head, I knew that was realistic. I had still not completely lost the hope that some miracle might come along but when I sat down and thought through all the things that were wrong with her – the osteoporosis, the shrivelled-up pituitary gland, the kidney and heart problems, the recently diagnosed liver dysfunction, the adrenal failure, the underactive thyroid and all the rest – I could not see how she could ever lead a normal life. And I knew that she had been getting closer to not just wanting to go, but actually *needing* to go.

She had stated her wishes to her doctors and to others in the family, she had written them out clearly and legally and had made the arrangements with Dignitas. I knew that if she was able to crawl out of that bed she would have put an end to what was a miserable life much sooner.

I thought that able-bodied people have the right to end their lives if they chose, why should she not have the same right? The only reason she could not exercise that right was that she was helpless and totally reliant on me.

Oh, but it was so hard to do what she wanted when it was going totally, utterly against every single feeling in my heart. Against what *I* wanted, for *me*. I wanted her to stay. How could I let her go? More than that, how could I actually, physically, carry out the actions that would help her to go when my every instinct screamed out against it?

She was my life. I was with her more or less 24 hours a day most days and my every thought was of her. Even when I was out, my thoughts ran along the same lines: '*I wonder if Lynn's okay. What can I bring her to make her smile? Oh, those are pretty pyjamas. Maybe I'll get her a pair.*'

When we were together we talked about everything. I knew her every mood and she knew mine. I knew her far more than a mother should know a 31-year-old daughter. Because of her illness, she was as dependent as a newborn baby and our lives were inextricably entwined. I longed to see her as an independent young woman doing all the things she dreamt about and to share in her joy. How could she, or I, give up on that dream that we had held for so long?

As the battle raged on between my head and my heart, Lynn gently but persistently nudged me to help her. At the same time she was making sure she said all the final, important things she wanted to say.

Her hands began to move again. She drew G, O, O on her left hand with her right forefinger. 'Goodbye?' I guessed. She nodded. Then D and S. 'Dad and Steve? You want me to say goodbye to them for you?' She nodded and went on, 'Tell them I am sorry and that I love them more than I can say.'

I was almost too choked to speak. 'They love you so much. They will miss you so much,' I managed to whisper. 'Can't you stay just a little while so you can say goodbye to them properly?'

Again her head shook sadly. 'I am sorry. It is too late.'

Looking down at her beautiful face, I thrashed around in my mind for more words, better words, words that would make her change her mind. I felt I was failing. I thought somebody else might be able to change her mind. '*Should I ring Richard?*' I asked myself. No, I shouldn't. Lynn didn't want me to. If he came he might get into serious trouble. And I didn't know if he could bear this scene. '*Is there anything he could say that I am not saying?*' No, there isn't. He understood as well as I did.

It was a very lonely place to be. I longed for Steve and Richard to be there. If we lived in one of the places the law allowed it and Lynn had been able to do things the way she wanted, she could have chosen her moment better – not in the middle of a freezing night. She would have had her family around her, everyone could have said one last good-bye to her and she to them. I would have been supported, she would have seen me surrounded by love and not been so worried about me. It would have been a much better, easier way for her to leave us.

'*I don't want her to go. I want her to be here. I want to keep her with me*,' I screamed inside. But I wanted her to stay for *me*, it was what *I* wanted. I was being selfish. I knew I must make myself do what is best for her.

Lynn made a stroking gesture with her right hand and looked around questioningly. I knew that meant she wanted me to fetch the cats to her. 'You want to say good-bye to Willow and Shadow?' I asked and she nodded.

I got up stiffly and rushed around looking for them. I wanted to be away from her side as little as possible. I ran down the corridor to my bedroom, calling them both, found Willow on my bed and raced back to Lynn with him. Then I hurried round to the spare bedroom, looked under the bed and in the kitchen and living room but I couldn't find Shadow anywhere, which was strange as he had to be in the house.

I thought Lynn would ask me to go back and search some more, but she just accepted that I couldn't find him and concentrated on stroking and kissing Willow. 'You will look after them, won't you?' she beseeched me.

I nodded dumbly as inside I was being torn apart. I had tried so hard to keep her going. These two young cats had been part of my plan. I had thought that when she fell in love with them she would not, could not, leave them. I had worked at thinking up so many things for her to look forward to. And she had gone along with it for well over a year.

But as I watched her taking her leave of the animal that had been one of the few sources of joy in her life, I admitted to myself that I had been getting round her for a long time, against her real wishes. I painfully acknowledged that it wasn't fair of me to continue to pressure her into staying, just because I couldn't bear to lose her and didn't know how I would live without her.

She had got to the point where she was saying, 'I have done what you wanted for long enough. Please, you must accept that I can't do it any more. I can't.' Agonisingly, I recognised that it would be plain cruel of me to keep on. She had put up with an intolerable life for all those years and she had the right to finish it if she wanted and needed to.

Willow snuggled comfortably down on the bed and Lynn turned to me again. She spelt on her hand F, R, I. 'Are you frightened?' I asked, feeling a fresh stab in my heart. My poor child, scared. I instantly wrapped her in my arms. 'What are you frightened of? Are you afraid of death? Of the unknown?'

She shook her head, no, and spelt out, 'I welcome death. Death is my friend.' Then she held up four fingers, meaning 'for' and pointed at me.

'You are frightened for me?' I whispered. 'You must not worry about me. I will be okay.' I knew that if I helped her I would have to go to the police station and answer questions about assisting a suicide but I didn't know what would happen after that. I really did not care at all.

She wrote F, R, I. again, then shook her head, which I knew meant 'not', then spelt out 'work'.

'You are scared that it might not work?' I murmured. Oh, my poor child. What could I say?

I hugged her in silent desperation. 'Thank you for everything you have done for me. I love you,' she signed.

The tears ran steadily down my face. 'I am so sorry this happened to you,' I sobbed. 'I don't know why it happened. It wasn't fair. You didn't deserve it. You have been so brave. I love you. I will love you for ever.'

We had been talking for over an hour and she had said all she wanted to say. As my sobs subsided, I stroked her hair and kissed her.

'Please, please help me,' she begged again. 'I can't stay. I need to go. I need two more syringes of morphine to be sure it will work. You are the only one who can help me.'

I didn't know what damage she might have done with the amount of morphine she had already taken. Could it have made her liver dysfunction worse, or even caused brain damage? If I didn't help her and she survived in a worse state than she already was, how could I live with that? More importantly, how could Lynn live with that?

As I looked at her beautiful, determined face and into her serious, pleading eyes, I finally accepted in my heart that she could not go on. There wasn't anything I or anyone else could say that would make a difference. One way or another, she was going to leave me.

I thought of what she had written in her Advanced Directive: '*I trust my parents to make the right choice for ME, and not for THEM.*' However much it hurt me, I had to respect her wishes and live up to that trust. I did not have the right to force her to continue to suffer. If I turned my back on her now, I was taking away the only bit of free will she had and that would have been an insult to her.

She was my life, but I had to let her go.

But even so, right up until the very moment when I whispered, 'Okay,' I didn't know which way I would decide. And I had no idea if I would be actually physically capable of doing what she asked. It was just so completely awful. I never could have imagined, or prepared myself for this: my Lynn asking me to go and get more morphine to allow her to escape her terrible life and to leave us for ever.

Now I had agreed, and now I had to do it. I went to the small spare bedroom where I kept the morphine. I was trembling and I felt utterly exhausted. I can't remember it very clearly but I know I opened up the toolbox I used to store the morphine and took out six vials, known as ampoules, of 60 milligrams each and two of 30 milligrams.

I carried them through to the living room and with shaking hands drew the liquid from the small ampoules up into two syringes. Then I remember very clearly walking back into her room and seeing her large eyes fixed on me, full of hope that I held her release in my hands.

I walked round to the far side of her bed to get close to the Hickman line, which was split into two at the end. With shaking hands, I went to connect the syringes, each now containing 210 milligrams of morphine. Lynn pushed my hand away, indicating 'I will do it' and took them from me.

I sat down on the small table beside her bed and leant over her to be as close as possible. She made the connections and, just as she was about to push the plunger on the first syringe, the lights went out in her room. The fuse serving the main lights had tripped though there was still a glow from her fish tank, which was on a different circuit. It seemed like some kind of omen.

'Wait a minute. I'll go and flick the switch,' I said, desperate to delay the moment. She shook her head firmly and pushed the syringes. One, and then the other. As the morphine surged into her bloodstream, her eyes closed.

I flopped across the top of her unconscious body sobbing. The words 'She's gone, she's gone' throbbed repeatedly through my head. Hoping she could hear me, I stammered out, 'I love you. Your dad loves you, everyone loves you. We understand. We don't blame you. We know what you've been through. You were so brave for so long. Rest easy now, my darling.'

For hours afterwards I just sat on the little coffee table beside her, holding her arm, stroking her hair, watching every breath she took, as the long night slowly turned into a chilly day. I hardly moved at all. I didn't eat, I didn't drink, I didn't sleep. She was still breathing and I wanted to be with her when she passed.

My mind churned as I raked through the agonising decision I had made, over and over again. How I knew she couldn't have gone on, that I had done what she wanted, what she had been saying to so many people she wanted for a long time. How she had written it down, how she had pleaded with me to help her, how I had to respect her… I had to keep repeating it all to myself like a mantra to stop myself falling apart.

The tears flowed endlessly as I talked to her, I didn't think they would ever stop. I didn't know if she could hear me or not, but I told her again how much I loved her and would love her for always and would miss her every minute of my life.

'I am sorry,' I whispered. 'You know your dad loves you and Steve loves you and they would have wanted to be with you. They will always miss you. You are not to worry about me. I will be okay.'

At first she seemed to be sleeping peacefully and I thought she was drifting gently away. But by the afternoon she started making gurgling noises and appeared to be having trouble drawing breath.

My heart raced and I felt so scared as I imagined what she could be going through. I couldn't understand it. She had had such a huge amount of morphine, it must have done terrible damage. '*Is she suffering?*' I asked myself frantically. '*Does she know what's going on? Is she in pain? Why hasn't the morphine worked?*'

I have since learnt that people make these noises when they are dying but at the time I didn't know what was happening and I felt rising panic. It was like going back to when her lung was punctured and she was in such terrible distress because she couldn't breathe. It had been so horrible and frightening that she insisted she never wanted to be in that position again. I could not bear the thought that she might be suffering now in the same dreadful way.

'Lynn, can you hear me?' I whispered urgently. 'Are you in pain? Are you fighting for breath?' She made no response but the gurgling noises went on. I didn't know what to do. Should I call Richard? Should I call the doctor or an ambulance, somebody who could come and tell me whether she was suffering or not?

Trembling, I went into the living room and lifted the phone. Then I put it down again. I hovered over it, thinking fast. '*I need someone here. I need some advice. But if I call an ambulance, they will whisk her away. They might put her on a life-support machine.*' I pictured her with that enormous tube being shoved down her throat again and I knew I couldn't risk it. I told myself that Lynn had said repeatedly that she did not want to be kept alive by machines. She did not want any treatment. I had to respect that. Yet she had also told me that she didn't want to suffer. I could not let her die in pain, but I didn't know what to do.

I was in mental torment. I went back into her bedroom and it looked to me like she might be in distress. What to do to help her? I suddenly thought I might be able to find something on the Internet. Clutching the intercom so I could hear her, I ran to the bedroom again to start up the computer. Feverishly, I googled 'overdose' and 'morphine', trying to find out what the effect might be of that amount of the drug inside her. Was there something going on in her body that I had no idea about?

I tapped something into the search bar, found a page, glanced down it and, if I saw something that might be help-ful, clicked on it and read through it rapidly. Then I went back into Lynn and she was still the same. Back out and on to the computer again, frantically searching for something, anything, that might help, running back to Lynn's room every few minutes to check on her. I went through loads of sites but was in most of them only for a few seconds. I was doing the same thing I had been doing for all the years since Lynn fell ill at 14: looking and looking for something to help and the right thing to do.

By now more than 12 hours had gone by and I suddenly thought that Lynn had not had her normal medications for spasms and nausea, adrenal failure and other things. I thought, if she can feel but the morphine has knocked her out so much she can't move to tell me, she might be suffer-ing and I won't know about it.

I thought the painkilling effect of the morphine might have worn off as well. The drug passes through the system after a certain length of time, which is why she was on a continuous supply. I thought the huge overdose might have done dreadful damage to her organs but might not actually be controlling her terrible pain any longer.

What did I do to keep her comfortable normally? I gave her medicines – so why not give them to her now? I hurried to the kitchen, counted out her usual tablets, crushed them in the pestle and mortar and diluted them, listening out for Lynn on the intercom. I added a few other tablets as well because I thought the breathlessness might be distressing her and they would calm her down. Back in the bedroom, I drew the diluted medicine into a syringe and slowly put it down her feeding tube in the usual way.

Then I made up another syringe of 210 milligrams of morphine and attached it to the syringe driver that delivered her normal daily dosage slowly into her thigh. I could have put this morphine down her Hickman line so it would have gone straight into the bloodstream but I didn't. I wanted her to have her normal, slow release, constant pain control. I must have thought that what she had already taken was a fatal overdose; it would certainly have killed most people. *I* wasn't trying to kill her. I was sitting with her, waiting for her to die. The main thing was, I could not allow her to suffer.

Once the drugs had gone down, Lynn's breathing settled and the awful gurgling noise stopped. Once or twice she moved her arms and head as if she was feeling something but it was not as upsetting as earlier. Night fell and I sat on by her bedside.

All through the night I sat there, feeling shattered by the agony of knowing I was going to lose her. Sometimes

I wept quietly, at other times I broke into a storm of noisy rage.

'Where is the fairness in this?' I cried to her. 'You may as well have given up ten years ago rather than go through everything that you have put up with. Why did you have to suffer so much to get nowhere? To get to this?'

At some stage, I can't remember when, I thought I had crushed and diluted some Sertraline tablets, the antidepressant she was prescribed after the first suicide attempt, which has a sedative effect. Just a few tablets – not enough to be fatal but I hoped enough to keep her in a deep calm state to make her passing as gentle as it could be. But strangely, no trace of this was found in her body. Maybe I never gave it.

After more than 24 hours had passed since Lynn had taken the morphine, I began to feel panicky again. What if she did survive? What kind of state would she be in? Who could I talk to? Who could I ask?

I searched my brain and suddenly remembered a group I had come across when reading about Dignitas, called Exit International, who believe in people having the right to choose to die. I looked them up on the Internet and found they had a 24-hour confidential helpline.

I dialled the number and a woman answered with a very soothing, sympathetic voice. 'It's about my daughter,' I blurted. 'She has been ill with ME for seventeen years and is bedridden and very severely ill and disabled. For two years she has been saying she wants to die and she has done an Advanced Directive.

'Last night she took a huge amount of morphine straight into a main vein but she is still alive. I don't know what is happening. Can you tell me what is going on? I am terrified she could be aware. Is there anything I can do to help her, to make sure she is not suffering?'

She listened and empathised, but then she said, 'I am so sorry but I can't help you. What you are doing is illegal as the law stands and if I gave you any advice at all, I would be breaking the law too.'

I returned to the bedroom and sat with Lynn knowing no one could help me. I had to manage this alone. Now and then I went back to the computer as another subject to search under occurred to me. At about 5.30 a.m. I was staring at the screen and I suddenly thought to myself, '*What am I doing? I don't know what I'm doing here. I don't want to be here. I just want to be with her.*'

I went back to Lynn and I didn't leave her side again. Her breathing was shallow and she was peaceful. At 7.10 a.m. on 4 December 2008, 29 hours and 25 minutes after she had knocked for me to come to her, she stopped breathing.

I was engulfed in a desolate feeling of loss and emptiness, mixed with a profound relief that she was finally at peace. Uselessly, I clung to her, yearning for her to come back to me. The force of grief shook my whole being. 'She's gone. My Lynn is gone,' I cried into the silence.

Part of me had died with her and I felt I had nothing left to live for. But at the heart of my agony was also the conviction that I had done right by my beloved daughter.

'*She is not in pain now, she is free,*' I kept repeating to myself. '*She had suffered all those years, she is not suffering now. She couldn't go on any more. She is where she needs to be. She's at peace.*'

I had to keep saying it to make myself accept that she had gone. And I truly believed it. My faith had died and Lynn was not a religious person but we both believed the spirit carried on and now I felt her spirit had been released.

As I lay there, totally heartbroken, one thought filled my mind. '*Her body was broken beyond repair. It was no use to her any more. That body is gone now and her spirit is finally free.*'

CHAPTER TWENTY
ARREST

I don't know how long I lay there with Lynn, desolate and forlorn, empty and weak. I had only had just over an hour's sleep in the previous two days. I still had not had anything to eat or drink, not even a glass of water, and I couldn't stop shaking.

But I could not give way to the vast tide of grief that threatened to totally engulf me. There were things I *had* to do. I forced myself to keep the raging waves of agony at bay and slowly sat up, struggling to concentrate. The first and most vital thing was that I had to get Richard to come as quickly as possible so he could spend some time with Lynn before the official wheels ground into motion. Fighting hard just to keep moving, keep functioning, I controlled my trembling fingers enough to send him a text. '*Please come now. Be careful. Don't rush,*' I typed.

I put that because I knew he would sense that what we had been waiting for had happened, not least because it was early in the morning. I thought he might drive too fast and crash so I wanted him to know that rushing would make no difference, without explaining why.

He rang me straight away. 'Why did you ask me to come? What's happening?' he enquired with alarm in his voice.

'I can't tell you now. I will tell you when you get here' I replied quietly.

He didn't push me to explain but promised to come as quickly as he could. I opened the side gate so he could let himself in then returned to Lynn's bedroom to be with my daughter.

It was still dark when I heard his car outside. I went to meet him at the kitchen door. I looked into his anguished eyes. 'She's gone,' I told him, as gently as I could.

He burst into tears. 'Oh no. How? What happened?'

'She took another overdose but it wasn't enough. It didn't work. So I helped her. I got her some more.'

Richard stumbled to her bedroom. When he saw her lying there, pale and motionless, like Sleeping Beauty, he became completely distraught. He dropped to his knees beside her bed and softly wrapped her in his arms. 'I am so sorry, Lynn,' he sobbed, hugging her tighter.

I knew he was not thinking that a wrong had been done to her. He was apologising because we had never been able to make her better. He felt like I did, that we, her parents, who loved her so much, had been utterly helpless in the face of ME. We had strived and struggled for all those years to do the very best we were capable of but he, like me, felt we had let her down and the medical profession had let her down. Everyone had failed her.

He didn't blame me. He had longed for her to change her mind and not leave us but he totally understood how she felt. Everyone in the family had accepted in their hearts that, however it happened, she had reached the end. But all Richard was thinking then was it meant he would never see her alive again or text her or phone her for one of their unique coded chats. And it was agony.

I stood beside him in silence, the weight of our heartache a tangible presence in the room. There were no words to say. Our tears flowed unchecked. After some time Richard managed to compose himself. 'You know we are going to have to phone somebody,' he said.

'Yes, I know,' I replied. 'I will ring Dr Woodgate at the surgery.'

'No, you have been through so much. I'll do it,' he insisted. I stayed with Lynn while he rang the coroner and the doctor.

Dr Woodgate came straight away. Richard met her at the door and she gave him a big hug, then she came into the bedroom and hugged me. She was being professional but couldn't hide the tears brimming in her eyes. 'Lynn was so brave. She fought for as long as she could. She put up with so much. She had just had enough,' she murmured gently to us. 'You and Richard did everything you could. No parents could have done more.' It helped a little that a professional who knew us so well could not see what more we could have done.

She examined Lynn to certify death formally and asked me what had happened. I recalled the events of the previous 30 hours as best I could while she scribbled notes on a scrap of paper. 'I don't know if I am remembering it all properly and I am not sure what time different things happened,' I said.

We came out into the living room and she wrote out what I had told her again in a neater version on a bigger piece of paper. I offered to photocopy it and I made two copies. She took the original scrap and a copy of the neatly written version and left the rest on the table. I thought they were for me and Richard.

Not long after she left, two policemen arrived, a sergeant and a constable. They were professional yet considerate. They knew Richard and the story of Lynn and they obviously understood that it was an utterly tragic situation for everybody.

I didn't realise at the time that Richard's call to the coroner's office had been misinterpreted. He had said that Lynn had tried to kill herself and that it didn't work and that I 'gave her' more morphine. When he used the words 'gave her' he meant that I had handed it to her, not that I had injected it, but the coroner took it to mean that I had actually administered it.

As a result, the coroner had alerted the police and a detective inspector had rung the officers as they were driving to see us and ordered them to treat the house as a crime scene and arrest me on suspicion of murder. The two officers didn't say anything about this and didn't caution me when they arrived so I assumed they were treating it as a case of assisted suicide.

They were there for about an hour, talking to Richard and looking around the place, while my head was somewhere else. All I could think about were the things I had to do at all costs for Lynn before they took me into custody.

She had insisted to me that her body should go to ME research and if that wasn't set in motion immediately, before the state pathologist got involved, I was afraid it would not happen. So I called Dr Shepherd from the ME Association, and asked him to get in touch with a pathologist who specialised in ME. And I had to organise somebody to look after the cats. I was so utterly exhausted and wrung out that it took every ounce of concentration to focus on the practicalities. One of the police officers described me afterwards as like somebody who was destroyed and on the brink of collapse but who was pushing herself to the extreme to try to keep it together.

The officers asked Richard what had happened and he related what I had told him. We were sitting in the lounge; I was there too, but I wasn't listening. One of the officers later said Richard was looking at me and I was nodding in agreement but it wasn't like that. My body was there on the settee but my mind was away, struggling through the fog of distress to work out who to call about the research and who I could ask to look after Willow and Shadow when I went to the police station.

I didn't need to listen because I had no worries about what Richard would say. I trusted him totally to describe exactly how it was. I knew assisted suicide was against the law but I was prepared to tell them openly that was what I had done. It never crossed my mind that I or Richard had to be careful about what words we used because the case was straightforward: I had done what Lynn wanted and had asked me to do.

I knew that in other cases of assisted suicide people had not been charged but they had taken their loved ones to Dignitas in Switzerland while Lynn had died at home with me, so I did not know if I would be treated the same way. '*But whatever they decide to do, so be it,*' I thought. I didn't care what happened to me. All that mattered was that I had done the right thing for Lynn.

After they finished talking to Richard, the police officers followed me everywhere I went. When I wanted to see Lynn again, they came with me. When I wanted to change my trousers, they wouldn't let me because that would have meant me being in my bedroom by myself. I can only guess they were worried I might harm myself. They came with me while I got an extra jumper and some shoes. I actually put on two odd shoes, one high and one low, which I only realised when I got to the police station.

'Please, can I just make a few phone calls?' I asked them.

It took me a while to make the arrangements and they started getting a little fidgety because they wanted me to go. Richard was irritated. 'Can't you give her a bit more time?' he snapped.

'It's okay,' I said. 'I know I have to go. I won't be long.'

I went in to see Lynn a couple more times. 'Goodbye,' I whispered one last time. 'I love you.'

She looked so peaceful, like she was just resting, as I softly kissed her creamy cheek. Then I turned to the police officers and indicated I was ready to go. In the living room I picked up the copy of the doctor's note and my address book. 'You can't take those,' one of the officers said hastily and took them from me. I still had no idea that I was suspected of murder.

We got to the police station at Brighton at about 11 a.m. and I was cautioned. I have the paperwork that says I was, but I don't remember it happening. By then I was in a complete daze. My normal state was to be chronically sleep-deprived as I usually only got a few hours' sleep a night. Now, not having slept at all and feeling utterly destroyed by the anguish of just having lost my beloved daughter, I went into autopilot, trying to go through the motions.

They took me to the custody block, where I had to hand over everything I had with me. Then I was shown to a cell and two female police officers came and strip-searched me. They took my shoes, socks and T-shirt but left me my jeans and a cardigan.

They photographed my body to look for bruises as evidence of any kind of fight. Two nurses took blood and urine samples and swabs. They even snipped bits off my nails – everything to look for signs of a struggle. At the same time I was still being treated with sympathy. 'I want you to know that we are all behind you here,' one of the nurses confided to me. 'We think it's terrible you have been arrested.'

I was then left alone for what seemed like ages. All there was in the cell was a bare, hard bed and I was absolutely freezing and shaking uncontrollably. Eventually my solicitor arrived and looked shocked at the state of me. 'You are shivering. Are you cold? Haven't you got a top or shoes or a blanket? That's disgusting.' She was kind and comforting and I took to her straight away.

She went off and got me a jumper, some plimsolls and a blanket then took me to a room where I told her everything that had happened. I can't remember the order of things too clearly after that. At some stage I was seen by a doctor who was supposed to assess whether I was a risk to myself and whether I was in a fit state to be interviewed.

He asked me little more than how I was, how long I had gone without sleep and did I feel suicidal. I answered his questions as calmly as I could and he obviously concluded that I was okay, but I can't have been. On top of no sleep and no food, I had just suffered the most devastating trauma that could have happened to anyone. It was not just that Lynn had died, it was the huge, prolonged battle I had fought within me to accept that she was actually going.

The police were anxious to interview me as soon as I had been pronounced fit to do so. My solicitor said, 'Just tell them how it was. There is nothing to worry about.' The questioning lasted just over an hour. They were gentle and sympathetic and I thought, *'Now that they have heard how it was, I'll soon be allowed home.'* It didn't happen. I was told I had to stay in overnight.

I was taken back to the cell, where I lay on the bare bed but sleep didn't come even though I was shattered beyond imagination. There was somebody shouting in one of the other cells. I remember lying there thinking that the cell reminded me of the time Lynn was in Guy's Hospital and they put her in a room with no window and no bell, like being in prison.

They had taken my watch so I didn't know what the time was. I didn't realise there was an intercom and I could have pressed the button to speak to someone. I thought about Lynn lying there in her cell-like room in the darkness and those people being so horrible to her when they were doing the experiment of not letting her know the time to catch her out in 'faking' her spasms.

Then this chap who was shouting called out, 'What's the time?' The answer came: 'Four a.m.' I thought about how I could get up and walk around and how awful it must have been for Lynn, paralysed, helpless and nobody coming to her aid. I was relating all my experiences to Lynn because all I thought about was her.

The next day I was interviewed again in the presence of my solicitor and an independent person who sits in when someone who is deemed a 'vulnerable' adult gives a statement. They are supposed to make sure you understand what is happening. The questions more or less went over the same ground.

Afterwards I was let out on bail but not allowed to go home as the police were still searching the house. Steve and Sarah had come over from Belgium and they picked me up and took me to a hotel near Eastbourne where we were joined by my brother Vinny and sister Dolie. Richard came over in the evening.

The next day they brought me back to the house. It felt empty and it was strange because I knew the police had thoroughly searched it so I expected it to be turned upside down. Everything appeared to be in its place but when I opened the cupboards I found they had pulled things out, then pushed them back in so all the stuff was mixed up higgledy piggledy, including all my paperwork. They had taken away Lynn's computer and mobile phone, my computer and phone, printers, cameras, videos, clothes and loads of documents.

More of my family came. I had lots of people around me but I couldn't settle down. The problem was Lynn – she wasn't there. Her bed was empty. I felt all the time that I should be doing something for her. When I was talking I would suddenly break off and get up, thinking I had to get Lynn's medicines ready or do this or that for her because that was what I had been doing for all those years.

That afternoon I went with Vinny and Dolie to see Lynn, who was being kept at the Conquest. She looked beautiful and she appeared to be at peace. I put my hand on her face. 'Oh, she's so cold,' I remember murmuring. Of course, she would be, but it was very upsetting, feeling that she was cold. But I think seeing her face just so peaceful did help me. 'She's free,' I whispered to myself.

When we drove back and came into the Close, there were about 20 or 30 media people outside the house. They took my picture as I went through my front door. We came in and shut the curtains and stayed inside for days. People slept in the living room or squashed into the other bedrooms together – we didn't use Lynn's room. Reporters kept asking for interviews and Vinny or my sister, Rosie, would answer the door to them, saying, 'No comment.'

I don't know how I got through those first few weeks after my beautiful daughter passed away. Richard and my family offered me all the support I could want. But I missed my poor Lynn so intensely. I missed her warmth, her kindness, her humour and her soft smile more than I ever imagined I would. It was impossible to think of my life going on without her in it. However much of a struggle it was, I knew I had to get through each day, each hour, each minute. I had to, for her.

CHAPTER TWENTY-ONE
ANOTHER GOODBYE

We couldn't hold Lynn's funeral until the coroner had released the body, which he did on 22 January 2009. I was pleased that my phone calls on the morning she died had been effective and the police pathologist agreed to preserve during the post-mortem what the ME pathologist needed to examine, principally her spinal cord.

I spent ages planning the funeral, mainly with Steve and Richard, but others helped enormously too. It was a bittersweet time of going back over Lynn's life with her old friends and family, remembering music she loved, things that were important to her and happy times she had.

My sister, Rosie, came shopping with me in Tunbridge Wells to help choose an outfit for Lynn to be laid out in. We found a pretty, high-collared blouse and a cardigan in shades of lilac – her favourite – and a straight skirt in a deeper purple. The assistant asked me if I was buying a present for someone special. I smiled back at him, thinking, '*She could not be more special*', but my eyes stung and I couldn't get the words out for the lump in my throat.

Richard and I talked it over and agreed she should wear the gold locket we had given her for her twenty-first birthday in which she kept pictures of us, and I asked the funeral directors to put on her wrist a silver Swarovski charm bracelet adorned with glass shapes and hearts that I had bought for her at an airport and which she adored.

The service was on 6 February 2009 at our local village church, St Peter's in Stonegate. It was as lovely as any service could be and the vicar was wonderful; he helped us make every bit of it meaningful.

Before we went in I was anxious about how I would get through it, and everyone was worried about me. All my life I have had a tendency to faint and at that time I was not strong and was having dizzy spells. Shortly after Lynn died I had passed out at home and ended up with a huge black eye from knocking myself on something.

Steve gripped my hand firmly as we arrived at the church behind the hearse. 'If I faint, you are *not* to take me out of the church. I *have* to be at Lynn's funeral,' I insisted to him. 'So just let me lie on the floor for a minute, then I'll be okay.' I didn't feel able to say or read anything but it was vitally important that I was there.

It was very, very difficult but Steve was strong and he stood beside me and held my hand and we all got through it okay. I felt Lynn's presence strongly and knew she was glad to be free. I have never had a second thought or a moment of regret about helping her to go and the knowledge that she is at peace is what keeps me at peace.

Because Lynn so often said, 'You can't fix me any more,' we chose the Coldplay song 'Fix You'. It was a most beautiful song that captured our emotions perfectly, about how we'd wanted to help Lynn so much in the most desperate of times.

We also played 'Lord of the Dance' because the lines about dancing with the devil on your back struck a chord with me.

Richard walked stiffly up to the lectern to introduce the next song – the one we thought of as our anthem, Labi Siffre's '(Something Inside) So Strong'. 'The words describe Lynn's feelings towards those who ignored her and were so cruel to her over the years, despite her being so terribly ill. Some people may think that she was eventually beaten, but they are wrong,' he said proudly.

The church was packed with family, friends and neighbours. Most of them understood the significance of the words and I felt all their spirits uniting and supporting us and remembering Lynn as the words rang out from the tape deck.

Courageously battling to control his emotions, Richard managed to read the beautiful anonymous poem, 'Rainbow Bridge', which Lynn had found on the Internet after her beloved cat Ollie died. It's about how you will meet up after death. '*There is a bridge connecting heaven and earth,*

It is called Rainbow Bridge because of its many colours…' it begins. It had us all in tears.

Steve spoke eloquently, recalling memories of Lynn before she was ill, how lively she was, how she would get him into trouble. He brought her to life. One of her best friends at school, Laura, spoke and her other best friend, Michaela, who went to live in New Zealand, wrote a special message which her mother read out.

And then to finish, we had the beautiful song, 'Run', by Leona Lewis. I clutched Steve's hand and felt as we listened to the wonderful chorus that the whole congregation was sending the same message as one to Lynn – we'd always be with her in some way.

Richard and I, with Steve and Sarah, accompanied Lynn's body to the crematorium, where we clung to each other as the vicar gave a short blessing before the curtain was drawn around her coffin. We then took ten minutes to compose ourselves before going on to the reception we had arranged in a local hotel. So many people came up to offer me their sympathy that the rest of the day passed quickly and I survived it.

I had already had shoals of messages from friends who wrote not only to say how sorry they were but also to offer support. They said they were behind me, they knew I was a good mother and that I looked after Lynn and loved her. Messages from Lynn's Internet friends also comforted me as they revealed how helpful she had been to so many of them.

They all said the same thing: '*I don't know how somebody so ill could be so positive and give so much to other people.*'

I was deeply touched by the response. By the end of it all I probably received a couple of thousand letters, plus loads of emails, messages on Facebook and a condolences page in the ME support group and not a single message was negative. It was quite incredible. All kinds of people I didn't know from around the country helped me get through each day with their caring words and thoughts. The police had warned me to expect some anonymous letters condemning what I had done but every single one of them, including ones from many friends I have who are very religious, offered me nothing but support, kindness, love and understanding. They were all lovely letters and some of them were deeply moving.

If they didn't know the address, people wrote '*The Bungalow, Stonegate*', having seen the house on the TV news. There were flowers and plants left on the doorstep. Once I came home and found a box of half a dozen eggs with a note saying: '*They were laid this morning, to give you sustenance.*'

At first after Lynn died I had thought, '*I don't know how I am going to get through this. I don't know how I will keep going.*' Those letters went a long way to helping me through. I took life like someone going to Alcoholics Anonymous – one day at a time. Each morning I thought, '*I will just get through this day and not think about tomorrow.*'

We planted a crab apple tree in the garden of the church in memory of Lynn, Malus Liset, hardy and strong to withstand whatever nature might throw at it. It's positioned on the short route she used to take from the school to the sports field. I sit by her tree and can see her running races on sports days, her long strong legs taking her out in front of her classmates, with the same look of determination she never lost, even through illness, even in death.

CHAPTER TWENTY-TWO
A LONG WAIT

On 16 April 2009 I was summoned to Brighton police station to be formally charged. I waited there with my solicitor, Kim Evans, for about an hour while phone calls were going back and forth, presumably with the office of the Director of Public Prosecutions, over the final decision about what the charge should be.

Finally the detective came back to the room where I was waiting with two other police officers and said he was going to charge me with attempted murder. Everyone seemed upset about it and Kim was nearly in tears but I didn't bat an eyelid. I just felt nothing. I suppose it was because that was the way I had dealt with everything for so long – I had learnt not to react to things, just to take it. '*And anyway,*' I thought to myself, '*whatever happens to me now doesn't matter, the worst has already happened – Lynn is gone.*'

I came out of the police station and walked over to where my family, Richard, Steve, brothers Jim and Vinny and sister Dolie were waiting. 'They have charged me with attempted murder,' I said. They were stunned and outraged. After about half an hour, once the initial numbness had worn off, I began to feel extremely cross and indignant too.

'*How on earth could they think that I would attempt to murder my daughter?*' I asked myself. '*Just how? Where did they get that idea from?*' It built slowly but the more I thought about it, the more I couldn't believe it. '*I don't understand it. It's wrong, it's totally wrong,*' I thought. '*I have to show them that I would never hurt Lynn.*'

The police had explained to me that the 'attempted murder' charge did not mean that I had tried to kill Lynn and failed. It was a legal term meaning I had taken steps to murder her, but they couldn't charge me with actual murder because they could not prove that what I had done had caused Lynn's death. She could have died anyway from the overdose she gave herself, no matter what I did or didn't do.

Whatever the technicalities, it was so horrible to have the word 'murder' associated with what I had done for Lynn when the only reason I had been involved was because she was physically incapable of carrying out her own wishes. I thought the authorities would soon come to understand the real situation. '*As soon as they read the details of the case more thoroughly, they are going to drop the charge,*' I told myself.

It took a few weeks to sink in properly how serious the situation was. I had already told the family that I would plead guilty to assisted suicide because that was what it was. Now I told them, 'I will never plead guilty to attempted murder. They can do what they want with me.'

I started going through loads of papers and researching on the Internet about court procedures and criminal law and picking bits out and thinking, '*Ah, when they see this they will surely drop the charge.*' But I felt I had no control over the situation. I really didn't care either. As far as I was concerned, I had done the right thing and if that meant I had to go to prison, then so be it.

It was my brother Vinny who nagged me into being more proactive. 'You might think it will be okay now, but wait till you are sitting in a prison cell,' he warned.

It slowly dawned on me that I had to start fighting or else they could actually find me guilty. And the maximum sentence for attempted murder was life imprisonment. Even assisted suicide carried a maximum sentence of 14 years. But more importantly I had to show them they were wrong. It was assisted suicide and nothing else.

Facing a possible prison sentence, I had to sort things out at home in case I was forced to rent out the house. In any case, Lynn had asked me to hold a sale of her things to raise money for ME research. Most of her stuff was stored in the loft and day after day, I tried to find the strength to tackle the job.

'*I'll just get one box and make a start,*' I told myself. I clambered up into the loft full of determination but each time I caught sight of something, like the old cot she used to keep her dolls in or her sailing shoes, I crumpled, completely overwhelmed by a fresh and intense wave of grief.

It was extremely distressing because I was driven by an urgent feeling that I must do the things Lynn had asked me to do – just in case. I tried to start again and again for three or four months but it was no good. So my sister Rosie came to stay for a couple of weeks to help. 'Shall we make a start?' she repeated each morning. 'Okay,' I agreed. 'Tomorrow.' After days of this she finally put her foot down. 'Come on, now. Make a date for the sale, book the hall and then you will *have* to do it.'

So I made the booking, which forced me to steel myself to start getting the boxes out and handing them down to her. I still didn't get round to going through them while she was with me so after she returned to Ireland she kept phoning and saying, 'Have you got started yet?' Her nagging helped me to get going and I found it got a bit easier as I went along.

We had brought down boxes and boxes that were now stacked up high in Lynn's bedroom and along the corridors of the bungalow. They were full of jewellery, clothes, soft toys, make-up, craft materials – mostly presents she had been given over the years, many of them still in their wrappers, unopened.

It was a hugely emotional process. Everything I took out brought a memory. One day I found some cassette tapes. I put them in the machine and I heard my daughter's voice for the first time in 17 years. A lively, giggly, girly voice. I had forgotten what it sounded like.

She had recorded the tapes while messing about in her bedroom with her school friends. On one she was pretending to be a presenter of a radio programme and was asking her friend questions and telling jokes and the two of them were laughing. On another she played a bit of piano and clarinet 'Stranger on the Shore', the tune I always loved so much.

It was so lovely to hear her enthusiasm but so sad as well. I sat there with tears streaming down my face listening to her sounding so happy and full of the joys of life. I could have dumped the tapes years earlier – I nearly did. Now I was so pleased I had kept them.

Her roller skates looked almost new. I held them in my hands, picturing her whizzing along the Close with an excited grin. She had got them for her fourteenth birthday in September 1991, and had mastered them quickly but had not used them much by the time she fell ill that November.

There were her musical instruments – her clarinet and guitar and a couple of keyboards. They brought back memories of her playing around trying different backing rhythms. I came across old exercise books and stories she wrote at school and her uniform and rucksack. There were sailing jackets, bats and balls and other stuff she and Steve used to play with, all shoved up in the loft and forgotten about during the years of illness.

I put aside some special mementoes for her friends and for family and the rest went to the sale. Organising that helped fill the time and keep my mind occupied. I had to round up people to help, design the fliers, get them printed and price what I was to sell. I was just about ready in time.

It was a marvellous day because of the wonderful spirit of everybody who came to help and worked really hard and who came to buy. The village community gathered together in memory of Lynn and they were so warm and supportive. It was successful too – I raised £1,400 and still had quite a lot of things left over. I was able to get through it because by then I had spent months handling Lynn's things and was used to seeing them, but Richard couldn't manage it. If he had come along on the day and seen all those memories laid out together, it would have destroyed him.

One of the hardest things I had to do was to clear out Lynn's big fish tank. It meant so much to her, it was another little world of colour and life in her room. I didn't want to touch it for a long time. I wanted to keep her room as much as possible as it was. Then I got to the point where I had to. There were loads of fish because they were always breeding.

I started catching the fish about 60 at a time and giving them away or taking them to the fish shop. It took weeks. Then there were only a few. That was very hard because every time I passed the room, it looked empty, which made that feeling of there being so much missing from the room much worse.

I finally managed to catch the last few then cleaned out the tank and advertised it for sale – I didn't ask for much. I was delighted when a young couple with a little girl came for it. The man absolutely adored fish and said he could never have afforded such a huge fish tank normally. I thought this was the perfect family to have it. In a way, Lynn's delight in her fish would live on in theirs.

In the early weeks after she died I sometimes managed to trick myself into thinking she would be back again soon, she was just in hospital for a while and I had popped home to pick up a few things. But then I would be hit by reality and overtaken by a tide of grief. Other times, while doing something ordinary like walking down the road, or washing up, the grief would come over me unexpectedly, like somebody had come up behind me and knocked me in the back of the knees, and I just gave way.

As time went on, that didn't happen so much. Instead I felt her loss more deeply and more constantly and there were a lot of triggers that sent me into meltdown. If I went into Marks & Spencer's in Tunbridge Wells and caught sight of a rack of pyjamas, I broke down and had to run straight out. During Lynn's illness I had looked out for nice pyjamas every time I went shopping because it was all she could wear. She had hundreds, but now I would never need to buy another pair.

Having to read through legal papers, attend court hearings, have meetings with my barristers and so on, meant I had to keep functioning rationally and could not give way to my grief. In some ways, it delayed my grieving process. Many times I just longed to be alone and not to have to deal with any of it.

I went out more than I had done for years – I visited my family in Ireland and they came to stay with me. I met Steve for a short break in France and visited him in Belgium. But each time I went away, I wanted to be back home after only a day or two. Lynn was with me everywhere I went, but I still felt closest to her in the house where our lives had been so intimately entwined.

When her birthday came, 20 September, everyone wanted me to be somewhere other than at home on my own. I agreed to go to Steve and Sarah's in Belgium for a couple of days but I wanted to be at home on the day. The whole week was very difficult. I told myself it was only a date, but I couldn't help the memories flooding back of the day she was born and how thrilled I was to have the little girl I always dreamt of and all the things I hoped for her. I travelled back on the Sunday, the day of her birthday, and sat by her tree in the churchyard, feeling the intense pain of my broken heart.

Three days later the Director of Public Prosecutions, Keir Starmer, QC, published his interim guidelines, setting out the 'public interest factors' that he said should determine whether or not people involved in assisting a suicide should be prosecuted.

He had been forced into this when Debbie Purdy – the woman whose case Lynn and I had followed so closely – won a significant legal victory in the House of Lords. She argued that it was a breach of her human rights not to know whether her husband, Cuban jazz violinist Omar

Puente, would be prosecuted if he accompanied her to Dignitas. The law lords agreed, saying the situation was a 'violation of the right to a private and family life' and ordered the DPP to clarify the law.

In response the DPP had drawn up these interim guidelines to apply while he prepared a formal set. In them he stipulated the factors against prosecuting someone, which included that the 'victim' had a clear, settled and informed wish to commit suicide, had told the 'suspect' this and asked for their help. The victim should have a terminal illness or an incurable disability or degenerative condition, the suspect should be 'wholly motivated by compassion' and be a close relative or friend of the victim 'within the context of a long-term and supportive relationship'.

The factors which would make a prosecution more likely included when the victim was under 18, they had a mental illness or learning difficulty, their wish to commit suicide was not long term and settled, they did not ask personally for the suspect's help or did not have an incurable illness. Prosecution would also be likely when it could be shown that the suspect could be motivated by standing to gain from the death or they pressurised the victim into it.

Mr Starmer made it clear that assessing the public interest in a prosecution was 'not simply a matter of adding up the number of factors on each side and seeing which side of the scales has the greater number. Each case must be considered on its own facts and its own merits.'

And it did not mean the law had changed. He said, 'I also want to make it perfectly clear that this policy does not, in any way, permit euthanasia. The taking of life by another person is murder or manslaughter – which are among the most serious criminal offences.'

When I heard about this announcement, I went through the guidelines carefully. Every single one of the factors against prosecution applied to me, while not one of those in favour of prosecution did. I was thrilled. I thought it meant the end of my ordeal. I rang friends and said, 'Surely they will drop the case now!'

I kept expecting the charge to be dropped, but it didn't happen. I went to see my MP, who said he would try to intervene with the DPP and the then Justice Secretary, Jack Straw, and Richard and Vinny and many others wrote protest letters to the DPP. Nothing did any good.

I had seven court appearances before my trial, the first to enter a plea, followed by a series of case management hearings. I was told quite early on that if I pleaded guilty to attempted murder, the sentence would be reduced.

If I had done that, it would have been telling the world that Lynn had no control over her own destiny. It would have been saying *I* decided her life should end when it was *her* decision. It would have robbed her of her dignity.

After I was charged the media came flocking back but most of them gave up after getting 'No comment' for a few days. A few weeks later an independent TV company, Grace Productions, got in touch again and said they would like to prepare a programme for transmission after the trial. I agreed so long as the programme would include the message about the acute need for more research into ME. I also decided to speak to the *Daily Mail* as they had published a sympathetic interview with me and Lynn during ME Awareness Week in 2006.

Grace Productions, who were making their programme for the BBC's *Panorama*, took me to meet Debbie Purdy to discuss the subject of assisted suicide. I found Debbie to be full of energy and humour, zipping about her terraced house in Bradford, Yorkshire, in her wheelchair. I thought she was incredible.

'I am happy now because I am sure my husband will not be prosecuted if he helps me,' she told me. 'I want to live. I don't want to die. So the judgement in my case means my life will be longer because I won't have to go to Dignitas early, when I am still capable of getting there under my own steam.'

'How can you be a hundred per cent sure?' I asked her. 'The guidelines are there, but I am still being prosecuted.'

'It is not just the guidelines but all the publicity around my case which makes me confident. But I am going to carry on working to change the law so everyone else will be protected,' she said.

Panorama also took me to see Chris Woodhead, the former Chief Inspector of schools who suffers from motor neurone disease, at his remote farmhouse in Snowdonia. He was another very strong personality and I took to him instantly. He is in a similar position to Debbie in that he wants protection from prosecution for his wife if she helps him to die when he is in the later stages of his disease. A national newspaper once reported that he said that when the time comes he wants to take his electric wheelchair to the edge of a cliff and push himself over it.

But unlike Debbie, he did not agree that the law should be changed to allow euthanasia. 'I don't trust politicians to frame a law that would suit every case. I think the law should stay as it is and doctors should be given the authority to decide when to help someone,' he said.

He thought guidelines on the factors that should decide when someone is prosecuted were a good idea but that the DPP's needed improvement. 'My wife stands to gain financially from my death. That would apply to most close relatives in this situation' he pointed out.

'I believe people should have a choice. I want that choice. I don't like the idea of going to Dignitas but I don't want to be in a state where absolutely everything has to be done for me and I am just waiting to die. I am frightened of choking or suffocating. I want to be able to choose my time.'

Like Debbie, he said he would be able to live longer if he was sure his wife would not face prosecution for helping him at the end.

The strongest voice from the other side of the argument came from Baroness Campbell, who was born with the degenerative disease spinal muscular atrophy and uses a wheelchair. She gave an impassioned speech in the House of Lords in July 2009, against a proposal put forward by Lord Falconer to relax the law on assisted dying.

She argued that changing the law would lead to a situation in which doctors would encourage people with disabilities to end their lives. 'Those of us who know what it is to live with a terminal condition are fearful the tide has already turned against us,' she warned. 'If I should ever seek death – and there have been times when my progressive condition challenges me – I want to guarantee that you are with me, supporting my continued life and its value. The last thing I want is for you to give up on me, especially when I need you most.'

The proposed amendment to the Coroners and Justice Bill, which would have changed the law to allow people to help a loved one with a terminal illness to travel to a country where assisted suicide is legal, was rejected in a free vote by 194 to 141, largely because of Baroness Campbell's speech.

When I listened to that speech, I thought that Baroness Campbell is severely disabled but she is well enough to get up, get dressed and attend the House of Lords. I wondered, 'Where was the impassioned argument on behalf of someone like Lynn, who wasn't?'

On the *Panorama* programme Jeremy Vine asked the Baroness, 'If you had been Lynn's mother would you have said no?'

'I would like to think I would have done,' she replied. 'I think about would I want to be helped and then I think, goodness, what would that do to my husband for the rest of his life? For me, it's as wrong to ask someone to kill you as it is for someone to kill you. It's not all one way.'

Listening to her made me cross. '*How* dare *she judge Lynn like this*,' I thought. Lynn was not wrong to ask me to help her. What *was* wrong was that she had no other option but to ask for that help. If the system that allows an able-bodied individual to commit suicide fully respected the rights of those who are too ill to carry out the act themselves and allowed assistance, Lynn would not have had to die worrying about what was going to happen to me.

Lynn's letting go didn't mean she was weak or selfish. She was not. When her hope had gone, when she had endured more than anyone had a right to expect her to endure, she summoned all her courage and strength to let go and to face death.

Thinking of my daughter's death reminds me of some words I came across once, I don't know who wrote them: '*Giving up doesn't always mean you are weak; sometimes it means you are strong enough to let go.*'

Baroness Campbell is concerned that elderly or disabled people will fear they are a burden on their families and will come under pressure to end their lives before they want to. I recognise there is a danger of unscrupulous people taking advantage and there must be very strong safeguards to protect the vulnerable.

As someone with a degenerative illness, Baroness Campbell said that she was someone whose boxes would all be ticked as a candidate for assisted suicide. But that is not true. The first and most important box would say: 'I want to die.' She doesn't – and nobody is going to force her. Everyone can choose to live until the very last natural moment, whatever pain or distress they are in. So why can't everyone be free to choose not to?

I never doubted that I had done the right thing for Lynn but when I finally read the long letter she had written to her Internet friends I felt like she was telling me so all over again. I would have respected her wish to keep it only for the eyes of the friends she sent it to, but my solicitor told me it was going to be read out in court. I would have collapsed if I had heard it like that for the first time so she emailed me a copy so I could prepare myself.

I sat at the living room table and clicked on it. It was dated 18 November 2008 at 4.46 a.m. My heart ached as I pictured Lynn, alone and sleepless in the night, trying to muster the courage to tell the people who cared about her that she needed to leave this world. And finally hitting 'send'.

I began to read and I began to cry and I didn't stop crying the whole way through. It took hours. I was totally distraught and had to stop at almost every sentence and lay my head on the table to allow my eyes time to clear the tears so I could go back to reading her words. They were so compelling and real. I understood what she was trying to tell her friends as considerately as she could. And the way she described her feelings was so powerful, it stripped me bare. It made me realise the depth, the intelligence of my daughter.

It was her voice, her spirit, vividly alive once more, connecting with me, pleading with me to understand her and forgive her. I did and I loved her completely but, oh, it hurt so much that she was now gone for ever.

CHAPTER TWENTY-THREE
THE TRIAL

The night before the trial I didn't sleep much. At about 5 a.m. I looked out of the window. It was snowing. It was Tuesday, 12 January 2010, and England was in the depths of one of the coldest winters for years. There was already about a foot of snow on the ground. My heart gave a thump. How was I going to get to the court through this? I prayed it would not be delayed. I couldn't bear waiting any longer to know my fate.

I pulled on a dressing gown and went through to the kitchen. Vinny was already up, making a cup of tea. 'I was just about to wake you,' he said. 'Have you looked outside?'

My terrific brother had already been out in the cold and dark to clear the snow off his car and the drive and I was so very grateful that he was there making sure I would get to the court on time no matter what.

As always, my family were out in force giving me fantastic support. Vinny and his wife Olive, my brother Nicky and sisters Rosie and Dolie had come from Ireland and my sister Marie had come all the way from Australia. Steve had leave from work and was staying with Richard and Jeanette in Eastbourne and my other two brothers and sister-in-law were making their way down from London.

It was about an hour's drive from Stonegate to Lewes Crown Court. Weather conditions being so atrocious, we decided to leave as early as possible. I faced the question – what do you wear when going to your trial for attempted murder? '*Something restrained*,' I thought and chose my charcoal grey trouser suit and a light grey top. It looked a bit severe. I didn't want the jury thinking I was a grim-faced misery. I picked out a pink and grey scarf and draped it round my neck, which softened the look a little.

The last thing I did was pick up the two precious lockets I would keep with me throughout the trial. Around my neck I fastened the silver locket that had a little bit of Lynn's ashes inside. Then I slipped the locket of white gold that held strands of her hair into my trouser pocket, where I could hold it unseen. '*Okay, Lynn?*' I silently appealed to her, touching the locket at my throat. '*Very smart, Mum.*'

The snow was deep and crunchy, making the roads lethal, but Vinny did a great job of getting us to Lewes by 7.30 a.m. We met Steve, Richard and Jeanette, Richard's brother, David, and two of Richard's friends who had come to support him. We all went for breakfast in the old White Hart Hotel across the road from the court, an ideal spot to stay out of the glare of the media.

I was nervous and my hands were shaking. I still felt indignant that the DPP could not see that this charge was wrong. And I was distressed by the thought of how much

Lynn did not want anything like this to happen to me, but I was not afraid. 'I just want them to get on with it now,' I said to everyone who asked how I was feeling.

Richard was more upset than me and was angry that I and the rest of the family were being put through this ordeal. He had been summoned as a prosecution witness, which traumatised him even further. Because of this, he would not be allowed to go into the court until he was due to give his evidence. He spent days anxiously pacing the corridors of the courthouse which were freezing because the heating had gone on the blink.

The call for 'All parties in the case of Gilderdale to go to Court One' came at 10.30 a.m. By then I was in a private room with my barristers, John Price, QC, and Fiona Horlick. They gave me an encouraging look. 'All right, Kay? Ready to go?' I nodded and took a deep breath.

Inside the court a female guard showed me to the dock in front of the public benches. I climbed the three wooden steps and she fastened the little gate after me. I felt exposed, perched up there, but I was comforted by the warmth coming from my family and friends filling up the benches behind me. And Lynn was there with me. I felt her spirit, anxious for me, supporting and loving me, and I drew on her strength.

The court usher ordered everyone to stand up as the judge, Mr Justice Bean, came in through a door behind his bench opposite me and took his seat. He was a lean figure, with a wise, foxy face and an air of authority, dressed in scarlet robes with deep, white fur cuffs.

Proceedings began with various discussions between the lawyers and the judge. One was about selecting the jury in a case that involved something on which people might hold fixed opinions. The judge decided he would say that the case concerned assisted suicide and ask anyone who had such strong views on the subject that they could not return an impartial verdict to make it known to him.

I was facing three charges: count one, attempted murder; count two aiding and abetting an attempted suicide; count three, aiding and abetting a suicide. There was an argument about count two – the judge kept asking, 'What is the point of count two?' He ruled after a bit of argy-bargy that the jury would find it 'baffling' and the charge should be dropped.

So now the jury would be faced with a straight choice – were my actions attempted murder or assisted suicide?

Before the jury came in there were a few days of legal arguments over what evidence should be admissible in the case. The barristers called witnesses to support their arguments – Dr Woodgate, the doctor who talked to me at Brighton police station and all the police officers involved.

PC Stuart Ball, one of the officers who came to the house, was asked why he and his colleague had not immediately cautioned me. He replied, 'If I am honest, it was an upsetting situation. I am familiar with Mr Gilderdale. I had worked with him in the past. Perhaps that was an error of judgement.'

After the barristers from both sides had put across their arguments, the judge decided to rule that the evidence of the two police officers who came to the house and of both the interviews I gave at the police station were inadmissible in the trial. Mr Justice Bean was quite scathing about the way I had been treated by the police when I was traumatised and sleep-deprived, particularly when they insisted on interviewing me on the afternoon of Lynn's death.

This ruling meant that the only account of what I did would come from Dr Woodgate's recollection of what I told her on the morning that Lynn died. Whatever the outcome might be, I felt a sense of relief that I was fortunate enough to have a judge who seemed not only astute, but reflective and fair.

On Monday 18 January 2010 the six women and six men who were to decide my fate were sworn in. I stood up in the dock, feeling 12 pairs of eyes upon me as the court clerk read the charge: 'That between the second of December 2008, and fifth of December 2008, Bridget Kathleen Gilderdale attempted to murder Lynn Gilderdale…'

After I sat down, Mr Justice Bean warned the jury that they had to try the case on the evidence and that meant only what was put before them in court. 'Don't be influenced by external matters such as media reports,' he said. 'Don't try to obtain information elsewhere such as the

Internet. Please resist the temptation to discuss the facts of the case with your family and friends.' That must have been difficult for them when the whole question of euthanasia and assisted suicide was such a hot topic at the time.

At 10.56 a.m., Sally Howes got to her feet and opened the case for the prosecution. 'This case is about a young woman called Lynn Gilderdale and the tragic events of the last two days of her life,' she began.

'These events led to her untimely death by toxic poisoning due to a fatal overdose. Central to these events will be the actions of her mother, Bridget Kathleen Gilderdale. There will be no dispute between the prosecution and defence that the defendant was a caring, loving mother who considered her actions to be in the best interests of her daughter.

'It will not be your task to judge the motives or the morals of the mother or where your sympathies lie. It will be your task to consider whether, having considered all the evidence, the actions of Kay Gilderdale fall outside the law, the law that appertains to us all, protects us all and protects us sometimes from ourselves.'

She went on to give a summary of Lynn's life, her illness, her wish to end her life and what she did about that, such as contacting Dignitas and writing her Advanced Directive. She moved on to the morning of 4 December 2008, and summarised Dr Woodgate's account of what I had told her. This included the statement: 'Between three thirty a.m. and five a.m. she gave her three syringes of air into her Hickman line with the intent of giving her an air embolism.'

Turning to face the jury, Miss Howes continued, 'The job that you have to do is to sort out whether the prosecution has proved its case…at no stage does [Mrs Gilderdale] have to prove anything to you…you have to be satisfied so that you are sure. But nobody wants to frighten the jury at this stage. You all know what it's like to make an important decision in your home, personal or work life and you know you have to be sure and it's the same here.

'She is charged with attempted murder despite the fact that Lynn died. This is because the evidence from the toxicologist is inconclusive – he can't say which dose it was, or which combination of doses, that actually resulted in her death. So we have to ask you to examine the actions of the defendant during the last thirty hours very carefully. Don't look at the end result; look at what happened. And in examining what happened, ask yourself: what did she do, and secondly what did she intend, at the time of those actions? In other words, what did she want to achieve?

'It is the prosecution's case very simply that when Mrs Gilderdale realised that those two large doses of morphine that she provided to Lynn, that Lynn self-administered wanting to end her life, had not done the job she wanted to achieve, when she realised her daughter's suicide had gone horribly wrong, she then set about performing actions with no other intention than to end her daughter's life. The further cocktail of drugs, the further injection of air, were all done to terminate her daughter's life. It wasn't done to make her better.

'The prosecution does not dispute for one moment that the defendant was a caring, loving, most devoted mother. We do not dispute that Lynn suffered from a profound illness with a quality of life that was almost unimaginable or that she wanted to end her life…I return to what I said to you at the beginning – it is not your task to judge the motives or the morals of what [Mrs Gilderdale] did or to choose where your sympathies lie. It is your task to decide whether the actions of Kay Gilderdale fell outside the limits of the law, the law that protects us all.'

The first prosecution witness was Dr Woodgate. She had been such a good doctor and friend to me and Lynn that I was sure she must have hated being there, but she gave her evidence in a very calm, clear and professional manner. She talked about how she had known the family since 1987 and the history of Lynn's illness.

On the morning of 4 December she said she had 'found Lynn lying in bed in her usual position. She looked dead. She was very pale, puffy-faced. I asked her mum what happened. She came into the bedroom with me and stood by the bed. She was quite unsure what had happened. She was quite stressed'.

She described how I told her about giving Lynn the morphine then that Lynn had become very restless. 'Kay said to me she was frightened Lynn would be brain damaged.' After I had talked about giving Lynn her normal medicines, Dr Woodgate said, 'She told me she had also given Lynn syringes of air into the Hickman line…She told me she had probably given her three doses of air…If you fill a syringe with air, it may kill someone.'

I knew what was going to be said so was not shocked by this but I have no memory of injecting air down Lynn's Hickman line, nor do I remember telling the doctor I had done it.

In cross examination, John Price asked the doctor to read out part of the extremely touching letter she had written to me on 9 December 2008. Dr Woodgate read: 'Surround yourself now with all that's good and helpful and encouraging. I will never forget the tangible sense of love I felt every time I entered [Lynn's] room.

'Ever since her teenage years she was surrounded by a deep love…I felt that same sense of deep love as you unfolded the events of that last night to me. I saw that all your motivation was deep love. So now look after yourself as your first priority. You and Richard were her most precious possessions. She will want you to be nurtured and supported as you go on.'

Later, in her re-examination, Sally Howes brought Dr Woodgate back to the normal medicines I had given Lynn, including the 24-hour dose of morphine. The prosecutor insisted forcefully that there was no reason for me to give that as Lynn had already had a huge amount of morphine.

Three times Dr Woodgate stood her ground and patiently explained that it was for therapeutic reasons because the earlier morphine would no longer be effective as a pain relief due to the amount of time that had elapsed. She said I had told her that Lynn showed signs of distress and could have been suffering and that my actions, in giving her her normal medications, would have relieved that suffering.

When the prosecution called Richard to the stand, he looked as if every nerve was stretched to breaking point. I had tried to reassure him beforehand. 'Don't forget you have experience of being a witness when you were a police officer. You can do it,' I said.

'Yes, but this is very different,' he replied grimly.

Strangely, Sally Howes only asked him to identify himself, then she sat down and left all the questions to be asked by my barrister, Fiona Horlick, who proceeded to take Richard through the story of Lynn's life. There was total silence and concentration in court as Richard poured his heart and soul into trying to make the jury understand how it really was for Lynn and us, and he did it brilliantly; she would have been so proud of him. As I listened, I had a difficult struggle not to break down.

He described how I had 'fought every minute' to improve Lynn's life and had cared for her devotedly. When he arrived at the house on the morning of her death, he said, 'Kay looked totally heartbroken. Her world was coming to an end. She was crestfallen, everything you could describe of somebody who had been to hell and back.

'It was all very surreal. She was functioning, but wasn't functioning. It was just an empty person standing there.

Her body had just collapsed.' He added, 'We are never, ever going to get over it. We are not just talking about December 2008, but the subsequent thirteen months of this procedure. It's torn every member of the family apart.'

I don't know how he got through it, but he was my best character witness.

Next came Lynn herself as Fiona Horlick read out her Internet letter. This was my daughter, speaking from her grave, telling the world how she felt and what she wanted.

> *Okay guys, I have something really important that I'd like 2 talk 2 u about; something extremely private & personal that I want 2 share with u, my closest friends; the 'chosen few'!*
>
> *After many months – years, even – of serious deliberation, I've pretty much come 2 a huge decision. I hope u will try 2 understand my reasons behind coming 2 this decision, even if u don't personally or morally agree with it, & I also hope that u won't judge me too harshly…*
>
> *I don't really know where 2 begin or how 2 say it, so I'm just going 2 come out with it & hope u can find it within your heart 2 understand what I'm about 2 say.*

Lynn was very vivid in my mind as I listened with my head bowed. I felt the silver locket warm against my neck and my fingers closed around the gold one in my pocket and I could feel her spirit watching, willing them to understand that she had been a real, whole person and had the same right as they did to have control over her own life and death.

Basically, as I think some of u have known (or at least suspected) 4 awhile, I've had enough of this miserable excuse 4 a 'life' that I've merely been semi-existing in 4 the last 16 & a half yrs…& I've been thinking about my long-term future more & more.

Yes, I've had enough & I want 2 die.

This is no whim, & it's certainly not just because of the reactive depression that I was diagnosed with a few months ago…I really, really, REALLY want 2 die. I've just had enough of being in such pain & feeling so sick every second of every day, & battling thru 1 serious health crisis after another.

I'm tired…so very, very tired. And I just don't think I can keep hanging on 4 that elusive illness-free existence, that could, technically, be waiting 4 me just around the corner…but 4 which I just can't keep blindly holding on 2 ever-diminishing (& now pretty-much non-existant) hope that I will, 1 day, be well again.

I just can't do it.

This is something I've thought long & hard about, & the more I think about it, the more I feel it's what I want – so much so, that I've discussed it (& continue 2 discuss it) with my parents at great length (as much as I'm able 2, anyway). And altho they obviously desperately don't want me 2 'go', they can see I've just had

*enough & they understand why I can't keep hanging on
4 much longer.*

She wrote about her first suicide attempt and being on
antidepressants and that she had not changed her mind,
and she described getting a DNR and doing an Advanced
Directive. There was total silence in court apart from the
sound of reporters flipping the pages of their notebooks as
they wrote furiously to record all the words.

*Yes, I know there's a (very slim) chance I could almost
fully recover & that I might be able 2 live – really live – a
somewhat relatively 'normal' life 1 day. But even if I woke
up 2morrow almost fully recovered, I still won't be able 2
live the life I've dreamt about living 4 the last 16 yrs…*

*My ovaries have packed up so I most likely can't
have children (my all-time greatest wish), & even if I
could, I'm already 31 yrs old, so by the time I get out
there & find the man I want 2 have my children with,
I'll be far past the age I wanted 2 be when I had my own
baby. I know a lot of women are absolutely desperate 2
have their own babies & they can't, for 1 reason or
another. But they are often otherwise healthy young
women who can look 4 other ways 2 fulfil their desire…*

*Yes, I could adopt or have fertility treatment, but it
all takes time – plus, u need 2 be relatively healthy 2 be
accepted in2 those kind of programs, & I can't see myself
ever being well enough 2 do either of those things…*

Also, my bones are so painfully osteoporotic that even a cough or a sneeze could cause a fracture, so how exactly am I going 2 be able 2 live the active life that I've dreamt of? The kind of life I had b4 it was all stolen away from me at age 14; swimming, sailing, running, cycling, walking, sports, etc.

And they are only two examples of what would hold me back.

I'm just tired…my body is tired, and my spirit is broken.

I've had enough – can u understand that? I hope u can, I really, really do.

I was glad that I had read Lynn's letter before the trial. I'm not sure how I would have coped if I hadn't have been prepared. It was incredibly difficult to hear Lynn's account of her illness, but her strength, compassion and kindness were at the fore, showing everyone in the courtroom that day just how intelligent and thoughtful my beautiful girl was.

I want u 2 know, that in addition 2 me not wanting any life-saving/life-preserving treatment, if I'm ever presented with an 'opportunity' 2 leave this world, then I have 2 admit that I will grab it with both hands…I'm so sorry if it hurts u 2 'hear' me say that – I hate causing u extra pain – but that's the way I feel & I know that it's not ever going 2 change, so I wanted u 2 know what the 'plans' 4 my long-term future are.

I understand that some ppl will think I'm just depressed, or think I'm being weak & opting 4 the easy way out (altho suicide is far from 'easy' in my opinion & recent experience), or think it's ridiculous 4 me 2 even consider suicide when there's still a chance I could recover or at least be better than I am now.

I'm also painfully aware that I have a couple of very special friends who may well be reading this, who have terrible diseases that will sadly lead 2 them inevitably passing away some time in the future. They're terminally ill, yet they never seem 2 stop fighting or trying their hardest 2 stay in this world 4 as long as possible – & I'm in awe of their strength 2 not have given up yrs ago, I really am. Those lovely ppl may well be disgusted at me now…But a long time ago I made a kind of pact with myself; if I was still 100% bedbound & so seriously ill when I reached the age of 30, then I would kill myself. Well, I was 30 last year & the desire 2 leave all this pain & sickness behind me has done nothing but increase.

I want 2 die…so, so much.

M & I have probably spent hrs, on & off, discussing everything 2 do with this, & despite her doing her best 2 try 2 get me 2 see things differently (trying 2 ensure that not being resuscitated is what I truly want), my resolve 2 leave this 'life' has done nothing but intensify.

I'm sorry, I know this may be a shock 4 some of u, especially as I feel as if I often come across as being permanently (annoyingly?!) optimistic & 'happy'. But my intention 4 posting this entry wasn't 2 cause pain 2 u, my wonderful, wonderful friends…

Please don't be angry; try 2 understand…

Try 2 put yourself in my situation. Reread the online newspaper articles about me 2 see – only a tiny part of – what I've been thru in the past 16 yrs, & continue 2 go thru every day…Spending every second of your life in intense pain, feeling permanently extremely ill (NOT just lying in bed resting – oh, if only!!), & being 100% relient on others 2 care 4 your most basic needs, only surviving because tubes & medications & pumps & feeds are keeping u alive artificially – without all this modern technology, I wouldn't still be here.

I did not have to imagine Lynn's physical torment; I had lived through it with her, every day. It was painful for me to revisit. But Lynn's strong sense of purpose came across in her eloquent words, she was stating her case clearly and firmly, better than anyone else could.

Imagine that u had led your life from inside 1 small room (apart from regular hospital stays), & from inside 1 single bed, for 16 LONG yrs, since u were only 14 yrs old…Imagine being 31 yrs old & never having kissed some1 properly, let alone done anything else…Imagine having the painfully thin bones of a 100 yr old woman & not being able 2 move without the risk of a serious fracture…Imagine not being able 2 get the spinning thoughts out of your head because you're unable 2 speak & are too ill/weak 2 properly converse with others in any meaningful way, except by slowly typing emails 2 ppl on a little PDA…Imagine not being able 2 turn yourself over in bed or move your legs without some1 lifting u…

Imagine having 2 use a bedpan lying down (not easy)…Imagine having never been in a pub or club at 31 yrs old…Imagine never being able 2 fulfil the 1 thing u want above all else (except your returned health), the thing that should just be a given right 4 all young women: 2 have your own child. As I've already said, obviously I know that a lot of women can't have their own children, for 1 reason or another…but that doesn't stop MY heart from aching with the need 2 hold my own baby.

Imagine wanting 2 die – knowing, with every fibre of your being, that it's what u desperately want – but being too ill 2 actually be able 2 end your life yourself, & therefore being imprisoned inside the miserable existence which is your 'life'…

Imagine that all of the above is only 4 starters; that there's SO much more going wrong in your body than u would have ever believed is possible, & u only discover the extent of what's going wrong as each new pain/symptom is investigated & shows up yet another serious abnormality…

The drs have no idea how 2 piece 2gether all the parts of the jigsaw that are my condition(s). Right now, they just don't make sense.

1 day, I KNOW they will. But not now; not yet; not 2day; not for me…

I don't have 2 imagine any of the above.

This is my reality.

And I've had enough.

My body & mind is broken…& I want peace. God, I'm SO desperate 2 finally end this seemingly never-ending carousel of pain & sickness & illness & suffering…

The courtroom felt incredibly still as Lynn's powerful and moving words were read out. Lynn was her best advocate, she could not have conveyed more clearly her wishes, just as her letter showed her to be the caring, thoughtful and intelligent person she was. I was happy that she had the chance to speak for herself.

I love u all, & I can tell u honestly now that had it not been 4 some of u, I would have given up a long, long time ago. You've made the last couple of yrs of my life so much more bearable than it was b4 I found u all, & I can never thank u enough 4 that…you've been my life-line. Literally. And I love u all dearly 4 it, I truly do – as I love my family. But altho the love of my friends & family has kept me going when at my absolute lowest, I can't stay here just 4 u guys any more…I just can't.

I have nothing left.

I'm spent.

And so, I end this entry by repeating something I said at the beginning…

I hope u can find it within your heart 2 understand.

As the trial went on I kept talking over with my barristers whether I should take the stand. At first I wanted to because I so much wanted to tell everybody exactly how it was. But because I had such a great legal team and because of the way Richard spoke and Lynn's Internet letter, I felt the truth was shining through and perhaps there wasn't a need to put myself through it.

'Won't people think I have something to hide?' I asked my barristers. I was thinking that when you watch a trial on TV, everyone is waiting for the accused person to go on the stand. People want every bit of you when you are in a situation like that and I was worried they would feel cheated if I didn't speak. Then I thought, '*All I have had since Lynn died has been support and kindness from total strangers as well as everyone who knows me. Perhaps I am wrong to think they will believe the worse of me.*'

I swayed one way and the other right up until the day when the decision had to be made. The advice of my legal team was that it was not necessary for me to do it, but it was my choice. It was a hard decision to make, but in the end I chose not to go on the stand. It was a huge relief; I think I would have broken down and I really didn't want to do that. I felt that would have been an insult to Lynn when she endured so much worse with strength and patience.

The defence was very short. I had a list of character witnesses, but there was no need to call them as several of the prosecution witnesses had already spoken in my defence. Then the barristers for both sides spoke eloquently in their closing arguments. The case was adjourned for the weekend and I went back to the bungalow with my family. It was good to have them around and the phone kept ringing and neighbours called in so I was too busy to give way to the gnawing anxiety about what was going to happen to me the following week.

On Monday 25 January the court reconvened for the judge's summing up and the verdict. We arrived early again and had some breakfast in the hotel across the road while the TV cameras and press photographers mustered on the pavement outside the court.

It all seemed to happen very fast at the end. I thought after the jury returned there would be quite a long procedure. After all, this was an important case as it would be the first time the ordinary British public, in the form of a jury, had the chance to express their views on the assisted suicide debate. Their decision would show where their sympathies lay for people like Lynn, trapped in an unendurable existence, and for me, whom she asked to help her.

Not that I was thinking of any of this as I stood in the dock, waiting for the verdict. I was only thinking of Lynn, my beloved daughter. Nothing mattered except that she was at peace.

'Foreman of the jury, have you reached a verdict on the charges against Kay Gilderdale on which you are all agreed?' asked the usher.

'Yes,' he said.

I felt a chill down my spine. I didn't know how I could cope with prison, the clanging doors, the separation from everyone I loved. But my chin rose as I thought, '*Whatever will be, will be. I wouldn't have done anything differently.*'

'On count one, the charge of attempted murder, how do you find?'

I had no idea which way it would go – the jurors gave nothing away. I braced myself as the foreman kept his eyes on the court usher. Then finally, he gave the answer: 'Not guilty.'

He had not even finished getting the words out before a huge roar rose like a tidal wave from my family and friends on the benches behind me and seemed to lift me up bodily. It was incredible; I felt as though I was going to fly across the court. The tears rolled down my face. I was so grateful, I wanted to shout out, 'Thank you!' then I thought, '*No, you don't do that.*'

Visions of Lynn came to me; of her running and laughing on the beach as a young girl, of her lying sick and exhausted in her shrouded room. I saw her smiling at me now with relief and pleasure that my ordeal was over. Now she could finally go to her eternal rest. And I could begin to grieve properly.

EPILOGUE

ONE LAST GOODBYE

On a dry, sunny day at the end of October 2010, Steve, Richard and I fulfilled Lynn's wish to take her ashes to a spot where we all used to be happy together. We chose the quiet end of Eastbourne Beach near the sailing club where she and her brother messed about with dinghies, windsurfers and canoes and Richard and I felt so content watching them being so happy.

The wind was coming off the sea and there was quite a swell so we had to find the right place where the ashes would be taken out to sea. Steve spotted it – a breakwater where the shingle was piled up high on one side and the water was much deeper on the other.

As we stood there, we knew it was perfect. It was windy and vibrant, yet peaceful and beautiful. The blue sky was dotted with scudding clouds. There were three windsurfers out on the water. The sundrenched sea danced and sparkled, like Lynn as a child.

We took it in turns to hold the cylinder-shaped scatter box which helped direct Lynn's ashes to where we wanted them to be. Richard first, then Steve, then me, each of us silently releasing her into the deep water and setting her free. We scattered flowers from her funeral which I had dried in a flower press – lilacs, delphiniums, irises and lavender-coloured roses – and they chased to and fro on the waves while I whispered my last goodbye to my daughter.

As her ashes drifted away I was thinking that the three of us could meet her again anywhere we were in the world, any time that we could stand on a beach and look out on to the sea that was now her final resting place.

We stood there together for a while not saying much. Each of us remembering Lynn in happy times and sad ones. It was a beautiful moment.

In the early months after Lynn died I wondered how I could go on when she was gone. In truth I still do. I know the sadness I feel will never leave me. I'm learning to walk alongside it, to accept it as my constant companion. Even when I'm laughing or joking, it's there. When I fear it will overwhelm me, I remind myself what Lynn taught me about being strong. And most of all I comfort myself with the knowledge that she is free.

At first, with the trial and media interest, there was a lot happening which delayed the time when I had to face life without Lynn. Everything was different. And nothing felt right. Even being able to walk freely out of my front door didn't feel right. Whenever I am doing anything, I feel I should be doing something for Lynn. The feeling is particularly strong when I go shopping – I have an almost irresistible urge to search for the kind of pyjamas or jewellery that Lynn would like.

The practicalities of life meant that I had to look for a job. It took time because I found it almost impossible to concentrate on anything except Lynn and my emotions were all over the place. Eventually I did courses in accounting and office admin and took on some voluntary work to get accustomed to an office environment again. It paid off when I managed to land an admin job last November.

My sister Dolie has been there for me every day since Lynn died. We're going to Australia to visit our sister, Marie, but otherwise I find I can't plan much. I just live from moment to moment, and I still don't like being away from home, the place I feel closest to Lynn, for more than a few days.

Meanwhile I have decided to carry on campaigning in Lynn's name to promote awareness of ME and to raise money for research. Research is the key to understanding this illness and Lynn has already made her own contribution.

When her body was examined by the pathologist who specialised in ME, he discovered 'dorsal root ganglionitis' – infected nerve roots – and nodules of Nageotte, which are little tombs of dead cells, in her spinal cord. These would have caused her terrible pain and sensory nerve damage. They found similar cells in the body of Sophia Mirza, an ME sufferer who died in 2005 at the age of 32, and I believe also in other sufferers.

These findings are proof that Lynn's ME was a neuro-logical disease. I should be happy that we were proved right all along, but how can I be happy when Lynn had to die to provide that proof? She knew the evidence would be there to be found. 'The answers are within me, Mum,' she used to say to me wistfully. 'It will be too late for me but it will help others.' I hope she was right and that some good will come out of her death and others will not have to suffer the way she did.

Many doctors still shy away from ME because they don't understand it. Others are only now acknowledging it has a physical cause. For instance, Dr Martin Scurr, who has been a GP for more than 30 years, wrote in the *Daily Mail* on 7 June 2010, '*By the way…at last I've been convinced that ME is real.*

'*I admit it, I was wrong. For many years I – like many of my medical colleagues – have blamed ME on psychological and behavioural causes. Then last month I attended the fifth World Conference on ME. There I spoke to a number of experts who were emphatic that the evidence shows the condition does have a viral origin.*'

He went on to discuss the evidence that sufferers are born with a genetic vulnerability to the disease and that it flares up when it is sparked off by one or more common viruses such as glandular fever. He concluded, '*This is an exciting time and some solace to those who have this awful illness and have never been believed.*'

If only all doctors would show such humility and admit when they get it wrong. Lynn felt very strongly about the lack of understanding from the medical profession and the inadequate portrayal of ME generally. 'Being disbelieved is almost as hard to bear as the pain,' she explained.

That's why she did whatever she could from her sickbed to improve public awareness, taking part in documentaries, news bulletins, newspaper articles and being the face of The 25% ME Group. She was determined that her good work would continue even when she was gone.

The annual World Conference on ME, which brings researchers together from all over the globe, is organised by Invest in ME. This group is doing a great job in changing attitudes and promoting study into this devastating and complex illness. Dedicated scientists are making progress in the UK and abroad but more money is vitally needed to support their work.

I feel so very sad about what happened to Lynn. I will never be able to understand why she was treated so badly. I feel very angry about that. My trial was nothing in comparison to the trial that was her life. I don't want anyone else to go through such torture.

It still seems hard to believe I was charged with the attempted murder of my daughter. Right from the beginning I pleaded guilty to assisting her suicide and was willing to accept the consequences of my actions, even though I still believe fully that I did the right thing in helping her escape her wretched life.

I don't understand why my whole family had to be put through such stress on top of trying to cope with the loss of Lynn. I am baffled and confused by it all. I am deeply and humbly grateful for the wonderful support I have had and am hugely indebted to my legal team and the judge and jury who believed that my foremost concern was to make sure that Lynn was not suffering on her journey to a better place.

My darling daughter is with me every minute, in my waking hours and in my sleep. I see her face and talk to her in my thoughts and wish with all my being that things could have been different. I remember these words I read somewhere: 'Goodbye isn't painful unless you're never going to say hello again.'

I draw comfort from the poem 'Rainbow Bridge' that Richard read out at Lynn's funeral. It tells the story of losing a pet and how the animal is restored to health and vigour on 'the other side'. The poem says that those who *were hurt or maimed are made whole and strong again, just as we remember them in our dreams of days and times gone by*'. I murmur the words and they help me imagine Lynn not broken any more, saying, 'Hello, Mum,' with a smile on her face.

I have been able to do some of the things Lynn wished for me. She wished for me to travel to beautiful hot places and discover new things. I've done this and will do it again, but it doesn't stop the pain.

She wished for me to have my biggest desire come true. This was for her to get better and, sadly, that was never going to come true. And she wished for me, that *all* my dreams come true, but how can shattered dreams be realised?

This reminds me of an exchange of emails we had mid 2007. She was very unwell and feeling sad, thinking she would never get better.

> I dont lik it at al. Feel as if it makes life harder for us al. Particularly u and dad. So I feel very bad about it...I AM trying to be happyer but its not exactly working yet ;)

I replied:

> Dear Lynn,
>
> Please don't feel bad about feeling sad. It is understandable that you do and it is clear that you are making a huge effort. It shows what you are made of, strong stuff (you must take after your mother of course!), but that doesn't mean you have to be super human.
>
> Dad and I are very proud of you, but realise what a hard time you're going through. You can lean on us as much as you need to. We will always be here for you, until the day you say, 'go away for God's sake and give me some peace!'
>
> I think dreams are a bit like what you were talk-ing about today with Dad, about having to do things to get to where you want to be, otherwise nothing

will change. Some people don't acknowledge their dreams because they are afraid they won't come true – 'don't dream and you won't be disappointed.'

Others know what their dreams are and acknowledge them but don't do anything to make them come true, they just expect their dream to land on their lap.

Some give up on their dreams because they feel they can't do anything to make them a reality, but that's where the trick lies, to believe in your dreams, act on them when you can, but don't expect something for nothing.

Something for nothing reminds me of something that was given to you when you were last in hospital, exactly because you didn't expect something for nothing and deserved it so much that it came to you. All the other things that you deserve so much will come to you too, but you must not stop dreaming, seeing possibilities and acting on them when you can.

Try to hold on to your dreams for a little while longer. Dreams do come true, but you've got to have a dream to make it come true.

Love,

Mum

Lynn sent me this reply:

I dont think peeple do get ther dreams very often...I mean, hav U had any ;) Maybe we wil both get ar dreams 1 day and they wil come tru...

My daughter was beautiful in her body and her soul. She was kind, she was loving and she was wise. Above all these, she was brave. While I never stopped pleading with her to hold on to her dream of getting better, she had the enormous courage to give up on it, face the bleakest reality and embrace the ultimate freedom that can only be found in death. She forced me to match her courage and to give up on my precious dream too so that I could help set her spirit free from the body that betrayed her.

With her help I am battling to summon that same courage every day; the courage to resist falling into bitterness and resentment – that would not be worthy of her; the courage to feel glad that she is free though her loss still hurts so much. And the courage to believe that our last goodbye was not a goodbye at all, only farewell until we meet again.

ACKNOWLEDGEMENTS

I'd like to say a huge thank you to my wonderful family who have supported and encouraged me throughout. I am extremely grateful to Gill Swain, who offered endless and invaluable advice without which this book might never have been written.

My thanks to Ebury, especially to my editor, Kelly Ellis, who has guided me gently and brilliantly throughout the publishing process. To everyone who supported me – thank you. And, most of all, thank you to Lynn for being such a special human being.

My loving and courageous daughter asked me once if I would write a book about how bad ME can be. 'No, I couldn't write a book, but *we* could – together,' I replied. That was in 2006 and, contrary to my first reaction to her suggestion, the book has now been written. Not in the way it was supposed to be, but nonetheless, we did do it *together;* because Lynn was in my heart and in my mind every step of the way.

ABOUT THE AUTHOR

Kay was born in Dublin in 1954. The youngest of ten, all she'd ever wanted was a family of her own. After leaving school, she trained as a nurse and went on to have two much-longed-for children, Stephen and Lynn, with her then husband Richard.

She now lives alone in East Sussex, where she works as an administrator, and is a proud grandmother of two. Kay is a dedicated supporter of The 25% ME Group. The charity exists to support those who have the most severe forms of ME and the people who care for them. For more information or to show your support, visit www.25megroup.org or write to 25% ME Group, 21 Church Street, Troon, Ayrshire, KA10 6HT.